Disruptive Learning Narrative Framework

Also available from Bloomsbury

Critical Education in International Perspective, Peter Mayo and Paolo Vittoria

Educating for Peace and Human Rights: An Introduction, Maria Hantzopoulos and Monisha Bajaj

Education for Social Change: Perspectives on Global Learning, Douglas Bourn

Educational Research: An Unorthodox Introduction, Gert Biesta

Global-National Networks in Education Policy: Primary Education, Social Enterprises, and 'Teach for Bangladesh', Rino Wiseman Adhikary, Bob Lingard, Ian Hardy

Identities and Education: Comparative Perspectives in Times of Crisis, edited by Stephen Carney and Eleftherios Klerides

International Schooling: Privilege and Power in Globalised Societies, Lucy Bailey

Post-Qualitative Research and Innovative Methodologies, edited by Matthew K. E. Thomas and Robin Bellingham

Race, Education and Educational Leadership in England: An Integrated Analysis, edited by Paul Miller and Christine Callender

Schooling as Uncertainty: An Ethnographic Memoir in Comparative Education, Frances Vavrus

Social Theory for Teacher Education Research: Beyond the Technical-Rational, edited by Kathleen Nolan and Jennifer Tupper

Syntheses of Higher Education Research: What We Know, Malcolm Tight

Disruptive Learning Narrative Framework

Analyzing Race, Power and Privilege in Post-Secondary International Service Learning

Edited by
Manu Sharma, Andrew Allen and Awad Ibrahim

BLOOMSBURY ACADEMIC
LONDON • NEW YORK • OXFORD • NEW DELHI • SYDNEY

BLOOMSBURY ACADEMIC
Bloomsbury Publishing Plc
50 Bedford Square, London, WC1B 3DP, UK
1385 Broadway, New York, NY 10018, USA
29 Earlsfort Terrace, Dublin 2, Ireland

BLOOMSBURY, BLOOMSBURY ACADEMIC and the Diana logo are
trademarks of Bloomsbury Publishing Plc

First published in Great Britain 2022
This paperback edition published 2023

Copyright © Manu Sharma, Andrew Allen and Awad Ibrahim and Bloomsbury, 2022

Manu Sharma, Andrew Allen and Awad Ibrahim and Contributors have asserted
their right under the Copyright, Designs and Patents Act, 1988, to be identified
as Authors of this work.

For legal purposes the Acknowledgements on p. xii constitute
an extension of this copyright page.

Cover image © franckreporter/Getty Images

All rights reserved. No part of this publication may be reproduced or transmitted in
any form or by any means, electronic or mechanical, including photocopying, recording,
or any information storage or retrieval system, without prior permission
in writing from the publishers.

Bloomsbury Publishing Plc does not have any control over, or responsibility for, any
third-party websites referred to or in this book. All internet addresses given in this
book were correct at the time of going to press. The author and publisher regret any
inconvenience caused if addresses have changed or sites have ceased to exist, but
can accept no responsibility for any such changes.

A catalogue record for this book is available from the British Library.

A catalog record for this book is available from the Library of Congress.

ISBN: HB: 978-1-3502-5378-0
PB: 978-1-3502-5382-7
ePDF: 978-1-3502-5379-7
eBook: 978-1-3502-5380-3

Typeset by Newgen KnowledgeWorks Pvt. Ltd., Chennai, India

To find out more about our authors and books visit www.bloomsbury.com
and sign up for our newsletters.

*With great honour and love, to my dearest confidant and closest friend,
Natasha Tennant.
And to my charming twins and husband, Saagar Sharma-Hassidim,
Keshet Sharma-Hassidim and Dr. Doron Yosef-Hassidim, who
make the impossible possible.
– Manu Sharma*

In loving memory of my elders – my mentor, Dr. Patrick Solomon, my mom, Thelma Allen and my sister, Olive Whitehead. You paved the way for me. Wish you were here.
– Andrew Allen

I dedicate this book to my wife, Dr. Hala Talballa, and to my daughter, Baian Ibrahim. With unconditional love and gratitude for your patience and continued support. You are humanizing me and for this, I am utterly grateful.
– Awad Ibrahim

Contents

Notes on Contributors		ix
Acknowledgements		xii
Introduction		1
	Manu Sharma	
1	Disruptive Learning Narrative Framework: Understanding Intense and Uncomfortable International Experiences	9
	Manu Sharma, Andrew Allen and Awad Ibrahim	
2	Investigating an International Practicum in Kenya: A Longitudinal Perspective of the Disruptive Learning Narrative	35
	Glenda Black, Rogerio Bernardes and Kevin Wilcox	
3	Transforming Student Imaginaries of Cuba: Disruptive Learning Approaches in Short-Term Study Abroad Programmes	55
	Aaron M. Lampman and Kenneth Schweitzer	
4	Disruptive Learning Narratives: Canada to Kenya Returns	73
	Hermia Anthony and Njoki Wane	
5	Linguistic Discomposure: Disruptive Learning Narratives and Lacan in a Short Study Abroad Programme	91
	Michelle Parkinson	
6	Navigating the Discomfort of International Teaching Placements: Resistance or Flexibility?	117
	Leva Rouhani and Ruth Kane	
7	Helping Future Teachers Negotiate the Paroxysms of Patriotism at Home and Abroad: A Parallax View	139
	Stephen Parliament and Geoffrey Scheurman	
8	International Experiences in the Bahamas: A Tropical Restoration Experience	153
	Kevyn J. Juneau	
9	Winterim in Cuba: Unlearning and Disruptive Moments	175
	Simon A. Akindes	

Conclusion 199
    Manu Sharma

Notes 203
References 205
Index 221

Contributors

Simon A. Akindes is Professor of Political Science and director of International Studies at the University of Wisconsin-Parkside, USA. He publishes on democratization, sociopolitical movements, civil-military relations, and politics in education, popular music and sports. His most recent article is 'Côte d'Ivoire: The Military, Ruling Elites, and Political Power' (2021).

Andrew Allen is Associate Professor of Education at University of Windsor, Canada. He is co-editor, with Patrick Solomon, Jordan Singer, Arlene Campbell and John Portelli, of *Brave New Teachers: Doing Social Justice Work in Neoliberal Times* (2011).

Hermia Anthony is Professor at Centennial College, Canada and Lecturer at the University of Toronto, Canada. Her publications focus on African indigeneity, indigenous knowledge and womanism.

Rogerio Bernardes is a secondary school teacher and Adjunct Professor at Nipissing University, North Bay, Canada. His research interests include critical approaches to intercultural education and physical education.

Glenda Black is Professor of Education at Nipissing University, North Bay, Canada. She is the co-editor with Kurt Clausen of *The Future of Action Research in Education: A Canadian Perspective* (2020).

Awad Ibrahim is Professor of Education at University of Ottawa, Canada. He is the author of *The Rhizome of Blackness: A Critical Ethnography of Hip-Hop Culture, Language, Identity and the Politics of Becoming* (2014).

Kevyn J. Juneau is Assistant Professor of Conservation and Environmental Science at the University of Wisconsin – River Falls, USA. He is the author of multiple scientific articles about invasive species ecology and management.

Ruth Kane is Professor of Education and director of Graduate Studies, Faculty of Education, University of Ottawa, Canada. Her current work includes research and participatory programme evaluation of Northern community-based teacher education in partnership with Inuit.

Aaron M. Lampman is Associate Professor of Anthropology and International Studies at Washington College, USA. He is co-author, with Ken Schweitzer, of

'The Challenge of Dispelling Post-Colonial Tourist Imaginaries of Cuba through Study Abroad' in M. Di Giovine and J. Bodinger (Eds.), *Study Abroad and the Quest for an Anti-Tourism Experience* (2020).

Michelle Parkinson is Professor of English at the University of Wisconsin – River Falls, USA. She is author of a book review of Daniel Juan Gil's *Before Intimacy* for the *Journal of the History of Sexuality* (2011).

Stephen Parliament is Adjunct Faculty in Teacher Education at the University of Wisconsin – River Falls, USA. He is the author of 'Renaissance of Social Studies: Looking Forward' in G. Scheurman and R. Evans (Eds.), *Constructivism and the New Social Studies: A Collection of Guided Inquiry Lessons* (2018).

Leva Rouhani is a part-time professor at the University of Ottawa, Canada. She is the author of multiple articles about gender and development, including *Using Digital Storytelling as a Source of Empowerment for Rural Women* (2019).

Geoffrey Scheurman is Distinguished Teacher and Professor of Teacher Education at the University of Wisconsin – River Falls, USA. He publishes and presents on inquiry-based practice and constructivist teaching and has served on several overseas appointments, including visiting professor in China and Fulbright Roving Scholar of American Studies in Norway.

Kenneth Schweitzer is Associate Professor of Music at Washington College, USA. He is co-author, with Aaron M. Lampman, of 'The Challenge of Dispelling Post-Colonial Tourist Imaginaries of Cuba through Study Abroad' in M. Di Giovine and J. Bodinger (Eds.), *Study Abroad and the Quest for an Anti-Tourism Experience* (2020).

Manu Sharma is Assistant Professor of Education at Thompson Rivers University, Canada; and currently serves as the Human Rights Co-Chair for Thompson Rivers University's Faculty Union. She is co-editor, with Amanda Zbacnik, of *Educators for Diverse Classrooms: A Case Study Approach to Equity and Inclusion in Education* (2020). Her research interests are in social justice, higher education, critical race studies, and educational law.

Njoki Wane is Professor at the University of Toronto, Canada, and is currently serving as the Chair of the Department of Social Justice Education at the Ontario Institute for Studies in Education. Wane's research interests focus on African indigenous education, black feminisms, anti-colonial thought and decolonization. She has authored and co-authored numerous publications, including *Decolonizing the Spirit in Education and Beyond: Resistance and Solidarity* (2019).

Kevin Wilcox is a classroom teacher with the Greater Victoria School District in Canada, holds a Masters of Education from Nipissing University, Canada and is a past instructor at the University of Victoria, Canada. His research interests include critical approaches to intercultural education and the role of technology in universal design for learning.

Acknowledgements

An honourable thanks to my mentor and good friend, Professor John Portelli; he is truly an inspiration in my life!

(Manu Sharma)

Introduction

Manu Sharma

When reflecting on current literature available in the field of international studies, with a focus on understanding the Canadian and American post-secondary students' international narratives while travelling and studying abroad or upon return to their homeland, much of it focuses on 'transformation' (Black & Bernardes, 2014; Corkett & Hatt, 2015; Larsen & Searle, 2017; Mwebi & Brigham, 2009). Often, the process and reasons for transformation are not explained using a critical theoretical framework that draws on an uncomfortable or disruptive experience but rather focus mostly on self-reflection and positive experiences. In light of this, we argue that short-term international educational experiences that are done without a critical intention often become an exotification of international travel, a 'saving the underprivileged' trip, and/or demonstrate a colonial privilege and gaze that recolonize those spaces. We also contend that an international space that requires students to remain deeply immersed in the culture, language, and everyday life as they live there for the duration of the travel is necessary in order to begin these deeper conversations about race, decolonizing, power and privilege.

As a response to some of the challenges presented by the aforementioned literature, the co-editors of this volume hope that the Disruptive Learning Narrative (DLN) framework addresses these critical, mostly colonial, issues. The DLN encourages educators who take their post-secondary students abroad to think through uncomfortable and disruptive experiences by examining and analyzing its three elements (disidentification, dislocation and displacement) and the nature of these in disruptive narratives. For example, we argue that, first, personal experience and narrative can be such fertile grounds for critical theorizing and, second, such intentional and critical experiences are necessary and crucial in helping, especially, white students from Western countries think critically about race (Kovach, 2009; Smith, 1999). Thinking through these experiences abroad helps these students rethink the power differences and inequities faced by racialized people back home, for example, in Canada and the United States.

The current volume provides a range of North American post-secondary critical short-term international experiences that are shared by university instructors who have conducted and facilitated the learning of their students in international settings. It is important to note that the identity formation of the student body and instructor(s) is different in every chapter. This is significant because, based on the identities present, the chapters reveal unique insights into the learnings that emerge after applying what we introduce as the DLN framework.

The DLN is a framework that emerged out of six years of conversation (2014–20) between the co-editors of this volume. The co-editors are all racialized academics who are dedicated towards helping their students to unpack and deconstruct primarily racial tensions in a healthy manner while programmes practice teaching in their study abroad and international service learning. All three co-editors are faculty members who are racialized as Black, African and/or East Indian in society; they call Canada home and have personal experiences with the impact and influence of racial identity markers in Canada and in international spaces.

Using insights from their own lives and the international shared experiences of their post-secondary students who they have taken abroad, they witnessed a need and call to address what the learning that comes from these critical international experiences does for their students when they return to North America. In May's (2006) words, 'we often know what we do and why we are doing it; what we do not know is what our doing it does' (p. 85). In the hopes of gaining insight into this eloquently phrased philosophical question, this collective volume has been formed.

Each contributing author was given the opportunity to read an earlier draft of Chapter 1 from this book, 'Disruptive Learning Narrative Framework: Understanding Intense and Uncomfortable International Experiences', which offers and explains the DLN framework as a theoretical tool to aid in unpacking their students' disruptive and often uncomfortable experiences while participating in a supervised post-secondary international experience abroad. The contributing authors were asked to analyze, critique and add new possible dimensions to the DLN framework, while using it as they saw fit to aid them in thinking through the student narratives or self-narratives (in some cases) that they chose to share. It is important to note that we wished to respect the contributing authors' autonomy in how they wanted to engage with the DLN framework and how much of their positionality they wanted to share in their chapters. As a result, some chapters use some of the key elements in the DLN framework more than others while still engaging with the overall themes of power and privilege. Moreover, each chapter engages with positionality as the individual author wishes; this sometimes means that there is a collapse of racialized or marginalized people into one category and the individualization of the white people, but because the authors' identities are not a mandated part of their chapters, understanding positionality throughout each chapter is complex. Thus, the contributing authors disclose their experiences in a way that make sense to them and their naming of different races and their embodiment is left to them to determine. In what follows, I provide a short overview of each chapter for the ease of our readers.

Chapter 1 (Manu Sharma, Andrew Allen and Awad Ibrahim)

Chapter 1, 'Disruptive Learning Narrative Framework: Understanding Intense and Uncomfortable International Experiences', has three main goals. First, it begins by providing what the authors hope is a deep understanding of what constitutes a critical international experience which challenges the common forms of international travel for service learning, which can be advertised as an exotic trip or mission trip to help save others in less developed and less fortunate regions of the globe. Second, it introduces the DLN framework and its three interdependent and overlapping elements, namely, (1) disidentification, (2) dislocation and (3) displacement. These elements are presented alongside two gestural vignettes based in Tanzania, and are analyzed by the DLN framework as a way to think about DLN as both an epistemic and a methodological framework. Third and finally, this chapter shares that the DLN framework was originally designed for teacher education programmes that had international practicum placements for their students. Over the six years of conversation, however, the co-editors have collectively agreed that this framework can be applicable to a variety of post-secondary international experiences, as it influences, to varying degrees, the professional and personal identities of the students who go abroad. Thus, the following chapters provide insights from a variety of disciplines in post-secondary institutions and international experiences that require different types of learning purposes.

Chapter 2 (Glenda Black, Rogerio Bernardes and Kevin Wilcox)

In Chapter 2, 'Investigating an International Practicum in Kenya: A Longitudinal Perspective of the Disruptive Learning Narrative', the longitudinal effects of a three-week international teaching practicum on teacher candidates in Kenya are examined with the use of the DLN framework. The international teaching practicum was done in conjunction with a non-government organization. The authors argue that while international teaching practicums centre the participant and their future students as benefactors, this approach may be both short term and lacking in scope. Thus, the authors contend that a social justice approach to relations between cultures must directly address the processes involved in othering, and interrogate how any programme or exchange encourages the recognition of critical aspects of power relations. In their concluding remarks, the co-authors offer a new element to be added to the DLN framework, namely, *interdependence*, which pursues action from the experience founded upon the praxis in the Canadian setting *and* in the international setting.

Chapter 3 (Aaron M. Lampman and Kenneth Schweitzer)

Chapter 3, 'Transforming Student Imaginaries of Cuba: Disruptive Learning Approaches in Short-Term Study Abroad Programmes', examines American post-secondary students who participate in a short-term study abroad programme to Cuba. The authors use the DLN framework to explore how student imaginaries are challenged and transformed through pedagogy designed to cultivate reflexive and critical thinking. They argue, based on the guided discussion they have witnessed and writing assignments they have received, that uncomfortable cultural and spatial *dislocation* encourages critical self-reflection about hidden and unconscious social norms. As a result of the analysis of their experiences with students abroad, the authors conclude that the DLN can be extended to explore how pre-existing imaginaries, including stereotypes and prejudice, are transformed through experiential learning in the study abroad context.

Chapter 4 (Hermia Anthony and Njoki Wane)

Chapter 4, 'Disruptive Learning Narratives: Canada to Kenya Returns', offers a different insight as it reports on the international experiences of four racialized students from a Canadian university who visited Kenya to participate as learners in cultural immersion, academic conferences, school visits and excursions. This chapter offers a decolonial lens on what can be understood as the miseducation of Africa in Canada (Smith, 1999; wa Thiong'o, 1992). Four narratives, when analyzed with the DLN framework, demonstrate a temporary disidentification, a strong dislocation when returning to Canada and a possible sense of displacement when considering the understanding of spirituality gained from travelling to Kenya. The striking insight is how the international experience itself in Kenya had a limited disruptive impact; yet it created the space for a silent catalyst upon the racialized students while in Kenya. As a result, the main disruption came in the form of dislocation in relation to other racialized bodies when these students returned to Canada. The authors conclude that a sense of unification, spiritual connection and appreciation for an accurate understanding of the wealth of knowledge, people and culture in Africa was brought back to Canada, and mobilized a unity amongst Black people in a positive manner.

Chapter 5 (Michelle Parkinson)

Chapter 5, 'Linguistic Discomposure: Disruptive Learning Narratives and Lacan in a Short Study Abroad Programme', examines a five-week study abroad programme done in 2016 and 2018 that took place in London, Paris, Berlin and Prague, respectively. The author shares an analysis of her students' experiences as Americans in European countries. She chooses to use the DLN framework to frame the unique situation of this international study and what it does at the macro level of power, privilege, race, ethnicity and identity. She also uses Lacan's (2006) work alongside the DLN to illuminate the micro-level linguistic changes and struggles that DLN entails. One of the central disruptive narrative themes she shares in this chapter pertains to linguistic disidentification. The author contends that Lacan's theory about the entry into language and his notion that it occurs continually throughout an individual's life can usefully extend this volume editors' DLN framework regarding its contribution to disidentification, dislocation and displacement.

Chapter 6 (Leva Rouhani and Ruth Kane)

Chapter 6, 'Navigating the Discomfort of International Teaching Placements: Resistance or Flexibility?', offers narratives of Canadian students who travelled to Uganda with their university instructor to participate in a teacher education programme. When these narratives are analyzed with the DLN framework, they demonstrate resistance to conforming to local teaching contexts of Uganda and illustrate the implications of pursing their own pedagogy in the host communities. The teacher candidates, as depicted in these narratives, did have intense uncomfortable experiences, but rather than these leading to disidentification, dislocation and displacement, some teacher candidates drew on their discomfort to reinforce their allegiance to Canadian norms and values. Thus, the authors contend that while international service learning placements can help teacher candidates build their competencies to support diverse classrooms, one of the challenges of building these competencies is that the short duration of the placements does not permit teacher candidates to break through power dynamics that govern their relationships with local schools and teachers. Moreover, the authors conclude that because of the significant consequences of these unintended outcomes on local host communities, it is important to take note of the unintended programme outcomes, in addition to those outcomes promoted in the goals of international placement.

Chapter 7 (Stephen Parliament and Geoffrey Scheurman)

In Chapter 7, 'Helping Future Teachers Negotiate the Paroxysms of Patriotism at Home and Abroad: A Parallax View', the authors draw on what they term a parallax experience for students, in which personal growth is dependent on dialogue between incommensurable perspectives (Žižek, 2009). They share a number of student-based narratives in both China and Ecuador, as well as the narratives of themselves as instructors who have travelled to different parts of the world. They argue that as their teacher candidates tried to make sense of their experiences, the result was a disadaptation or a maladaptation of the subject to his or her environs, an outcome that they incorporate into the DLN framework. After using the DLN framework to analyze the students' narratives and their own narratives, the authors find that there is evidence of 'patriotic paroxysms' – immediate explosions or expressions of emotion created by one's sense of national identity – while living and teaching in foreign cultures

(Scheurman & Parliament, 2018). The authors conclude that it is not until teacher educators use the DLN framework to analyze their own intense and uncomfortable experiences that they are able to deeply analyze the disruptive learning that lies beneath the international vignettes of teacher candidates. Finally, the authors claim that a parallax view of teaching is the philosophical basis of inquiry that is necessary and critical to learning, whether overseas or in their local context.

Chapter 8 (Kevyn J. Juneau)

In Chapter 8, 'International Experiences in the Bahamas: A Tropical Restoration Experience', the author provides a rich historical context for a two-week course he supervised, created and led in Andros Island in the Bahamas for his students. The author gives attention and acknowledgement to the political history and racial positionality of students and himself as instructor. As a result, the author shares that, when creating this course, he wished to develop an ecological restoration course in a tropical or subtropical biome, but was mindful not to take a 'white saviour' mentality or a colonial approach to address these environmental issues. The author shares two main experiences: one that occurred during a particular visit to a community in Andros Island, and the other as an ongoing disruptive experience and unease with the daily living quarters that the students slept in. After reflecting on the DLN framework and his overall thoughts on the course, he shares that it is essential for instructors who take students abroad to resist the temptation of viewing communities and people through the lens of a tourist, as this would help avoid the exploitation of marginalized groups of people.

Chapter 9 (Simon A. Akindes)

In Chapter 9, 'Winterim in Cuba: Unlearning and Disruptive Moments', the author describes his experience of taking a group of students to complete a course in Cuba with a particular visit to Santiago. He explains that the purpose of the trip with respect to the course was to study what they could in twelve days (16–28 January 2019), by seeing Cuba, listening to Cuba and experiencing Cuba. The chapter shares reflections that provide a deeper insight into the intricate political history between Cuba and the United States and how that impacted student interactions with local people, as well as what social justice issues Cuba is still working through. The author presents multiple narratives and shares how they enter into the dialogic space of the three different elements in the DLN framework. He draws on the assignments that his students completed for him during this course; in particular he uses students' texts provided in their final projects, writing assignments, podcasts and movies. After a thorough examination and analysis of the narratives, the author explains that the learning from this course can be seen as a string of 'accidents' and 'moments' with possible short- or long-term implications. Moreover, he claims that this learning can have a disruptive nature, which presents as an upsetting and emotionally charged experience that can be a precursor to powerful self-reflections and new behaviours. In addition to these disruptive learning opportunities, he shares that a comforting experience could also lead to transformation in oneself; so he adds that it is important to acknowledge the positive experiences as well.

Thus, it is with this collection of eight contributing chapters using the DLN framework as described and explained in Chapter 1 of this volume that the significance and importance of this new theoretical framework becomes evident. The thoughtfulness and sincerity of each of the contributors to this volume helped provide new insights into the DLN framework. The fact that every contributing chapter and its author(s) articulate their own interpretations of any narratives they experienced themselves, or that of their students, makes this theoretical framework adaptable to different models of international post-secondary experiences that are often created and offered by public institutions in North America. In closing, this collective volume demonstrates critical reflection on how the context of constructing the international experience, the identities of the students and instructor(s), the historical context of the international country and the home country to which students and instructor(s) return to, and the importance of recognizing the varying degrees to which different students and instructors are impacted by each of the three elements of the DLN framework (disidentification, dislocation and displacement) helps give insight and meaning to May's (2006) statement of 'what we do not know is what our doing it does.'

1

Disruptive Learning Narrative Framework: Understanding Intense and Uncomfortable International Experiences

Manu Sharma, Andrew Allen and Awad Ibrahim

What happens when professors take teacher candidates to an international teaching placement, such as Tanzania, for their pre-service teacher education practicum? Moreover, how do the teacher candidates and the professors understand their lived experiences abroad? Theoretical in nature, the aim of this chapter is to answer these questions by proposing a theoretical framework, which we are calling the Disruptive Learning Narrative (DLN). The DLN is built on three overlapping elements: disidentification, dislocation and displacement. These three elements emerged as a pattern from years of observations and listening to stories and reflections shared by teacher candidates with respect to the international practicum. We show how the DLN enables us to gain insights on what happens to teacher candidates' understanding of what it means to be in a position of dominance or marginality. While unpacking the DLN, we also present two of our own brief and unique faculty supervisor narratives to exemplify how the DLN framework works. We acknowledge that the DLN framework would be very useful to other professors in the field of teacher education and to professors who take students to international settings to do experiential work. We conclude that the DLN framework helps expand, complicate and deepen the process of understanding the students' experiences in international placements.

In teacher education programmes, it seems, there is a growing trend to offer international practicum placements (Crabtree et al., 2014; Malewski & Phillion, 2009). Pence and Macgillivray (2008) explain, in addition to attracting and recruiting new students to their regular programmes, teacher education programmes are increasingly seeking these international opportunities as these are valuable for teacher candidates and provide a space for personal growth through multiple interactions with new and unfamiliar contexts (cf. Quezada, 2004; Willard-Holt, 2001). Although exposures to other cultures are beneficial, in this chapter, we argue that an international placement which challenges a student's level of comfort, and requires that they robustly engage with a different culture and ways of being, challenges their disposition of power or marginality in a new space, and would thereby provide a greater opportunity for growth and learning.

In particular, the international context we have in mind goes beyond volunteering and a 'feel good' experience, as it provides the dimension of waking up and staying immersed in a reality that is estranged for all our teacher candidates. Consequently, the resulting experience is intensified in such a way that cannot be replicated to the same extent at a local (Canadian) level or a 'voluntourism' experience abroad (Bailey & Fernando, 2011). As a result, the intense experiences that often arise out of such critical international experiences, as described above, are the ones to which the DLN is most applicable and helpful.

To that end, in this chapter we share two of our brief teacher educators' vignettes. Both of these vignettes are based in an international setting, while teaching abroad in Tanzania, where our teacher candidates grappled with discomfort around their identity and the new power dynamics. In retrospect, we use the DLN framework to analyse both of these narratives based on our observations of our teacher candidates in the hope of unpacking an understanding of their intense, disruptive and uncomfortable experience. It is important to note, although we examine the international experiences abroad through the field of teacher education using the DLN, this framework is applicable to all international experiences that promote a critical and experiential learning opportunity.

Disruptive Learning Narrative: A Theoretical Framework

The DLN is a theoretical framework that we have developed out of an urge to understand and seek clarity about intense and uncomfortable international experiences. These uncomfortable experiences are unique because they often challenge the core value systems and traditional ways of thinking for students. When we started reviewing observations of our teacher candidates prior to, during and after their international experience in Tanzania, these reflections provided new insights that were powerful in making sense of the conflicts and tensions in their international placement and how these later impacted their perceptions of what it means to be a teacher.

Upon a closer examination of our teacher candidates' reflections, we noticed there was a high level of emotional and cognitive dissonance. This dissonance made us, as teacher educators, curious to investigate what was underlying these deep personal conflicts in our students' experiences. Most, if not all, of our teacher candidates' narratives became 'counternarratives' that brought up unexpected topics and categories of race that rarely get discussed in teacher education programmes. As a result, we identified three common elements in all of the counternarratives that we witnessed and learned about while in Tanzania. It is in each of these counternarratives that we find three elements which make up the DLN framework, namely, (1) disidentification, (2) dislocation and (3) displacement. We explore the DLN framework to further deepen the critical analysis of our observations of the consciousness of our Canadian teacher candidates upon reflecting on their international placement experiences.

Methodologically, we as teacher educators use observations of teacher candidates' experiences as we present attempts to discern their interactions in their international practicum placement. We use a narrative research methodology (Clandinin & Connelly, 2000). This methodology is also known as narrative inquiry, and captures personal and human dimensions of an experience over time, thus assessing the relationship between personal experience and cultural context. For Creswell (2014), narrative research is a design of inquiry in which the researcher(s) studies the lives of individuals and this account is retold and storied by the researcher(s). For the purposes of this chapter, we use only two brief narratives of a larger data collection based on interviews and journaling of multiple trips to Tanzania. Since the international teaching placement initiative upon which this chapter is based on was started in 2008, we have accumulated a great deal of research data and narratives. In light of the history of this initiative in Tanzania, we would like to provide an overview of how teaching practica were created as learning opportunities.

Origins of the International Practicum Placement Initiative

The idea for the international teaching placement initiative originated in 2008 out of an application for a large research grant in Tanzania involving Dr. Grace Puja from a university in Tanzania and four faculty colleagues from a university in Canada – Drs. Nombuso Dlamini, Clinton Beckford, Chris Clovis and Andrew Allen. While travelling across Tanzania and visiting schools, the Canadian faculty members explored the condition of the schools and learned of the local students' passion for education. As colleagues, they were particularly moved by their experience of visiting a group of forty-five children who lived at a small centre for orphaned and vulnerable children in a rural community in central Tanzania. When they asked the children at the centre to list their needs, they asked for assistance with food, tutoring, textbooks, school supplies, school uniforms and school shoes. Consequently, the vision of the initiative to implement an international teaching placement grew out of a desire of the Canadian faculty to do more and to help support children at the centre. The children at the centre identified very basic human needs of food, water, shelter and clothing that they needed support in receiving. Thus, originally the initiative to take teacher candidates to Tanzania had two foci: (1) to practice teach in local schools in Tanzania and (2) to work with the children at the centre for orphaned and vulnerable children by helping to provide for their basic human needs.

Contextualizing the Community Placement and the Centre for Orphaned and Vulnerable Children

To understand the context of the work that was done by the initiative in Tanzania, it is important to understand the Tanzanian land and its people, the community where the centre for orphaned and vulnerable children is located, and where we take teacher candidates to practice teach in the local schools. The country of Tanzania is divided into thirty-one regions. The particular region of Tanzania that we visited (and continue to visit annually) is located in a remote rural area, making it mainly a vulnerable community within Tanzania itself because of its isolation. The children at the centre live just outside a small town with a population of less than two hundred thousand. The surrounding community is mostly poor and under-resourced. Three of the four schools that the teacher candidates teach at have no running water or electricity and the buildings are in need of repair. The schools lack basic teaching and learning supplies and the students consistently perform poorly on the national exams each year. Most of the elementary school classrooms consist of rows of wooden benches with a chalkboard and can have as much as up to eighty or a hundred students in each class. The centre for orphaned children is equally in need of repair with respect to its physical infrastructure and daily resources.

International Teaching Placement Initiative in a Teacher Education Programme

With a respectful disposition towards learning and working with a diverse community, this initiative is promoted among incoming teacher candidates at a Canadian university at the beginning of each academic year. Over the years, since 2008, a group of alumni teacher candidates who have travelled to Tanzania stay involved to provide information sessions on what the international teaching placement initiative is about and what can be expected in terms of preparing for the placement. The alumni often make it clear that the trip is a working placement that continues to serve and work with the local community members in Tanzania. They also emphasize that teacher candidates must pay for their own travel, accommodations and food while in Tanzania. The alumni took the lead in helping with several fundraising events to raise funds and collect items to take to Tanzania strictly for the use of the needs of local Tanzanian children.

In addition, in order to be involved in this international placement, each teacher candidate submits a resume and a cover letter stating why they should and would like to be a part of this alternative international teaching placement. After the alumni and faculty supervisors (Manu Sharma and Andrew Allen in 2014) screen the resumes and cover letters, interviews are set up with the chosen teacher candidates. The interviews are 45 minutes in length and have semi-structured questions that the teacher candidates answer. After the interviews, the faculty supervisors and alumni discuss the applicant's strengths and suitability for this particular initiative. Finally, we offer the teacher candidates the opportunity to participate in the initiative if they pass the application and interview screening. It is important to note that this international teaching placement is in addition to their required Canadian teaching placements that would have already been completed, thus allowing for a local and international perspective on practicum experiences.

Details of Teacher Candidates' Activities in Their Placement in Tanzania

Once in Tanzania, the team of teacher candidates and faculty members stayed at a local hotel in the community that was able to accommodate the group. The local government provided a small bus to transport the group to and from the schools and the centre. On the ground, in Tanzania, teacher candidates taught for most of the day on all weekdays. They were placed in pairs per classroom, either at two elementary schools or three secondary schools that the children attended near the centre, and asked to collaborate with the local teachers. After school and on weekends, throughout the international placement, teacher candidates worked at the centre for orphaned children. They were divided into four teams: food and nutrition, health and well-being, education and construction/renovation. Each teacher candidate assisted in one of these groups to ensure that the needs of the children at the centre were being met. Each day, teacher candidate groups would go to the market to buy food, take children to the hospital for check-ups and treatment, buy textbooks and school supplies at the market, and engage with local contractors to renovate and refurbish the centre's buildings.

Each year, groups of between eight and twenty-seven teacher candidates have been involved in several projects, such as building a water tower, fixing the water harvesting system, creating a vegetable garden, buying livestock, building enclosures for chickens, cows, and goats, and so forth. Generally, upon arrival at the centre, teacher candidate groups are asked to inspect the site and speak with the caregivers to perform their own needs assessment of the children and the centre. To carry out tasks that are identified by the needs assessment of the site, the teacher candidates were divided into the aforementioned four teams and were expected to engage and collaborate with local community members to help ensure the sustainability and feasibility of the tasks.

In addition to working in these four teams, teacher candidates provided tutoring for the children at the centre to help develop their English language skills, help with homework, and engage in sports and recreational activities. After leaving the small rural community close to the orphaned children, the teacher candidates would co-teach with teachers at a privately funded American school for Maasai children in another region of Tanzania. Thus, given all that was expected of teacher candidates in this international placement, it is not surprising that our teacher candidates ended up developing very strong caring relationships with the children – especially since they take on a parental and an advocate's role that moves beyond their role as simply 'teachers' and as they attempted to meet the basic needs of the children.

We acknowledge here that attempting to do any kind of relief work on the continent of Africa by bringing Canadian student teachers opens us up to the critique of reinscribing the dominance of the West in coming to save the people of the 'dark continent'. However, Robin Crabtree (2007), in pointing out the potential negative impact international service learning programmes can have on communities or countries, reminds us to also look at the tangible manifestations of the material and spiritual impact we have had in Tanzania. For example, the local principals of the school where we teach tell us that the school attendance increases dramatically once we arrive in the community and many students continue to attend afterwards. We continue to receive messages even today from former students in Tanzania who thank us for our tutoring and for helping them with their homework and to let us know what they have accomplished educationally. It is not uncommon for the so-called orphaned children at the centre to run up to us when we arrive every year to show us their report cards. In addition, we have provided immediate and well-needed medical attention for several children as well as have improved the living conditions for the children at the centre. The work that we have done has inspired others in the community, including alumni of the centre, to begin to take up that work themselves and to want to help other orphaned and vulnerable children in Tanzania.

Furthermore, Crabtree believes that one way to help to mitigate the past colonial or neocolonial legacy of dependency on foreign aid is to partner and collaborate with grassroots organizations. She says that these organizations can best determine local needs and help design sustainable participatory development projects aimed at capacity development, self-reliance and knowledge sharing. In this way, the purpose of the work that we do in Tanzania is to eventually exclude ourselves and to have the locals sustain practices and initiatives that we may have started with them, but ultimately have them decide whether they wish to maintain these themselves locally. We help build this bridge between local sustainability efforts by working with various community organizations and we have hired local contractors and purchased local supplies for renovating the centre. Moreover, instead of bringing school supplies and shoes/clothing with us from Canada, we purchase those items from local shops to support local businesses and to help create a local connection between the children we work with and these local business partners. These are just a few of the ways that we have reconceptualized our work over the years on the ground in Tanzania.

Team 2014 in Tanzania

In the team of teacher candidates that went to Tanzania in April 2014, there were four racialized males and three racialized females and eleven white female teacher candidates in our group. We as the teacher educators (Manu Sharma and Andrew Allen) self-identify as a racialized female and a racialized male. Beyond our racial composition as a group, it was important to note that within our racialized teacher candidates, five of them identified as Muslims. It is important to note that Islam and Christianity are the two main religions in Tanzania. In addition, teacher candidates' race, language and religious identification had an (un)conscious impact on their interactions with local Tanzanian community members. For example, our Muslim students who are also racialized (either of African descent, or originating from the Indian subcontinent as well as the Middle East), expressed feeling very comfortable in Tanzania and they participated in local religious observances like Jumaa and went to the mosque for Friday prayers with some of the children at the centre. It is important to acknowledge that although Canadian racialized bodies are read differently by local Tanzanians (as being privileged), there was a strong desire for a connection with locals that our Canadian racialized students felt was unlike anything they felt in Canada amongst other racialized bodies. We believe this is worthy of noting in the discourse on race in different global contexts because we observed how all our racialized students in particular made extra efforts to learn the words and phrases of the local Kiswahili language to endear themselves to the local people and how they would often enthusiastically greet them with hugs, extended handshakes and fist bumps.

Having said that, we have intentionally collapsed the racial identities of our students into two categories of racialized and white teacher candidates because of the tendency of the students themselves to form into these two groups during their personal time and in the informal spaces on the ground in Tanzania (such as at dinner or on the bus), and we noticed that the general themes of the students' responses and reflections emerged out of these two categories. In addition, we never intentionally asked our teacher candidates to identify themselves racially during the whole programme. However, we noticed that those teacher candidates who we believed as having a background from places such as India, the Middle East or from the Arab world seemed to share experiences of and reflections on Tanzania that were similar to those of our Black students on the trip. This is not to say that all our racialized students or even our Black students somehow fully understand what their racialized or Black bodies mean on the continent once they are in Tanzania. The ideas presented in this book are a way of making sense of our student teachers' experiences of going to Tanzania and being in a situation where race or being racialized is intensely more salient than what they are used to back in Canada.

We are also aware that although other racialized and Black students can enact anti-Black racism and attitudes, we simply have not observed any of those attitudes or incidents during these trips to Tanzania. Moreover, as the vignettes will demonstrate, the conversations and reflections that happened with either our racialized or white students were quite different from each other. At the same time, we wonder how often these same group-specific personal conversations happened on campus back in Canada because of the low number of Black and other racialized teacher candidates. We only became more aware of these conversations because we were in Tanzania and we found that apart from race being salient, as faculty instructors ourselves, we were in students' spaces because we travelled, ate, taught and worked all day together as a large group.

In light of this contextualization of the participants, ourselves and the placement, there were a number of variables at play for disrupting the normativity of what would be taken-for-granted or common-sense knowledge in Canada. To be precise, by Canadian common sense knowledge we mean values and behaviours which are held by white middle-class families who are Christian and hold the dominant position of power, in contrast to racialized, non-Christian, and working-class people. As teacher educators who are curious about the learning process of teacher candidates with diverse students, we asked the following questions: In what ways are identity factors such as but not limited to race, religion, language, and ethnicity addressed in this intense cross-cultural experience by different groups of teacher candidates? How can we make sense of the tensions and dissonance experienced by teacher candidates? How do these experiences impact the teacher candidates in their future classrooms full of diverse learners? To better grapple with these questions, in the next section, we share two brief illustrative vignettes that emerged from the April 2014 international teaching placement experience. After sharing these vignettes, we will explain the three elements in the DLN framework as they pertain to each of the vignettes, with the hope of demonstrating the usefulness of this framework to provide insights into such narratives.

Observations and Two Illustrative Vignettes

As mentioned above, we have noticed over several years of taking teacher candidate teams to Tanzania that both our collective groups of racialized teacher candidates and white teacher candidates tend to form two separate subgroups based on their racial identity make-up. As a result, when the teacher candidates were working, teaching and eating, they often generally sat in these two groupings. For decades now, teacher education programmes in Canada tend to consist of predominantly white and middle-class teacher candidates (Solomon, 1997) and, from our observations, that is still reflected in our programmes. Consequently, we have noticed that it is not uncommon in our teacher education programmes for Black and other racialized teacher candidates to form these two groups because of the relatively few Black or other racialized students within our faculty of education.

An example of this group dynamic occurred upon arrival in Tanzania where we observed two racialized teacher candidates taunting their white peers. They shared exaggerated accounts of spontaneous wild animal attacks while in Tanzania. They were apparently drawing upon the stereotypical 'exotification' of (East) Africa, which some of the young white females may have been exposed to, based on what knowledge is shared about East Africa in Canada. For example, one white teacher candidate reported that she was afraid to sleep and stayed up all night on the first night because she believed she heard animals outside her window.

These observations set the tone for the narratives that we also witnessed. To better contextualize the vignettes that follow, it is worth noting that the whole delegation, including us as teacher educators, made sure we at least had one meal together. The shared meal took place at dinner time. This shared eating time was also used as a working meal, during which we went over the happenings of the day, reports from project teams and the activities for the following day.

Anchoring the Vignettes in the Disruptive Learning Narrative Framework: Take II

We acknowledge that the two illustrative vignettes below, which came from our own notes, are not exhaustive vignettes nor are they 'thick descriptions', but rather they are intentionally gestural. Our objective behind citing them is simply to anchor our analysis using the DLN framework, and for our reader to imaginatively 'see' how useful the DLN framework can be. Thus, keeping these vignettes in mind, in what follows, we will provide an insight and analysis of Vignette 1 and Vignette 2 using the DLN framework. We will deconstruct each vignette in relation to the three elements of the DLN framework, namely disidentification, dislocation and displacement. The three elements are informed by Britzman's (2012) work on teacher identity, Foucault's (1986)

> ## Illustrative Vignettes: Take I
>
> #1. At one of our nightly group meetings, a racialized male teacher candidate suggested that '[Our regular taxi driver] today said that a Mzungu [Kiswahili for white (Caucasian) person or person of European descent] should not go shopping in the market anymore, because they caused a commotion and they are unable to bargain for the best prices'. In response, a white female teacher candidate who had gone to the market that day to buy food for the children suddenly got up and ran out of the room in tears.
>
> #2. A small group of our teacher candidates (predominantly white females) were having a discussion during the first few days in Tanzania. While watching this small group, we saw one of the racialized Black males walk away in protest from the group of white teacher candidates. We were surprised when we heard him say, 'How come you never spoke to me all year at the university and now that we are in Tanzania, you are complaining that I don't sit next to you or talk to you?'

work on heterotopias, and also consider Sigmund Freud (1955) and Anna Freud's (1974) approach to displacement theory. As a result of the analysis of the vignettes, we argue that the DLN framework helps us understand and explore how this placement impacted and possibly enriched or complicated teacher candidates' understanding of personal identity and, thus, in turn their teacher identity.

Disruptive Learning Narrative Framework
Element One: Disidentification

Britzman (2012) describes the most provocative question in all of educational research by Willard Waller as 'What does teaching do to teachers?' In relation to teacher candidates, she asks further, 'What does learning to teach do and mean to student teachers and those involved in the practice of teaching?' In the following paragraphs, we build on these two questions by Waller and Britzman to ask more specifically, 'What does learning to teach in this particular international practicum placement do to our teacher candidates?' Britzman claims that such questions open up the underside or vulnerabilities of teaching, the personal and private struggles as teachers construct their teaching practices, and their own teaching voices and teacher identities. For teacher candidates especially, the issues are made even more complex as the practicum placement is where they first confront the multiple meanings, constraints and possibilities in the process of constructing their own teacher identities (Britzman, 2012). Immersing them in an international setting, and particularly one that poses such a great contrast to what they are used to as Canadian teacher candidates, induces great discomfort. Both the teacher candidates' personal and professional teacher identities are continually being reshaped as they attempt to identify with the unfamiliar teaching environment in Tanzania. Issues of race and poverty, and power and marginality in teaching, are unavoidable; they underpin all aspects of teaching and learning in this context. Therefore, disidentification through the DLN framework is also concerned with how these issues move to the foreground of the consciousness for our teacher candidates and how they attempt to make sense of or identify with the unfamiliar.

We argue that teacher candidates' experiences in Tanzania cause them to disidentify within the new cultural and social norms of Tanzania or to dissociate themselves from their customary or familiar identities in Canada. We are proposing the term *disidentification* to refer to the process of becoming either increasingly or dramatically less identified with one's own familiar social and cultural norms. Through this disidentification process, teacher candidates lose or are unable to identify several familiar frames of reference in Tanzania, and they experience dissonance and tensions in trying to make sense of their experiences. In such cases, teacher candidates are forced to reframe, recast and/or reconstruct their own identities in relation to their new and unfamiliar surroundings and the ways in which they are being perceived differently in Tanzania.

For example, the norms and familiar ways of identification are challenged for both racialized and white teacher candidates in the context of Tanzania, where the majority of the people they see around them are racialized as Black and African. Consequently, race and racial identity are taken up very differently by the group in Tanzania, and particularly as teacher candidates who are in the unfamiliar context of Tanzania. Teaching is a dialogic process and thus teacher candidates are being shaped by their teaching (and, by extension, their learning to teach) as they shape their identity as a teacher. Britzman identifies several dialogic discourses and tensions between knowing and being, thought and action, theory and practice, knowledge and experience, the technical and the existential, the objective and the subjective as important to learning to teach (Britzman, 2012).

Within the cohort group of teacher candidates in Tanzania, Britzman's dialogic discourses and tensions were both collectively and individually experienced. We noticed moments of disidentification within the group through various interactions amongst different team members, particularly with respect to race-based issues as seen in Vignettes 1 and 2. In addition, what Maxine Greene (1984) in Britzman's work calls 'the immediacy of the felt encounter' resonated with the teacher candidates in Tanzania (p. 26). The 'immediacy' magnified the process of disidentification, making teacher candidates even more aware of their own discomforts. Furthermore, there is a resulting 'double consciousness' (Britzman, 2012) of the new emerging identity, which is being superimposed over the familiar. The process of disidentification is deeply personal and is experienced differently for each teacher candidate. Before teacher candidates leave Canada, they bring their own meanings, perceptions and notions of being, and teaching, on the continent of Africa for the very first time. Regardless of their backgrounds, teacher candidates find that these pretravel beliefs and values are challenged, questioned or even contested upon actually being in Tanzania, and the felt encounter in the new culture is nothing like what they expected.

For example, as briefly mentioned previously, teacher candidates often bring with them stereotypical perceptions of 'Africa' based on very persistent and pervasive media images of a place that is diseased, dangerous, uncivilized and overrun by wildlife. They express surprise when we land at an international airport, stay at a hotel equipped with Wi-Fi and travel within our first city in Tanzania to do banking and go to a restaurant. It is at this initial contact on arriving in Tanzania that the felt encounter of being in Africa presents the starkest contrast with everything they originally believed that they knew about Tanzania. In order to cope with this cognitive dissonance and tensions caused by their experiences in the whole international placement, we argue that a new consciousness or teacher identity emerges for teacher candidates, which can manifest itself in different ways. For example, as seen from Vignette 1, our white teacher candidates sometimes experience discomfort when race is mentioned. We also find that white teacher candidates often feel discomfort when engaging with issues of race for the first time in Tanzania. As a result, they experience disidentification when race comes up in any conversation. In other words, it is easier for race to be either taken for granted or ignored in our seminar courses and practicum placements in Canada. However, in

Tanzania, issues of race are unavoidable because our white Canadian students are put into an unfamiliar minority position in which they are confronted by issues of race and power in this new positional dynamic. Thus, in moments when race is brought up in conversations, it can be painful and very difficult for teacher candidates who previously are used to (un)consciously avoiding discussions about race.

What adds to the complexity about conversations regarding race in Tanzania is that the perception of race is a powerful class marker. This is because most whites or European people are seen to be tourists or foreign nationals who (unlike the locals) are assumed to have power and privilege. Consequently, even though our teacher candidates felt discomfort in their daily interactions in the local community (e.g. buying groceries or asking for directions), due to a lack of language or social and cultural capital, there was a competing complexity of how their race was perceived by local Tanzanian people. Tanzanian perceptions of whites in Tanzania are based mostly on the tourists they see and on the images of the West through the distorted window of the media. It is not uncommon for Tanzanians to talk openly about race as a statement of fact. As a result, when whiteness and its privilege is named or even implied, it becomes a source of discomfort as it conflicts with the values and sensibilities of visiting Canadians who tend not to talk about race and are less comfortable discussing the privileges that race affords them.

At its most powerful impact, disidentification also involves teacher candidates trying to imagine their own reflections of themselves held up against the distorted window of the media-based perceptions of the local Tanzanians. We have seen a number of occasions where our teacher candidates have strongly defended themselves against the perception that they are all wealthy, wasteful, live in big houses and so forth. We chose to use Vignette 1 in our analysis because of several reasons. First, we felt that this story best exemplified how all three aspects of the DLN framework operated within our group of students. We see here how issues were initially ignored or avoided until race and, by extension, privilege were named and located for the first time in conversation in the group. We also see how the utterance of naming race opened up feelings of white fragility and white guilt. We also believe that utterance became a watershed moment for the group as it brought out those previous in-group conversations out into the open in the large group. We argue here that DLN has to be named, located, identified and discussed as a way of helping our students to make sense of their experiences in Tanzania.

Vignette 2, on the other hand, raises some other interesting questions about the consequences of the silence or lack of discussions about race back in our Canadian teacher education programme. This experience in Tanzania created the space and the context for difficult conversations about race or racial identity and the tensions it created between teacher candidates that were unlikely to happen in Canada. In other words, several inequities and tensions related to racial identity go unsaid and unnoticed in our domestic practicum placement as there is no space for them, but in an international teaching placement that forces these issues and tensions around racial identity to come to the surface, they cannot be ignored.

In Vignette 2, the Black teacher candidate became more acutely aware of the social norms in the Canadian teacher education programme. We argue that because of this teacher candidate's experience with disidentification in Tanzania, in contrast to what he experienced in Canada, he was able to find the courage to speak up, to identify and express how he felt. He was empowered by the racial dissonance to state and question why he was being treated differently in both contexts. As a result, this international teaching placement provides a rare but valuable experience that allows teacher educators to shed more light on teacher candidates' emerging identities as they engage in this intense level of the unfamiliar.

Thus, we understand disidentification as an element in the DLN in the international practicum placement because of the way in which teacher candidates disidentify from their familiar Canadian social and cultural norms. This element of the DLN leads to the opening up of missing discussions about race in our teacher education programme. The experiences and vignettes of teacher candidates are far more nuanced through the DLN and, as constructivist teacher educators, we see the moments of dissonance and tensions as key teaching and learning opportunities.

Disidentification in the DLN framework disrupts or brings forth a contrast to the familiar as part of the counter-vignettes of teacher candidates developing personally and professionally as teachers. It is the shifting between the familiar and the unfamiliar, and the identification and disidentification, which promotes the emergence of new learnings for teacher candidates about themselves as new teachers. Thus, it is the analytical writing or reflective sharing of these vignettes, which use the DLN framework, that provide insightful learning opportunities for teacher educators, teachers and teacher candidates around issues of racial identity and its privilege. Yet, we also argue that disidentification only represents one element of the DLN framework and the next two sections provide the other two elements that are often present in such international experiences.

Disruptive Learning Network Framework Element Two: Dislocation

Another element in the DLN framework is dislocation as it relates to teacher candidates' change in physical location and how they locate themselves within the group dynamics while staying in Tanzania. The concept of dislocation is helpful in guiding teacher educators and helping teacher candidates to reflect on their teacher identities with respect to how the geographical location impacts them. The complexity involved with the geographical shift is in understanding dislocation, with respect to how power moves within and across people on an individual and group level in the new geographical space. We need to consider two forms of dislocation: (1) a physical geographical dislocation (e.g. from Canada to East Africa) and (2) dislocation within a group dynamic (e.g. from a group leader role to becoming a submissive participant). Both of these forms of dislocation create a shift in power relations; in the first form when geographical locations are considered, social privileging emerges based on race with respect to the context of the vignettes mentioned earlier in this chapter.

The first form of dislocation acknowledges the geographical change, which immediately changes what is normative in terms of racial identity and its connection to social and cultural capital. In Tanzania the large majority of people are Black and only a few are very wealthy, whereas in Canada the majority of people who are wealthy are white. As mentioned earlier, white people in Tanzania are seen mostly as travellers of European descent and denote a sign of wealth, as it is understood that they are there to visit and travel. It is important to note that racialized people who travel to Tanzania are also seen to be privileged, in terms of socio-economic background and having the means to travel, and are viewed through a colonial lens. However, some common identity markers with the people in Tanzania based on race, culture, religion and ethnicity created a welcome social opportunity to build local connections. This small but reassuring connection allowed for racialized teacher candidates to assume greater social cultural capital in contrast to their white teacher candidate peers. As a result, racialized teacher candidates used this social capital that put them in better alignment with the local Tanzanians to feel empowered to make decisions and to take up a leadership role amongst their white teacher candidate peers. Thus, there is a complex role of understanding how race and other identity markers impact the power dynamics amidst the teacher candidates in the international setting of Tanzania.

The second form of dislocation calls for a more intimate and subtle level of power shifting, as it is embedded in social interactions within the group dynamic of the teacher candidates, which can be generally classified into two groups as either racialized teacher candidates and white teacher candidates. Racialized and white teacher candidates behaved differently with one another, verbally, physically and indirectly, while in Tanzania. For example, we noticed that racialized teacher candidates often decided how decisions were made, how brainstorming ideas occurred and often took the lead, in contrast to most of the white teacher candidates who took on a less dominant role in decision-making. Thus, acknowledging who was making the decisions and who was following them, and who was speaking and who was not speaking in the group discussions, demonstrates a dislocation of power within group interactions. In light of these two forms of dislocation, we argue that being dislocated in this context refers to becoming estranged from the geographical spaces and group dynamics with respect to how power operates when considering what are 'normal' routines, decision-making procedures and 'common' behaviours, while being 'thrown' into these unknown spaces, unknown routines and unknown behaviours.

Reflecting on Vignette 1, there were moments in which dislocation was apparent. The statement in the vignette referencing the comment from the taxi driver represents that skin colour is an easy identifier in Tanzania and that white teacher candidates are often seen by most local vendors as rich tourists who might be unable to navigate the local market and barter for the best prices. It is important to mention here that there is a small population of East Indians, Middle Eastern and Arab people living in Tanzania and any of our racialized teacher candidates could visually, religiously, ethnically and culturally 'pass off' as a local. Calling out a member of the group or implying that this teacher candidate is eliminating the bargaining opportunities for food presents both forms of dislocation in an interdependent way. It is clear that the geographical location (unknown space) allows for a change in power distribution and this, in turn, creates teachable moments that arise due to these DLNs. The fascinating point is that such race-based conversations that unpack the power dynamics of a dominant culture in Canada are not accessible in many teacher education programmes because the white teacher candidates often take their position of privilege for granted. However, in Tanzania, where there is a shift of geographical location, which also shifts the power dynamics and level of comfort, those who are seen to be part of the dominant social group in terms of the majority population swing in favour of racialized teacher candidates over white teacher candidates. As a result, white teacher candidates in Tanzania are confronted with holding a positionality that lacks authority and is uncomfortable for them. It is important to note that both racialized and white teacher candidates still have colonial power but, when solely looking at the power dynamics within this group of teacher candidates in Tanzania, the 'social' power shifts from white to racialized teacher candidates.

In particular, racialized teacher candidates tend to feel more comfortable and empowered to call out harm done by white teacher candidates. Such a call-out is a rare occurrence in Canada because racialized bodies do not have opportunities to bargain using social capital as they are not part of the dominant white culture. Thus, such conversational possibilities as expressed in Vignette #1 in Tanzania provide an opportunity to show white teacher candidates that their social capital, which is heavily based in their racial privilege, is not valued or helpful, and that a teacher candidate who identified as being racialized might be able to exercise more social capital and power amongst local Tanzanians. Having said that, we acknowledge that white people are still seen as rich and privileged and the comment from the taxi driver was meant to protect who he saw as an unsuspecting naïve white female being taken advantage of by vendors in the market. As a result, the element of dislocation within the DLN framework allows for an educational opportunity for both white and racialized teacher candidates to acknowledge how the geographical space and power and privilege dynamics within group interactions have serious implications on daily actions and everyday life decisions of dominant and marginalized groups of people.

Thus, given the context of dislocation, we recognize that the racialized cis-gendered male teacher candidate who has been forced to be in a non-dominant position without power in Canada may have intentionally tried to challenge the white female teacher candidate who has held some measure of power and privilege over him while in Canada. Moreover, the racialized male teacher candidate later in conversation shared that 'it was about time that what [he] is able to do has the value of doing something noteworthy such as going to the market,' in contrast to the white teacher candidate. As teacher educators who witnessed these conversations, we thought the reason behind the behaviour in Vignette 1 was that the racialized male student was potentially using internalized rage and resistance to challenge the white female in this unfamiliar physical space and unfamiliar group interactions. When we followed up with this racialized male, he confirmed that he wanted to 'call out' the other white teacher candidates on their obvious discomfort and uneasiness in Tanzania. We agree that power is implicit within group interactions even when it is not stated, as it seems to find company in the invisible measure of behaviours, especially in unknown spaces.

Do the two forms of dislocation (i.e. the physical geographical change and power dynamics within group interactions) give root to new forms of power in which resistance is implied and inescapable, we wonder? If this is indeed the case, what happens to the psyche of the teacher candidates when they are embedded in these forms of power and resistance? As May (2006) states, 'We often know what we do and why we are doing it; what we do not know is what our doing it does' (p. 85). Thus, the lasting effects on the participants present at the dinner conversation as outlined in Vignette 1 are still left somewhat unknown.

In Vignette 2 also, there are elements of dislocation. Both the dislocated geographical location and the dislocated group dynamic impacted and created the space for this verbal exchange. The difference between Vignette 2 and Vignette 1 is that in Vignette 2 there is a direct verbal dislocation, whereas the first vignette operated in an indirect verbal and behavioural dislocation. In light of this difference, let us examine the direct verbal exchange in Vignette 2 with Foucault's (1986) notion of heterotopias in mind.

Foucault defines heterotopias as follows:

> Places of this kind are outside of all places, even though it may be possible to indicate their location in reality. Because these places are absolutely different from all the sites that they reflect and speak about, I shall call them, by way of contrast to utopias, heterotopias. (Foucault, 1986, p. 24)

This definition of heterotopias fits what we believe the teacher candidates are experiencing, by way of a reality of Tanzania but by 'flipping the switch' on them with respect to culture, power dynamics and privilege, thus making the current reality in Tanzania feel unreal and foreign to them. Moreover, this unreal but real reality is creating new dissonances and different behaviour/action interactions, which are demonstrated in Vignette 1 and Vignette 2. More precisely, in Vignette 2 we find Foucault's example of a mirror that depicts a self-reflective moment, capturing what was going on in the mind of the racialized male student teacher. In the words of Foucault (1986),

> ... the mirror functions as a heterotopia in this respect: it makes this place that I occupy at the moment when I look at myself in the glass at once absolutely real, connected with all the space that surrounds it, and absolutely unreal, since in order to be perceived it has to pass through this virtual point which is over there. (p. 24)

Thus, we argue, that our teacher candidates, while in Tanzania, shifted into this heterotopic space, which is unreal for them, but at once deeply real to them, as it creates an inner dissonance that cannot be denied. This heterotopic space is evident in the words: 'How come you never spoke to me all year at the University and now that we are in Tanzania, you are complaining that I don't sit next to you or talk to you?' In these words, there is an acknowledgement of past experiences and now a call for future interactions to be different due to the dislocation in physical space and group interactions. In hindsight, as we reflect on this verbal exchange and grapple with Foucault's notion of heterotopia, as teacher educators, we wonder how impactful and necessary this international teaching experience is for teacher candidates? We acknowledge that Foucault (1986) contends that 'the heterotopia begins to function at full capacity when men arrive at a sort of absolute break with their traditional time' (p. 26). We see moments of 'absolute break' happen in Tanzania given these power shifts in geographical space and group dynamics, which then afford us the opportunity to begin to have meaningful and deeper conversations about race, power and privilege as we use the DLN framework to guide us. We are grateful for these learning opportunities that come from this unexpected experiential journey and acknowledge how, without them, there is often no catalyst to allow meaningful and personal conversations to occur with respect to race and power.

In retrospect, we wonder: Does dislocation provide a necessary critical insight that lends to teacher candidates learning, which in turn helps develop a deeper and intimate first-hand experience of a heterotopic space, which creates an opportunity for race- and power-based conversations? Foucault (1986) states that the role of a heterotopia is 'to create a space that is other, another real space, as perfect, as meticulous, as well arranged as ours is messy, ill-constructed, and jumbled. This latter type would be the heterotopia' (p. 27). Does the jumbled unreal but real experience in Tanzania then provide deeper reflective learning on power, privilege and race? Moreover, can analyzing the element of dislocation in both of its forms based on their experiences in Tanzania help educate teacher candidates by aiding them to grow with respect to being prepared for teaching diverse racialized students?

In conclusion, it is after analyzing these two vignettes in relation to the two forms of dislocation that the opportunities to learn about the impact such experiences had on teacher candidates' personal and teaching identity become apparent. We hope, with the use of the DLN framework, that educators are able to dig deeper into the undertones of power, privilege, resistance and heterotopic spaces created by dislocation.

Disruptive Learning Network Framework Element Three: Displacement

The third element of the DLN framework is displacement. Displacement deals mostly with the psyche; we describe it as the intense moment of rendezvous between disidentification and dislocation. Indeed, displacement is often the ultimate result of going *through* the simultaneous process of disidentification and dislocation. Framed within a Freudian framework (Freud, 1955; 1974), displacement is seen as a psychic event where there is a shift in action from a desired target to a substitute target. This 'displacement' happens when the desired target is not reachable or is unacceptable, and the substitute target emerges as acceptable or less threatening. Further discussion on Freud and his student, Jacques Lacan, will be taken up in Chapter 5.

We see displacement in Vignette 1 when the white female student, instead of confronting her lack of experience, her white privilege, her disidentification and dislocation, 'displaces' all of these by *running out of the room in tears*. In this vignette, displacement was thus an internal struggle, a burst of emotion, which the female teacher candidate did not know what to do with – and as it happens so often with displacement, it was released unexpectedly and rashly.

According to Sigmund Freud (1955), displacement happens when there is an internal struggle between the Id (basic human needs), the Ego (the beginning of our moral codes) and the Super Ego (the solidified and highest moral codes). Ultimately, Sigmund Freud argues that displacement occurs because the Id wants to do something the Super Ego does not permit. It seems as though the white teacher candidate desired to engage with the comment made by the racialized teacher candidate, but she felt uncomfortable in the particular context. The discomfort of participating as a white woman who is part of a professional programme in an international practicum where her racial identity and level of power in making decisions was not privileged was the cause of her internal struggle. In other words, her inability to respond to the comment using her white privilege made the situation very uncomfortable as she realized that her whiteness did not have the social and cultural capital required to do this bargain shopping; thus, she fled from the table.

To better understand displacement in Vignette 2, we need to broaden our knowledge about defence mechanisms that come about when the human psyche is displaced. According to Anna Freud (1974), defence mechanisms are triggered when we cannot escape a heightened emotional experience, much like the experiences in Vignette 1 and Vignette 2. These mechanisms include denial (denying what is true as false), displacement (substituting targets), intellectualizing (thinking more objectively), projection (attaching negative feelings to others), rationalization (justifying what is false), reaction formation (overreacting), regression (retreating to babyhood or child-like acts), repression (pushing feelings down to the subconscious), and sublimation (diverting the impulse (sexual or otherwise) into a moral or aesthetic direction).

In Vignette 2, we see a number of defence mechanisms manifest. We see, in particular, intellectualizing, reaction formation and repression. First, uttering his statement, 'How come you never spoke to me all year at the University and now that we are in Tanzania, you are complaining that I don't sit next to you or talk to you?', in the form of a rhetorical question meant that the racialized male student had thought about it before (intellectualizing). Second, the male teacher candidate might have overreacted but, according to Anna Freud (1974), reaction formation happens emotionally when our emotion cheats us, when we find ourselves uncontrollably overdoing or oversaying something. What the racialized student did and said demonstrates this reaction formation; Anna Freud would state that these statements contained repressed feelings that may have been there for a long time. The most interesting thing about displacement, Anna Freud explains, is that it brings that which is repressed to the surface, where the visible act shows and speaks about that which is subconsciously repressed.

It is important to note that we never intended to psychoanalyze our teacher candidates' behaviours and actions, but we found the idea of displacement helpful as a culmination that follows disidentification and dislocation. In particular, displacement sends the human psyche into places that it did not even know existed. Moreover, such displacement leaves individuals feeling overwhelmed, confused and lost at times by feelings of the unknown whilst in the midst of experiencing their disidentification and dislocation.

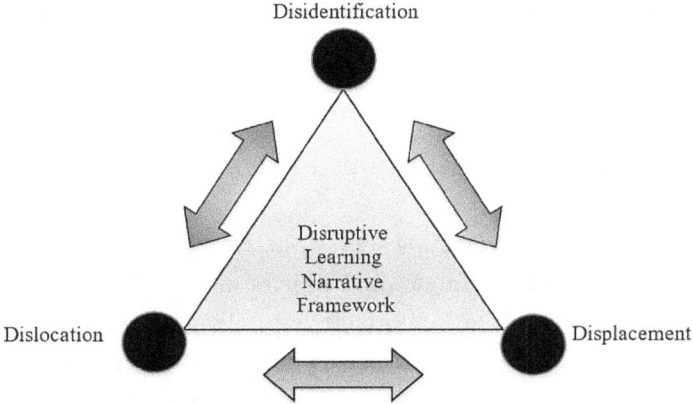

Figure 1.1 Disruptive learning narrative framework
Source: Manu Sharma.

Further to our discussion above, it is worth noting and adding that, within the axis of displacement, the two vignettes also shed light on how Tanzania displaces identities, of both white and Black/racialized students. For Black Canadian students, Tanzania provided an opportunity for them to be considered part of the dominant majority, which is not something they have experienced before. Thus this was an experience of displacement on a human psyche level. In such a human psyche level, displacement influenced the male Black teacher candidate's way of interaction with others, especially with his white colleagues: 'Our regular taxi driver today said that a Mzungu [Swahili for white person] should not go shopping in the market anymore, because they cause a commotion and they are unable to get the best prices'. This is not a simple linguistic utterance, but a displaced identity and location from which the racialized student is speaking. It is a form of displacement that empowers this teacher candidate to speak in ways he is not familiar with, in a language that is made possible because of the shift in his human psyche.

As for white students, Tanzania shook the ground from under their feet. Nothing was familiar anymore: neither language, culture, people, colours, streets, smells, air nor water. Thus, the disidentification and geographic dislocation caused the white teacher candidates to feel displaced in their psyche. In conclusion, displacement pushes us to speak a language that we didn't even know we had or knew how to speak. As teacher educators, it is the deployment of the DLN framework that enables us to decipher and make sense of displacement and its deep impact on the human psyche. In light of discussing all three elements, Figure 1.1 is a diagram that helps visualize how the three interactive, dynamic and complementary elements anchor the DLN framework.

Pedagogical Implications towards a Conclusion

Thus, the three elements, disidentification, dislocation and displacement, provide the foundation of the DLN framework. In light of using the DLN framework to analyze the intense and uncomfortable gestural vignettes in this chapter, we recognize how each of the three elements provides a continual, and sometimes overlapping, thread of examining that deepens our understanding of personal and professional identity. With respect to our vignettes, these three elements in the DLN framework provide different ways to explore what is happening to teacher candidates' personal and teacher identity formations as they engage with the international teaching placement experiences in Tanzania. Thus, in trying to understand the messiness and complexity involved in such intense and uncomfortable experiences while teaching abroad, the DLN framework is insightful in providing educators with an entry point to help facilitate dialogue amongst post-secondary students, including teacher candidates, upon their return home. DLN also gave us a way to answer our own question: What happens when professors take students (in our case teacher candidates) to an international practicum?

We contend, therefore, that using the DLN framework helps us shed light on healthy tensions and dissonances that sometimes are left unanswered, but touch a deep part of us that forever becomes transformed. Understanding such an international experience that challenges, disorients and estranges a teacher candidate from all that they know leaves an impression and indentation on how they understand themselves, and later becomes an imprint on how they view what it means to be a teacher to diverse racialized students. We have used the DLN framework as a tool for analyzing our own narratives from our observations and journals as teacher educators, and we record particularly those moments that run counter to or disrupt the traditional narratives of the domestic practicum in Canada or 'regular' teacher education programmes; for example, 'My Associate Teacher didn't say hello to me this morning, I think I'm going to fail' or 'My Associate wants me to teach 100% of the day and I am not ready'.

The DLN goes beyond these surface practicum issues and seeks out those thorny issues that often get ignored; for example, issues of race, class, gender, sexuality, and even power and marginality. We argue that these moments become teachable moments in teacher education or in post-secondary education in general, and the DLN provides a theoretical framework for analysis. Often times, such issues of power and marginality are rarely explored, taken up or analyzed in teacher education. For example, Ian Menter (1984) identifies the phenomenon of the 'practice teaching stasis,' where the triad of supervising teacher, teacher candidate and practicum advisor all have a strong tendency to avoid conflict or confrontation. Therefore, they avoid any issues that may cause any tensions or difficult thorny issues in the practicum. Thus, the DLN unearths the covert tensions underlying the teacher education programme and lays them bare for analysis in our teacher educator observations and narratives. We propose also to introduce our teacher candidates to the DLN framework to help them use it as a tool to analyze their own narratives and stories/journals. Teacher candidates can then name and locate those tensions they encounter through the DLN and through reflection, thus bringing them to a better understanding of their own experiences in the practicum.

Suggestions for Using Disruptive Learning Network as a Tool for Teacher Candidates

We have found over the years that one of the most challenging aspects of the international practicum is preparing our teacher candidates for the challenges on the ground in Tanzania. We argue that beyond just preparing lesson plans and learning Kiswahili, one of the greatest challenges for teacher candidates is the personal and internal conflict of venturing into unfamiliar physical spaces and into parts of their psyche where they have never been before. In this chapter, we have proposed a new framework grounded in key critical theoretical lenses for analyzing the practicum experiences of our students. We have used our own teacher educator narratives and observations because, at first, we were trying to make sense of the experiences of our students in Tanzania as a way of responding to issues and tensions when they came up in the international practicum.

We wanted to develop a new way of looking at our narratives and observations of the experiences of our teacher candidates. We now also see possibilities for using this framework with teacher candidates for analyzing their own experiences and reflections/narratives. Teacher candidates could be introduced to the DLN framework at the beginning of their teacher education programme in Canada before they go to Tanzania. Knowing full well that each experience is unique and different, we could share not only our narratives from over the years but also how we seek out and analyze stories that disrupt the traditional narratives. Teacher candidates could then be introduced to Menter's (1984) notion of stasis, particularly the practice teaching stasis. We could also identify ways that they can learn more about themselves as teachers through the DLN. In addition, we can follow up with teacher candidates on the ground during the international practicum and after the teacher candidates return to Canada.

Allowing teacher candidates to name and locate power and marginality that they identify in their own reflections and narratives has much to offer in any critical teacher education programme. We believe that teacher candidates could identify their own struggles with disidentification, dislocation and displacement and come to understand how a critical constructivist approach in teacher education draws learning from the tensions, conflicts and contradictions that arise in learning to teach. It would be valuable also to compare and contrast both international and domestic practicum experiences and narratives. Furthermore, teacher candidates could analyze stasis in their placements in Canada and apply the DLN framework to see if they can unearth some of the issues of power, privilege and marginality that go ignored or unnoticed in the practicum in Canada.

We hope for a future of teachers who teach to be surprised by all their students, who work to demystify the conservatism inherent in teaching the same lesson and in telling the same story over, even as the student population changes. We sincerely encourage teacher candidates to reflect and analyze their own stories by using the DLN framework. Again, we also believe the DLN is applicable to other professional disciplines that offer critical international practicum experiences, though the focus on this chapter has been primarily on teacher candidates.

Thus, it is not until teacher educators use the DLN framework to analyze these intense and uncomfortable experiences that they are able to trek on the path of uncovering disruptive learning that lies beneath international vignettes. It is when this disruptive learning comes to the surface that the quest of deep learning becomes meaningful and rich, giving a voice to silenced tensions and discomforts. As teacher educators we must begin a new and courageous dialogue that chips away at the complexities buried deep in the multiple realities of teaching, which become even more relevant when educators teach racialized students.

2

Investigating an International Practicum in Kenya: A Longitudinal Perspective of the Disruptive Learning Narrative

Glenda Black, Rogerio Bernardes and Kevin Wilcox

The pedagogical cornerstone to any teacher education programme is the practicum experience. Institutions are challenged with providing teacher candidates with carefully chosen experiences that integrate theory and practice and are responsive to the diverse social and cultural contexts of their students. Reflecting on their experience as a teacher candidate on an international practicum in Kenya, Logan's vignette reflects the goals of their three-week international teaching placement. They were to become culturally aware. In desiring to become a well-rounded, culturally sensitive educator, Logan is not fully aware of the impact associated with this concept. Finney and Orr (1995) highlight this concern in relation to the stratified nature of Canadian society, recognizing teacher education students 'are isolated from a significant portion of the population they are likely to teach' (p. 328). Attempting to facilitate experiences that may improve connections with diverse populations, institutions with teacher education programmes are increasingly providing a variety of teaching placements, study visits, community service learning as well as immersion field experiences. The Study Group on Global Education (2017) reported 11 per cent of Canadian university students in 2014 engaged in an international learning experience of some kind.

The institutional purposes and practices underlying these endeavours must be critically scrutinized if education is to help create a more just and equitable world, instead of maintaining the status quo. As Freire (1996) observes, education offers people the possibility to exercise a critical reading of the world, enabling them to intervene rather than to accommodate reality without questioning it. In our analysis of a one-time three-week international teaching practicum, we are sceptical of unequivocal claims that experiences offer transformational benefits (Dunn et al., 2014; Kearney et al., 2014; Maynes et al., 2013; Mwebi & Brigham, 2009; Tangen et al., 2017). To elucidate an understanding of students' intense and uncomfortable experiences on an international practicum, we apply the Disruptive Learning Narrative (DLN) framework (Sharma et al., this volume) to our longitudinal study.

Background of the International Practicum

For more than two decades, the university under discussion in north central Canada organized an ad hoc international practicum experience for teacher candidates. In 2003, the dean of Faculty of Education developed a partnership with a Canadian non-government organization (NGO) to facilitate an alternative international practicum (Miller, 2006). The dean believed the benefit of this unique experience for teacher candidates 'is a heightened social conscience and an understanding of their roles as teachers and as global citizens', and this notion was supported by faculty who volunteered their service (Miller, 2006, para. 23). This option for international teaching practicums continues today.

The decision to partner with the NGO was based on popular support the organization had garnered nationally in Canada, its productive work in the Kenyan region and its ability to package a safe experience for the participants. The partnering NGO continues to organize the international and local travel arrangements, accommodations, meals, and communicates with the local elementary school communities to arrange placements for the teacher candidates. The teacher candidates taught three to four hours in the mornings, while afternoons and weekends were reserved for activities and structured cultural excursions organized by the NGO. Feedback from the teacher candidates and faculty facilitators, however, consistently reported that risk management (i.e. personal safety), imposed by the NGO meant that the cultural experiences within the community were restricted. This reflects Tallon's (2012) work, outlining that young people have been educated to think of NGOs as helping in a stereotypical, deficit-based manner, sensationalized for Western stakeholders – notions discussed further in our results. The most restrictive regulation from the NGO was the prohibition on developing friendships with the local people, including host teachers. The NGO purported that developing friendships and communication outside the school yard would unsettle existing relationships within the community and would not be equitable.

In this chapter, we explore the longitudinal effects of a three-week international teaching practicum on teacher candidates in Kenya. In 2011 and 2012, a total of forty-six white teacher candidates (twenty-two candidates in 2011, and a new group of twenty-four in 2012) and two faculty facilitators (the authors) from the university under discussion had the opportunity to participate in a three-week teaching practicum in Kenya. The NGO was instrumental in coordinating the trip and practicum. Our practicum placement was in a western Kenyan rural primary school, and we worked with students from grades three to seven. The NGO selects school sites from within the communities they support. Upon arrival at the school, the teacher candidates immediately began teaching duties. The local curriculum was a modified British syllabus partly adapted to the social, economic and geographic Kenyan context. Thirty to sixty students in each classroom sat three to a desk, and shared notebooks and pencils. Classrooms were equipped with a chalkboard (black paint on a cement wall), chalk, a teacher textbook and shared textbooks for the students. Preparation for the international practicum included formal and informal gatherings of the participating teacher candidates and faculty facilitators. At these gatherings, previous participating teacher candidates, faculty facilitators and, when available, a speaker from the NGO shared their international practicum experiences.

Context in the Literature

International Teaching Practicums

Education must be intercultural, given the diversity of Canada's population. The concept of intercultural is dynamic and interactional, referring to evolving contextual relations, negotiations and processes with political and social justice motivations (see Aikman, 1997; Holm & Zilliacus, 2009; Leeman, 2003; Portera, 2008; Trilokekar & Kukar, 2011). Compared to multiculturalism, interculturalism is 'regarded as a more appropriate response to the new context of globalization and the increasing convergence of different languages, religions, cultural behaviour and ways of thinking' (Portera, 2008, p. 483), with a greater concern for acknowledging and responding to the exploitation of Indigenous peoples along with the suppression of their knowledge and practices (Aikman, 1997).

Since the 1960s, research has supported intercultural experiential learning to enhance teachers' cultural perspectives (Armstrong, 2008; Buchanan, 2004; Cushner, 2007; Grierson & Denton, 2013; Larsen & Searle, 2017; Lee, 2011;

Maynes et al., 2013; Mwebi & Brigham, 2009; Pence & Macgillivray, 2008; Taylor, 1969; Trilokekar & Kukar, 2011; Wilson, 1982). More recently, literature emphasizes that teachers who engaged in a variety of intercultural experiences became more culturally *aware* but little evidence demonstrates they became critical global citizens who actively engaged in social justice actions in response to inequities inside and outside the classroom (Larsen & Searle, 2017; Major & Santoro, 2016; Smolcic & Katunich, 2017; Trilokekar & Kukar, 2011). To paraphrase Merryfield (2000), experiences alone do not make a teacher an intercultural educator. This is because 'new patterns of thinking about teaching [are] not reinforced by the expectations and school structures of their home context' (Johnson & Battalio, 2008, as cited in Smolcic & Katunich, 2017, p. 52). More distressingly, cross-cultural experiences may reinforce colonizing attitudes and stereotypes due to a variety of factors including a lack of critical self-reflection on one's own positionality (Major & Santoro, 2016; Trilokekar & Kukar, 2011) or limited experience in the host country (Marx & Pray, 2011, as cited in Smolcic & Katunich, 2017). It is imperative that colonizing attitudes are increasingly problematized, especially given the spirit of reconciliation in the Canadian context between Indigenous peoples and settlers.

While international teaching practicums centre the participant and their future students as benefactors, we argue their approach may be both short-term and lacking in scope. Possibly, past positive evaluations of these programmes' successes have focused on what was deemed to be most institutionally rewarding, all the while perpetuating long-standing systems of oppression both in Canada and abroad. Our own previous contribution (Black & Bernardes, 2014) reported that planned learning opportunities could, in the *short term*, improve teacher candidate commitments to build community, notions of global-mindedness and personal confidence in teaching. Specifically, we noted the study's limitations, as it did not address power relations or provide an 'analysis of Western ways of being and thinking imposed on Indigenous students and communities' (Black & Bernardes, 2014, p. 3). In this longitudinal follow-up study, we contend a social justice approach to relations between cultures must directly address the processes involved in othering (i.e. treatment of groups of people as different from us or implying they are not one of us (see Said, 1978)) and interrogate how any programme or exchange encourages the recognition of critical aspects of power relations. Significantly, we heed the call for research involving teachers' overseas cross-cultural experiences to pay attention to 'hierarchies and power relations which offer differential benefit to people [and institutions] engaged in these programs' (Smolcic & Katunich, 2017, p. 56).

Theoretical Framework

The DLN framework is a comprehensive tool for unpacking the physical and psychological events that inform an individual's concept of self and of the other during an international experience (Sharma et al., this volume). This framework involves the triad of disidentification, dislocation and displacement. Disidentification is one's ability to identify with and/or disidentify from familiar social and cultural norms in the face of difference. Dislocation refers to the experience of a physical change in location and the teacher candidates' place within the ebb and flow of individual and group power dynamics. Finally, displacement is an apex, where disidentification and dislocation inform and reframe identity relative to different experiences in an attempt to contextualize meaning and meaningfulness. Both whiteness and the DLN problematize social occurrences. Whiteness studies focus on the historical and continued implications of whiteness while elucidating its fluidity, since one may evolve and enhance their cultural perspectives. The DLN provides concrete points of reference to unpack whiteness through its focus on identity, norms and location. Displacement itself represents the space for potential change, where identity can be reformed through experience, where whiteness may be reconstrued. Similar to DLN, transformational learning theory is a lens for interpreting personal experiences. In this theory, through a *disorienting dilemma* and *self-examination*, one is transformed to a deeper level of processing (Mezirow, 2000, p. 22).

Whiteness Studies

A socially constructed system of race-based logic involving institutions, individuals, and ways of thinking and interacting, whiteness is a *normative* standard employed by white folks for measuring *others* (Carr, 2017; Solomona et al., 2005; Twine & Steinbugler, 2006). This is realized through 'construct[ing] difference as 'Other' and as deficient when compared to the dominant group's standards' (Martin & Pirbhai-Illich, 2016, p. 360). Acknowledging and referencing the systemic influence of whiteness in Canada offers emic insight into the power relations involved when white bodies move in international space. Learned social behaviours associated with white empowerment can be disrupted.

Incorporating whiteness studies framework facilitates inquiry into research conducted since the 1960s supporting inter/multi/cross-cultural experiential learning as opportunities to enhance teachers' cultural perspectives (Armstrong,

2008; Cushner, 2007; Grierson & Denton, 2013; Larsen & Searle, 2017; Lee, 2011; Maynes et al., 2013; Taylor, 1969; Trilokekar & Kukar, 2011; Wilson, 1982). Predicated on contact, awareness and cultural exchange across groups, intercultural experiences often focus on being mindful of diversity (difference), and an approach that presumes equal power relations are present (Gorski, 2008). However, superficial processing from a position of privilege may further assert the superiority of one's own culture (Marx & Pray, 2011, as cited in Smolcic & Katunich, 2017) and entrench misconceptions of deficit perspectives (i.e. a focus on what others in a group lack, causing one to see differences as impediments and lowering expectations accordingly) within colonial discourses (Henfield & Washington, 2012; Sleeter, 2008).

Transformational Learning Theory

Transformational learning theory is an adult learning theory based on the fundamental principle that adults make meaning and learn from personal experiences (Mezirow, 1991). In this theory, life experiences are filtered, mediated and made sense of through one's values, beliefs and assumptions (Mezirow, 1991). New meanings can be created through the reinterpretation of experiences (Taylor, 2008). The process of transformational learning begins with a 'disorienting dilemma' (Mezirow, 2000, p. 22) creating a significant level of cognitive dissonance, whereby a new experience is recognized as inconsistent with previous understandings. It prompts one to engage in a process of 'self-examination' (Mezirow, 2000, p. 22). At this point, the experience may be processed at a *superficial* level, which does not lead to new understandings, or at a *deeper* level of processing, which may lead to new understandings (Gregoire, 2003).

Africentric ways of knowing have been positioned in opposition to Eurocentric perspectives that value the history, culture and knowledge of people of European descent (Harris, 1992), based on the idea of control over nature and people (Warfield-Coppock, 1995), and closely associated with the values of materialism, individualism, competition, outward focus, social status and power over others (Merriweather Hunn, 2004). Similarly, transformational learning theory focuses on the individual's capacity to use rational processes and critical reflection to make meaning and it does not consider the interconnected relationships within the cultural context (Taylor, 2008; Ntseane, 2011). To be inclusive of cultures outside of one's context, transformational learning must be culturally sensitive and address the influence of 'other individuals, family, community, and overall cultural values in the process of transformational learning' (Ntseane, 2011, p. 310).

Methodology

Our chapter uses the DLN framework to navigate the effects of a three-week international (Kenyan) practicum from a critical perspective. For our examination of the DLN, we followed a qualitative methodology, specifically framework analysis to describe and interpret what is happening in a particular context (Ritchie & Spencer, 1994). The analytical process 'involves a number of distinct though highly interconnected stages ... which involves a systematic process of sifting, charting and sorting material according to key issues and themes' (Ritchie & Spencer, 1994, p. 174). Stages of the framework analysis included familiarization, identifying a thematic framework, indexing, charting and mapping, and interpretation (Ritchie & Spencer, 1994, p. 174).

Participants

Three participants were selected for this chapter. These participants are representative of the forty-six teacher candidates who, in 2011 and 2012, travelled to Kenya for a three-week teaching practicum and who had not pursued further international development. Teacher candidates who travelled afterwards, pursuing their international development, are not represented. All three teacher candidates are white: Jayden and Logan identify as female, and Kelly identifies as male.

This chapter offers longitudinal insights towards understanding the impact of international practicums, vis-a-vis the DLN framework, especially since Kelly, Jayden and Logan continue to work in education. The participants represent both public and private education in eastern Ontario. Kelly and Logan teach in the public school sector and Jayden currently teaches at a private school. All three participants have been active educators since their international practicum. Therefore, their data elucidates what lasting impact international practicums may have on teachers and, by extension, on students and communities in central Canada. We use vignettes and themes from our participants' transcripts, which are woven into the fabric of the international practicum longitudinally, for each component (e.g. disidentification, dislocation and displacement) of the DLN.

Discussion

Disidentification

> Co-teacher candidates have some really great ideas about learning activities and teaching strategies. Each day when we came back to the compound and had a big group discussion, I found this very useful. ... I am much more adaptive with resources, [I] make do with what I have. ... I don't stress over getting all my students to achieve a level 3. (Kelly)

The DLN framework notes that disidentification 'is the process of becoming either increasingly or dramatically less identified with one's own familiar social and cultural norms' (Sharma et al., this volume). Our participants' experiences with disidentification are rooted in the vignette above. Yet DiAngelo (2011) claims, 'Many white people are unprepared to engage, even on a preliminary level, in an exploration of their racial perspectives that could lead to a shift in their understanding of racism ... result[ing] in the maintenance of white power' (pp. 65–6). Through the DLN framework lens, the practicum teachers' experience in Kenya forced them to reconcile personal and private struggles, which ultimately informed their teaching practice and teacher identity. While defining their teacher identities on their trip, participants routinely relied on Canadian preconceptions about what education looks and sounds like, what they expected to gain from individual interactions, and delineations between we and other, or us and them. This was perpetuated as the NGO had entrenched Western practices into the Kenyan community, leaving teacher candidates to (re)frame their identities in relation to this new, though familiar, setting.

Kelly's disidentification is a snapshot of a wider reflection on the opportunities that impact his teacher identity. Exposure to rote learning, different learning outcomes and teaching without technology during his Kenyan practicum impact Kelly's current teacher identity. Comparatively, learning opportunities also came from within as a result of personal challenges and peer dialogue. The vignette experience reflects the influence of disidentification on Kelly's identity (re)formation. Given Kelly's exposure to progressive teaching strategies in his programme (Hutchison, 2015; Pellegrino & Hilton, 2012; Trilling & Fadel, 2009), witnessing rote learning disrupted his value system, as it related to education. Given exposure to Canadian standards, Kelly disidentifies from rote learning, conceiving of the approach as deficit, or less than, though still informative. Alternatively, the strategies developed within, with his peers, were very useful – seemingly cutting across borders, into the Kenyan context but still applicable relative to Canadian educational values. Finally, within the DLN framework, this approach allowed Kelly to (re)form his identity, despite disruptive experiences, based on Canadian values.

Consistent across participants' reflections is their reliance on deficit framing when disidentifying and (re)forming their identity. This deficit-informed (re)formation of identity is often cited in international service learning scholarship. Framed around opportunities 'to be the cultural other' (Addleman et al., 2014, p. 195) or experiencing a taste of the subaltern, individuals seek to do without (Razack, 1998). The participants create stark divisions by disidentifying from values disruptive to their identity. Nonetheless, Logan and Jayden had unique experiences with disidentification.

> With so many biases, stereotypes, miscommunication, and cultural differences we forget that we all have similar dreams and goals. I learned this through conflicts with my teaching partners, we all had the same goals ... through talking with community members. While our lives may be different we still have the same feelings with similar hopes and dreams. (Logan)

Using the DLN framework, Logan's disidentification manifests in distinguishing between their goals and their peer's goals and the community members' hopes and dreams. As Logan recalls, these two groups (re)framed their identities. However, this vignette represents Tallon's (2012) concern with NGOs sensationalizing their work in the *developing world* when shared amongst Western audiences. Not only does Logan speak of biases and differences in the same context as dreams and goals, they also determine who has which and how they informed them. Logan shared the following goals with their peers: impacting community and learning to teach. Community dreams were *basic* needs, which the NGO can meet. Paradoxically, Logan's pedagogical (re)formation was informed by communication with members of the community; they now created learning goals with their students. Logan believes the Kenyan community members spoke of hopes and dreams, whereas their northern counterparts held and pursued goals. Ultimately, Logan's perspective is derived from both an inaccurate and a deficit perspective fuelled by not investing enough time to know and understand the local community members, while themselves being influenced by northern deficit perceptions. Logan's disidentification culminates in a doubling down on Commonwealth philanthropic values (Tallon, 2012) framed in us-them identity politics (Said, 1978), where Kenyan folks are to be helped, not understood. The subtle distinction between same feelings and similar hopes and dreams delineates empathy and recognition, adhering to identity politics.

> Oh, I'm teaching this? Okay, good. Give me two minutes… being able to adapt quickly to things where you just say to yourself – 'What's going on? Okay, I can do this,' and I don't need to look at the teacher's manual in depth and research this and figure this out. (Jayden)

The vignette above describes Jayden's experience with who, situationally, may be understood as the associate teacher for their practicum and their lesson planning. Jayden's situational associate teacher left the classroom soon after the group's arrival and orientation, leaving Jayden with text materials and a rough idea of the students' curricular progress. The lack of oversight provided Jayden an opportunity to quickly digest content, collaborate with peers and deliver lessons to their students – a highlight of their identity (re)formation (Sharma et al., this volume).

As a partnership between university and NGO, the international practicum experience was a different partnership than those typical in Canada (Darling-Hammond, 2014). Furthermore, a typical student embarking on a domestic practicum would be informed of the school where they are assigned, who their associate teacher is and they would be provided contact information (Darling-Hammond, 2014). For this international practicum, however, students were not assigned associate teachers. In fact, the NGO discouraged communication between participants and community members prior to the practicum, which led to a last-minute sharing of resources and curricular outcomes. This rushed experience influenced Jayden's perception, which created a deficit perspective of their experience – which then was projected upon the community. Disidentifying from the community experience, the forced flexible planning caused Jayden to highlight struggles amongst the students; they were disconnected from the instruction, the teacher candidates did not want to overwhelm them, and they were distracted by the situation's novelty. Instead of Jayden critically understanding where decisions had been made by the facilitators who organized the practicum, they assigned responsibility to their students (Moore, 2014; Schwarz, 2015). In this instance, Jayden perpetuated their privilege through a perception that Kenyan students could not meet expectations, instead of recognizing that the students were affected by the limited practicum preparation.

In these experiences, we see teacher candidates focus within to define what they may do without. These delineations leave one to inquire: Are we to look at the difference in social values and identity as an impact on teaching identity, or should we focus on pedagogical ingenuity and inquiry? If we compared their practicums from a pedagogical lens, would students in the international teaching practicum have increasingly transformational experiences or are those in domestic practicums just as likely to have similar experiences? What identities related to the practical act of teaching are created?

Dislocation

> While in Kenya, the first best thing that stands out about the trip was being able to learn so much about the community; from talking with community members, touring hospitals, schools and homes, and participating in daily routines. We also learned a lot about the community, as we saw firsthand the problems that face them (environmental, governmental, cultural) ... the worst thing about my Kenya experience is the concern that we did not positively affect the community or provide sustainable teaching strategies with our teaching placement. (Logan)

Within the DLN framework, dislocation 'relates to teacher candidates' change in physical location and how they locate themselves within group dynamics' (Sharma et al., this volume) during the international practicum experience. Generally, individuals recognize they are bodies in a new place, or bodies on the move (Razack, 2005). Razack's discussion is framed around Canadian, northern bodies; what is interesting about northern bodies on the move is the persistence of power, which makes privilege implied, possibly unescapable. Even if (invisibly) perceived, their perceptions of power impacts both the people in the space and themselves (Carr, 2017). For Logan, upon meeting familiar power dynamics within the NGO's compound, the saviour complex was actualized (Krabill, 2012; Matias, 2016). The intangibility of place contextualizes participants' experience with heterotopias. Foucault's (1986) discussion on heterotopias recognizes mind-body separation and, further, the ability of the mind to create spaces layered on top of those physically experienced. Using a mirror, Foucault juxtaposes 'the place that I occupy' with 'the moment when I look at myself in the glass' as being both real in the physical surrounding and unreal in that it is the perception of a virtual point, or that perceived by the mind (Foucault, 1986, p. 24). With northern dynamics supplanted onto the Kenyan community, the space becomes all the while familiar, but ultimately unreal. Instances of dissonance impacted the participant, leaving a presumptive sense of reality. These heterotopias impacted the teacher candidates, often manifesting in a questioning of their impact on the community (i.e. whether they benefited the community, since they had no tangible understanding of being in that space, just the tangible perception offered by the mirror of heterotopias).

Logan's geographical disillusionment is supported by concepts of power, framed in terms of problems facing them – the other (Said, 1978). Instances where power dynamics were challenged resulted in resistance by participants as they infringed on their assumed identities. However, when experiences were ascribed to presumed power dynamics, they were often lauded. Logan's vignette connects space and power. Positioning the Kenyan space as home to problems, or deficit, Logan juxtaposes this by inquiring into the difference they made. Logan ascribes to power dynamics associated with the saviour complex, presuming they *can impact* the space (Matias, 2016). To Logan, Kenya and its problems are ideologically located in northern language (Moore, 2014; Razack, 2005). Logan's impact is subjective; it is weighed in the North – the very architect of the structures witnessed in the NGO partnership dynamics. Completing the experience and humbly questioning one's impact perpetuates northern power while serving as a marker on a resume, often conferring power anew to one teacher candidate over another.

In another instance of being located in both a physical and hierarchical space, Kelly recalls they felt as if they were in a bubble, or in an experience crafted by the NGO. Entering the experience, Kelly presumed what community is in the Kenyan context. However, Kelly experienced disruptions to these presumptions of power when interacting with the students. Kelly believed increased access to education would result in increased urbanization, with students 'land[ing] a career as a doctor, teacher, pilot, driver, etc.[,] all of which are very urban based occupations'. Upon realizing these educational outcomes, students would no longer support and grow the community where they grew up. Despite limited understandings of the social dynamics and effect of access to education on Kenyan communities, Kelly presumed these aspirations to be burdensome. To attain these goals, the community would suffer as the individual must leave the community to pursue their goals. Furthermore, these standards and their ceiling existed relative to success markers to which Kelly himself ascribed. Despite indicating his pride in becoming one of the community members through immersing himself in a culture, Kelly's presumptions do not result in critical impact. Kelly measuring the Kenyan people as 'lovely and very successful people in their own way' is a flippant demonstration of northern bodies' impact on southern communities; (un)consciously contaminating conditions.

Through the DLN framework, dislocation focuses attention on 'change in physical location and how [individuals] locate themselves within group dynamics'

(Sharma et al., this volume). Informed by invisible privilege (McIntosh, 1989) and understood relative to heterotopias, participants demonstrate how space and power may be constructed during international practicums. In this instance, heterotopias mitigate deeply disruptive experiences as situated power dynamics means minimal resistance was required to divert disruptive experiences, despite a change in space.

Ultimately, this space is ideal for a stagnation among individuals, affirming Menter's (1989) *practice teaching stasis* in the international setting. Though rarely explored by participants, their experience with dislocation demonstrates the impact of power and marginality. Participants' experience of the unreal but real did not facilitate deeper reflective learning. Instead, participants' presumptions about space and power were reaffirmed. These experiences must be considered alongside Nakayama and Krizeck's (1995) work. As Schwarz (2015) explains, 'it may be that participants have an unconscious or unexpressed desire to maintain the status quo, as they have a vested interest in preserving their own power and privilege' (Schwarz, 2015, p. 10).

Limited critical appraisal of experience impacts the teacher candidates' perceptions of power. The limited exploration of concepts of power facilitates longitudinal festering that ultimately impacts the Canadian education system. This gap in critical reflection underscores a concern that 'many white people are unprepared to engage, even on a preliminary level, in an exploration of their racial perspectives that could lead to a shift in their understanding of racism … result[ing] in the maintenance of white power' (DiAngelo, 2011, pp. 65–6). Existing literature on the benefit of these placements shares a common belief: teacher candidates may become prepared to educate individuals of all races and creeds through exposure to a brief opportunity to teach racialized students in an international setting (Dunn et al., 2014; Grierson & Denton, 2013). Given this utopian ideal, the findings presented here elucidate a different reality. Thus, this work narrows the focus by inquiring: What experiences with space and power affect the teaching of diverse racialized students? Given the difference in affect, how may teacher candidates be exposed to space and power to provide meaningful teaching to diverse racialized students?

Displacement

Displacement, according to the DLN framework, is an internal emotional struggle, the 'culmination that follows disidentification and dislocation' (Sharma et al., this volume). Freud's (1955) theory on displacement describes the psyche's reaction when the interests of the Id and Super-Ego diverge. A disruption to the psyche shifts action from the desired target, deemed unattainable or not reachable, to an attainable, less threatening substitute (Freud, 1955). This reaction manifests as an outcome, courtesy of the ego or self. The culmination of the experience, the outcome, will be discussed in relation to the participants' (re)framed identity and their space-based experiences with power. Furthermore, as the DLN framework provides a lens to understand its displacement and deep impact on the human psyche, the longitudinal nature of this study will provide insight into how these deep impacts cause lasting effects.

Longitudinally gathered, participant data reflects heightened emotional experience not as a gestural vignette, but as a lasting displacement persevered across eight years. These longitudinal deposits are representations of reconciled conceptions, informed by disruptive event(s). By revisiting acts predicated on the experience, we are able to elucidate the participants' displacement longitudinally. In an effort to provide a deep depiction of the participants' experience across the DLN framework, displacement will be applied across the following three different vignettes.

> The students that I teach love stories and they love when I can relate stuff with life … the Grade 8 class that just graduated, things came to them quite easily and they had come from well-to-do families. So, [their teacher] said, 'I need some information'. I was able to relate it to her so that she could share it with her geography class, just about what it was like to get to school and the kids with the no shoes and the uniform that was bare threads. 'Okay, you know what? There is life outside of our little sandbox here … again, just to not take things for granted whether it's what you've got in terms of your resources to, 'Hey, you get an education … you get lunch' and all of those different things. (Jayden)

Jayden perceived the opportunity to partake in the international practicum as a welcome change. Having experienced education in the Ontario context, they desired to travel abroad, to experience new challenges, gain gratitude and become empathetic. Actively pursuing this opportunity, Jayden ascribes to the narrative advertised by the NGO and the institution. Following the DLN framework, the culmination of Jayden's disidentification and dislocation, was a sensational narrative, demonstrating that the only displacement they faced was grounded by either entrenching the narrative or disrupting the narrative. Thus, when they face the idea of whether their trip had meaning, Jayden experiences displacement: they can choose the threatening requiem of their deficit-based understandings or continue to perpetuate their unreal experiences of power.

Ultimately these experiences can demonstrate displacement but the gradation of such experiences varies. Feeling they must share their new knowledge with their students imposes this reality of Kenya – clarifying and/or informing their students' privilege.

The NGO offers minimal, or dosed, disruption, as it constructs experiences (Jefferess, 2012; Moore, 2014). In its very entity, supplanting education through the NGO necessarily situates northern progress and modernization as a standard of measurement or achievement. Thus, aspects of the participants' experiences are not only framed in the northern experience, but they are also (re)creations of northern dynamics. This perpetuation diverts attention from interactions of power, privilege and space, as discussed above in the participants' dislocation.

> *I believe the community members we worked with were hard working, ambitious, kind, and generous. I believe they appreciate the work the NGO does within the community, but I do not underestimate their passion and determination to better their lives themselves. (Logan)*

As the culmination of their experience with disidentification and dislocation, Logan's displacement occurs through focusing on a more suitable target. Participants often hold high ideals of fostering social and pedagogical change through transformative experiences on their international practicum (Grierson & Denton, 2013; Larsen & Searle, 2017). Taking part in an international practicum precludes that Logan desired to work in tandem with the community members to better themselves; it was their duty to act and provide betterment. According to Logan's vignette, folks desired to better their lives.

In their interview, Logan contends that impressive work has been done by the NGO and teacher candidates. However, they continue to question whether they had *enough* of an impact, a line of reasoning and questioning developed to frame Logan's substitute target. Consistent with the DLN framework, displacement occurs in Logan's experience as they recognize initial, expected outcomes may be neither as immediate nor as impactful as anticipated. Logan avoids potential dissonance when considering their impact on the community by shifting their expectations. Through the normalization of deficit (Henfield & Washington, 2012), Logan is empowered to simplify the work behind outcomes, reducing betterment, in their own words, to 'simple investments such as wells and sanitation'. Logan's experience refocuses the narrative on space and the fluidity of the white body (Carr, 2017; Razack, 2005). Despite being a dislocation from their initial ideals of personal pedagogical empowerment and social influence, Logan's substitute target, of impacting the community through mere involvement with the NGO, allows for the experience to remain impactful as they provided betterment and improved themselves. In this instance, displacement amongst white bodies demonstrates that participants can refocus their ideals to be free of disruptive, transformative experiences (Mezirow, 1991), while still feeling transformed.

> Initially I felt as a group we were a newer version of colonialism, where we showed up at their doorstep in a vehicle with all these resources and teaching ideas that didn't take into account their cultural norms and needs. ... My students were witnessed to privilege and materialism. A good example was myself having a pair of shoes on my feet and a watch on my wrist on the first day. My students were fascinated with my watch and none had shoes on their feet. The remaining three weeks I didn't wear a watch as I did not want to appear more advantaged than them, nor did I want them to be focused on aspiring to materialistic things. (Kelly)

Kelly's cumulative experience manifests physically. As a rendezvous between disidentification and dislocation, Kelly's displacement is the heightened emotional response to a challenge to power. Kelly ascribes to an us/them model of identity politics, which was situated in deficit, causing Kelly to lower expectations accordingly (Henfield & Washington, 2012). Ullucci (2010) finds this to be common among white teachers. Kelly's perception, that they may permeate the individual and community's identity, reflects an experience of the reality of lower-class lifestyle, as it focuses on how to live without many material goods (Razack, 2005). What Kelly perceives to disrupt this opportunity was a materialistic marker. By removing what they associate with privilege, Kelly demonstrates the culmination of his disidentification and dislocation, as the bubbled life they are in, both physically and invisibly, allows them to conclude that power is materialistic. As Allen (2004) describes, 'white privilege is structural and cannot be erased' (p. 130). Kelly's attempt to physically erase his privilege was a simplistic response to the disruptive experience. White privilege may be overcome, but acknowledging larger history and contemporary impact is necessary. Kelly's experience reinforces the perception that Westerners have and aspire for material things; however, people in Kenya neither have nor should they aspire to have material things. Limited in critical exploration of his own privilege, Kelly removes his watch in an attempt to decide what Kenyan folks may see of the Western world. This act contributes to the maintenance of white power vis-à-vis a deficit perception of Kenyan people.

As with the other participants, Kelly's displacement occurs through his experience with disidentification and dislocation. Within the DLN framework, displacement is culmination of these experiences: 'a psychic event where there is a shift in action from a desired target to a substitute target' (Sharma et al., this volume). Kelly's uncertainty about permeating the lower-class status, potentially jeopardizing the expected pedagogical and social outcomes of the programme (Grierson & Denton, 2013; Maynes et al., 2013; Larsen & Searle, 2017), results in heightened emotion. In this 'intense moment of rendezvous between disidentification and dislocation' from the DLN framework (Sharma et al., this volume), Kelly's response is to remove his watch, displacing his privilege so that he may become *one of them*, thereby achieving his intended outcome.

Alongside his peers, Kelly's experience demonstrates the ease with which participants may leave an international experience with a superficial transformation (Mezirow, 2000). This superficial understanding affects the individual's development, as represented longitudinally above. Although the international teaching practicum disrupts learning, this disruption occurs across a spectrum. Kelly's experience does not transform his thinking as it does not lead to new understandings. To get the most out of these experiences, we propose using DLN and a productive process to actualize transformation from disruption.

Implications

Adding Another 'D': Interdependence

We agree, based on our analysis, that while the DLN framework lays bare the disruptive experiences of an international practicum, what lies beyond is a consideration of overcoming limited transformation across participants (Mezirow, 2000). Longitudinally, the participants' transformations, represented through the DLN framework, do not produce critical pedagogy focused on disrupting narratives in the classroom (Schwarz, 2015; Smolcic & Katunich, 2017; Trilokekar & Kukar, 2011). We concur with Ntseane (2011) on the need to extend Mezirow's (2000) transformational learning to include critical reflection on cultural context. Taylor (2008) also points to the role of relationships in transformational learning, which includes the role of support from individuals, family, community and overall cultural values, which are described as part of an Africentric paradigm. Incorporating an interrogation of cultural values in transformational learning (home-and-away contexts) will assist learners in developing cultural sensitivity. Culturally sensitive individuals need to be aware of their own cultural values and how these are experienced by those with whom they are interacting (Ntseane, 2011). Culturally sensitive knowledge falls short of diffusing systemic issues of power and privilege, unless it is mobilized. This aligns with Tallon's (2012) critique of the messages students receive due to NGO sensationalization in the Commonwealth (New Zealand), as it leads neither to culturally sensitive knowledge nor meaningful action.

We propose that the DLN framework ought to be followed by a praxis-based opportunity, *interdependence*. Adding the *interdependence* component to the DLN framework allows for the inclusion of Africentricity or Ubuntu philosophy (Taylor, 2008; Ntseane, 2011). This approach challenges the Western neoliberal model, which constructs identity as unitary, sovereign and separate. The *interdependence* component is a community-oriented notion of the individual and how many African (sub-Saharan) cultures identify themselves in relation to the community.

Engaging in the DLN framework, which includes *interdependence*, would require teacher candidates to consider their own culture and context as well as their host's culture and context and how their presence is interpreted by their host. This furthers a call to make international practicums part of a larger credit course, offering opportunities for teacher candidates to critically reflect and evaluate disruptive teaching experiences among peers before and after such international placement opportunities. This shift would represent an institutional investment in the pedagogical development offered to their student population during international practicums.

The DLN framework allows us an understanding of what our doing does, and we are interested in what one may do once one knows what one's doing does. As a capstone to the DLN, *interdependence* pursues action from the experience; praxis in the Canadian setting *and* in the international setting. Participants' doing is participating in the NGO-university partnership and enterprise; underprepared by the institution and restricted by the NGO. Participants knew they desired a taste of the (subaltern) (e.g. Jayden's choice of the university, Kelly's desire to be one of them). They made inquiries and informed presuppositions prior to, during and after the experience. Longitudinally, their displacement enforces conceptions of *other* that are neither critical nor necessarily productive. Per our recommendations, it is imperative that students undergo formal work related to gaining culturally sensitive knowledge with an understanding of how it may be mobilized. Schwarz (2015) has similar findings in their data noting, 'participants' encounters with discomfort did not arouse wider commitments to understanding systemic injustice or to advocating for societal transformation' (p. 10). It is clear from the data that the participants experience a 'disorienting dilemma' while on their practicum (Mezirow, 2000, p. 22). As the DLN framework lays the experience bare, the longitudinal impact of resistance and heightened emotional experience results in simplified and sensationalized perceptions of the *other* (Tallon, 2012; Said, 1978), demonstrating a superficial pedagogical transformation (Mezirow, 2000; Trilokekar & Kukar, 2011).

We propose *interdependence* to interrupt passive DLNs. *Interdependence* is displacement pedagogically actualized. *Interdependence* creates space for mindful dialogue about international practicums and service learning within higher education as a mechanism for place-based learning, 'the process of using the local community and environment as a starting point to [learn]' (Sobel, 2004, p. 6). In response to participants' hyper focus on community and social impact, we must ask how international practicums fundamentally impact teachers and host communities. We may ask: What are the most impactful experiences in practicums? How are they framed? What deficit framing persists in domestic and international placements? Considering the limited transformation of participants' pedagogy based on the Kenyan experience, are the potential power impacts justified? *Interdependence* centres the following question: Can DLNs critically impact teacher candidates' pedagogical development in such an international experience as the one shared in this chapter?

3

Transforming Student Imaginaries of Cuba: Disruptive Learning Approaches in Short-Term Study Abroad Programmes

Aaron M. Lampman and Kenneth Schweitzer

Introduction

Participation by American students in study abroad programmes has increased dramatically over the past few decades. The Institute of International Education (IIE) reports a 300 per cent increase in US college students studying abroad since 1990 (IIE, 2017). Short-term study abroad experiences, defined as eight weeks or less, now account for 63 per cent of the students from the United States who engage in international education (IIE, 2017). Proponents of study abroad suggest that international experiences transform student world views, making them more open to cultural difference, more understanding of the power dynamics of race, class and gender, and more aware of the structural causes of inequality (Caton et al., 2014; Davis-Salazar, 2016; Palacios, 2004; Pan et al., 2011). This transformation in student perceptions is thought to result from interaction with new peoples, places and cultures, and from challenges encountered and overcome when crossing borders both geographic and personal (Bellamy & Weinberg, 2006).

The Disruptive Learning Narrative (DLN) (Sharma et al., this volume) offers a new framework for examining and understanding the transformations that occur in student perspectives during study abroad programmes. The DLN framework builds on observations that the intense and uncomfortable experiences that occur when engaging in robust ways with different cultures can challenge the core value systems and customary ways of thinking for the student. The DLN framework offers a method for reflexively thinking about such experiences in a way that will make sense of the conflicts and tensions that emerge when studying abroad, and how these tensions reshape the personal identity of the student.

In this chapter we argue that the DLN framework provides insight into how encounters with unfamiliar places and social norms can bring previously unquestioned assumptions to the surface for critical reflection and ultimately lead to revisions in personal beliefs about otherness. We will utilize the core features of Sharma, Allen and Ibrahim's (this volume) DLN, disidentification, dislocation and displacement, to discuss ways in which students shed pre-existing notions of Cuba and Cuban people and begin to consciously examine preformed perspectives about political and cultural differences. This process, we believe, leads to the emergence of new perspectives of the other. We will also investigate the ways in which student identities undergo transformation due to challenges to core and unquestioned assumptions they had about Cuba prior to the trip.

The 'Cuba Music and Culture Seminar' is a short-term study abroad course that blends pretravel classroom learning with a two-week immersive experience in Cuba. The course is run by a cultural anthropologist and an ethnomusicologist who work at a small liberal arts college in the mid-Atlantic region of the United States. Before travelling, we introduce students to the history of Cuba and teach extensively about Afro-Cuban music and culture. In January, during the winter break between semesters, we travel to Cuba where we live in a working-class neighbourhood outside the tourist district and introduce students to music venues dominated by Afro-Cuban expressive and religious forms of music and dance. Our pedagogical approach prioritizes extensive interaction with the host community and learning through critical reflection about daily experiences. Throughout the process our students find their comfort zones challenged by interactions that highlight race, class, poverty, privilege and previously held assumptions. In some situations, the students experience 'heterotopia' (Foucault, 1986, p. 24) as the tourist gaze (Urry & Larson, 2011) becomes inverted and they find themselves subjected to the gaze of Cubans. We argue that the DLN can be extended to explore how pre-existing imaginaries, including stereotypes and prejudice, are transformed through experiential learning in the study abroad context.

Our research is based on systematic thematic analysis of the travel journals and post-trip reflection papers of eighty-four students who participated in the Cuba Music and Culture Seminar between 2015 and 2019. Students in the Cuba Music and Culture Seminar are required to write about their experiences in reflective journals every evening. We ask them to split these journals into three sections that include 'observations', 'emotional reactions' and 'emergent insights/new questions'. We examined these travel journal entries in order to assess student narratives about the questions and tensions that emerged from their experiences. To identify and analyze student perceptions, we systematically coded these texts while searching for emergent themes (Bernard et al., 2016; Gibbs, 2008) that are patterned and shared across the group. The most prominent themes that emerged include transforming beliefs about Cuban people and society, breaching of comfort zones and responses to such breaches, feelings of discomfort and uncertainty associated with differing cultural norms and heterotopia, perceptions of immersion and 'being there', indications of liminality and borders, and transformation of pre-existing stereotyped or romanticized perspectives of the other.

Disidentification and Tourist Imaginaries

The 'tourist imaginary' can be defined as the ways in which tourists, including student edu-tourists, collectively imagine, or fantasize about, a place or people (Salazar & Graburn, 2014). Socially transmitted through discourse and media-political representation, these shared imaginaries function as pre-existing schemas of interpretation of otherness that shape student perceptions before and during the study abroad programme (Strauss, 2006). These imaginaries influence the perception of the experience by imposing socially constructed order on experiences and interactions with local people (Urry, 1990). Picard (2011) argues that preformed Western tourist imaginaries are quite difficult to challenge, and that travelling to foreign locations can ultimately confirm, renew and reinforce pre-existing notions about otherness and legitimate the imagined superiority of modern life back home. We argue that study abroad courses can mitigate this process by bringing the powerful cultural lens of pre-existing tourist imaginaries to the forefront to be challenged through group discussion and critical reflection.

In the DLN framework, disidentification is the process of becoming increasingly identified with one's familiar social and cultural norms, or, as we argue, becoming less identified with these norms (Sharma et al., this volume). When disidentification occurs, the student experiences dissonance as they try to make sense of their experiences, forcing them to reframe or recast pre-existing assumptions. A core claim of the DLN is that deep immersion in the 'elsewhere' of a foreign culture (Sharma et al., this volume), with different social norms and power dynamics, can create discomfort that leads to disidentification from unconscious biases and, we suggest, pre-existing imaginaries of otherness. Most tourists in foreign locations are likely to feel such discomforts, but if there exists an immersion spectrum, then study abroad courses that regularly place students outside the 'tourist bubble' (Bosley & Brothers, 2008) are likely to produce substantially more discomfort than tourism focused inside the tourist district replete with the familiarities of home. We argue that pedagogical approaches which immerse students deeply in a place and a culture raise the educational stakes for the student-tourist by assailing their comfort zone and challenging pre-existing perspectives, essentialisms and imaginaries.

Cuba, which lies only 90 miles off the coast of the United States, represents a fiercely forbidden otherness to the average American student. Pre-exposed to collective political discourse and media representations, students have a powerfully preformed 'imaginary' (Salazar & Graburn, 2014). This imaginary emerges in part from the long colonial relationship between Cuba and the United States. This relationship begins with American intervention in the struggle for Cuban independence from Spain in the late nineteenth century and the passing of the *Platt Amendment* in 1903 (Staten, 2015), which gave the United States control over the political decision-making process in Cuba. The early twentieth century saw a series of puppet dictators who served American interests, and the insertion of powerful American corporations that created vast wealth through control over land and labour on the island. In the mid-twentieth century, American organized crime developed a glamorous, corrupt and racially divided tourist mecca for Americans in Havana.

These interventions in Cuban affairs ultimately triggered a small band of rebels to engage in an unlikely revolution that succeeded in the first days of 1959. This revolution, which rejected American legal and political authority on the island, expropriated the land and financial wealth of powerful American interests, and led to retaliation in the form of the US embargo, which has remained in effect for more than sixty years. Since 1959, almost all political rhetoric has portrayed Cuba as an enemy of American interests and a bastion of the 'dark powers' of communism.

Narrative analysis of student journals indicates the power of these colonial imaginaries to create fear of Cuban otherness prior to the trip. One of the most commonly expressed themes was that political difference correlates with personal enmity. As a result, students imagined Cubans to be scary and unfriendly. One student wrote:

> The only thing that we are told about that country is that we are enemies and they are communist. That in itself is enough to make you think we would be walking into an extremely militarized state full of oppressed people and poverty.

Another student indicated, 'I had grown up with this idea that Cuba was off limits. I thought that Cubans hated America and wanted nothing to do with us. I believed that I would be unwelcome in their country'.

These very powerful tourist imaginaries of Cuba set the stage for culture shock and dissonance. The on-the-ground reality of Cuba is almost the opposite of what students expected. One student writes about his attempts to reconcile the disidentification of his expectations with his experience:

> I was already conflicted about the embargo because I thought it was the cause of poverty in Cuba. One day as I was eating lunch, I was turning my experiences over in my head, and here was my line of reasoning: I thought, if a woman who does not even know me can welcome me to her country with hugs and kisses, then America can afford to lift the embargo. This, of course, only proved to be the beginning of the breaking of the chains of misconceptions that imprisoned my brain.

A clear theme emerged that students were emotionally relieved about the reality of being a tourist in Cuba, but a much stronger theme is that their pre-existing perception of Cuba and Cuban people was fundamentally transformed through the process of disidentification from preformed imaginaries. While they imagined a surveilled and oppressed communist state that viewed the tourist with anger and jealousy, they discovered a country that is thriving with intellectual and artistic vigour and met people who enjoyed engaging with tourists on a human level. As an example, one student wrote:

> After spending ten days in Cuba, I found a deeper understanding for the term experiential learning. While traveling to Cuba, I carried some biases that were placed in my head from family, friends, and the media. I had the idea that this would be a poorly developed country, there would be police everywhere, and that Cubans would hate Americans. The cultural experience transformed my knowledge and previous views. The people there were honestly full of life and everyone seemed to be a part of a tight knit community.

Tourist imaginaries of Cuba are also rooted in colonial fantasies about the Caribbean. Media images from the mid-twentieth century onwards portray utopian fantasies of a pristine 'Garden of Eden' (Picard, 2011), peopled with exotic and primitive others. The image of the mulatta, for example, was a racialized mid-century standard for advertisements designed to attract tourism to the island. The typical images of the mulatta present a lightened woman of colour in the act of dancing before a crowd. Scantily clad in colourful clothing, the mulatta offered Americans a fantasy of mysterious beauty and forbidden desire, and the scandalous possibility of racial mixing at a time in which miscegenation laws were the norm in the American south.

These types of essentializing fantasies of Caribbean otherness are part of the collective American imaginary even today. For example, one of our students wrote: 'Before the trip I read that the people who live there are a vibrant and passionate people who are out dancing, making music, and "living life". Not like Americans who binge watch TV in their spare time'. There are subtle subtexts in this statement that hint at larger tourist imaginaries of the Caribbean as a 'hot' or 'steamy' place of sensual music and dance, both in terms of geography and in terms of an imagined essentialized character of the people. Free from the confines of a nine-to-five job and the prison of technological advancement, Cubans are imagined as free to spend their time making music and dancing or, as the student indicates, 'living life'. After two weeks in Cuba, however, the same student reflects on his preconceived notions and the following statement indicates that his tourist imaginaries underwent disidentification due to surprising and authentic interactions with the host community:

> The gradual, almost unconscious sedimentation of continuous, tiny observations did a lot to reshape and solidify my mental landscape of Cuba. The people with whom I spoke were an integral part of this change. Alina, for example, proudly showed me her framed university degree. But she also showed me the ration books that are used to obtain the weekly allotments of food staples like rice but also necessary products like diapers. She told me, without my prompting, that she's grateful for what her country has given her, but that sometimes things are difficult – even so, she's happy with her life, the people in it, and what she has. These conversations provided data – less easily quantifiable data, certainly, but valuable nonetheless – that expanded and humanized Cuba for me.

After the revolution and the imposition of the American embargo, Cuba developed a special relationship with the Soviet Union that culminated with the missile crisis, an event many worried could start a third world war. American visions of Cuba shifted towards perceptions of a surveilled, oppressed and impoverished population. The sudden withdrawal of the Soviet Union from Cuba at the end of the Cold War, when combined with the American embargo, resulted in a near halt to any essential commercial goods reaching Cuba. From 1990 to 2000, the Cuban populace went through extreme economic hardship. All existing commercial products on the island, no matter how old or damaged, were rebuilt or repurposed so that the population could survive. This included cars imported from America in the 1950s, and homes that would generally be condemned due to safety concerns. The impact of these historical events on the American imaginary is of a Cuba that is unchanged by modernity. As one of our students wrote prior to the trip, 'I imagined a land stuck in time'.

According to Echtner and Prasad (2003), the notion of undeveloped nations as unchanged and frozen in time is one of the most prominent imaginaries held by Western tourists. This deeply ingrained and often unconscious imaginary was originally constructed as part of the global colonial project intent on invasion, exploitation and remaking of Africa and the Americas in the European image. The imaginary can also be linked to early theories of social evolution, which posited that all societies would inevitably advance from stages of primitivism to civilization (see Tylor, 1871). More recently, this imaginary is deeply embedded in the basic assumptions of post–Second World War modernization projects intent on global development and economic progress, and adventure tourism packages promising exotic encounters with local and native peoples. More than half of our students wrote in their journals that they imagined that travelling to Cuba would be like travelling back in time.

Rosaldo (1989) argues that the tourist myth of people frozen in time often transforms into longing for imagined traditional cultures that survive intact despite the ravages of colonization. He calls this longing for a simple or more spiritual pre-modern people 'imperialist nostalgia'. For many of our students, some form of imperialist nostalgia seems to have motivated them to travel to Cuba before it is irrevocably transformed by capitalism. As an example, one of our students wrote in his journal prior to the trip, 'The opening of Cuba and the flood of people from the United States might bring a selfish aspect to Cuba that could tamper with the deep beauty and spirituality of its people'. After two weeks of interactions with Cuban people and critical discussion and reflection, we can see transformation in some student perspectives. One of our students, for example, wrote at the end of the trip:

> Before we traveled, I heard a podcast that discussed some people's fears that Cuba will become too touristy or Westernized as a result of the opening up of relations between the US and Cuba. I now think this fear is pretty revealing: it seemed to be usually expressed by tourists themselves, whose concern seemed to stem more from a desire to maintain the product they were consuming – that is,

a very specific image of Cuban culture, replete with mojitos, old cars, and nightclubs – rather than from uncertainty about the ramifications of that change on the Cuban people themselves. I share a similar fear that the opening of relations will have a rapid and negative impact, but my concerns stem more from the difficulty of balancing Cuba's very real need for tourism as its primary industry with a wariness of economic, cultural, and even sexual exploitation by people from the U.S. and other foreign countries.

Ultimately, the result of colonial history is that Cuba and its people are preconceived by Americans as the radical other. These perceptions tend to lead to the formation of dichotomous categories for our students, including hardened perceptual distinctions between capitalist/communist, impoverished/wealthy, oppressed/free, weak/powerful and Latin/Anglican. It is difficult to dispel such powerful imaginaries through classroom teaching. We argue that experiential learning through study abroad often leads to disidentification, dislocation and displacement of such ideas, allowing for radical transformation of world views.

Spatial Dislocation and Power Inversions

Dislocation happens when one becomes estranged from familiar social and cultural norms, and when one is immersed in unfamiliar spaces and surrounded by unfamiliar people, languages and power relations that regulate social interactions (Sharma et al., this volume). Whereas the spatial element of dislocation creates physical and emotional discomfort, the social element of dislocation brings unquestioned assumptions about behaviour to the surface. These processes of dislocation facilitate critical reflection about self and other.

In general, Western tourists in other countries maintain a position at the top of the socio-economic power structure while touring, especially when they remain in the tourist bubble which is designed specifically to provide the comforts and services of home. Most tourists unconsciously expect to 'gaze' at the people, natural places, and cultural and historical sites of a foreign country. This tourist gaze (Urry & Larsen, 2011) comes from a place of power and privilege, as it is the tourist who has come to this place to gaze upon otherness. Inevitably the power status of the tourist is challenged in a multitude of ways, which causes stress and discomfort. It can be disempowering, for example, to be unable to communicate effectively when navigating seemingly simple and routine tasks in another country. More serious inversion of the normal power structure can happen when the tourist steps outside of the tourist bubble and engages with local people in more authentic ways. Complete inversion of the power structure, which happens when local people invert the 'gaze' at the tourist, can lead to profound discomfort and reflection and exploration of pre-existing beliefs about the world.

The Cuba Music and Culture Seminar actively promotes a sense of spatial dislocation and discomfort among our students by requiring them to live in a working-class neighbourhood outside the tourist bubble. The sights and sounds in this neighbourhood make no concessions to tourist desires. We promote social and cultural dislocation by requiring the students to participate in structured activities that are deeply unfamiliar on multiple planes. Among the most challenging of these activities is a series of dance classes, offered by members of one of Cuba's most prestigious dance troupes, Conjunto Folclórico Raices Profundo, which specializes in African-derived dances such as those associated with the religions Santería, Palo-Monte and Abakua. Founded in 1975 by former members of Cuba's Conjunto Folclórico Nacional, Raices Profundo has performed across the globe, with multiple tours to Latin America, North America, Europe, Asia and Africa. We argue that dance can engender a visceral sense of embodied dislocation that leads to profound and critical exploration of one's social, cultural and physical norms and assumptions.

Each year, the dance classes begin on our first morning in Havana. Still weary from the previous day of travel, the students have an early breakfast and set out from the homestays for the five-block walk to the permanent workshop and rehearsal space of Raices Profundo. Navigating crumbling streets of Centro Havana, we dodge hundreds of Cubans on their way to work and soon arrive at the entrance to the workshop. From the street the workshop looks abandoned, resembling something that would have been condemned in the United States. Passing through the doorway, the students enter a large, vaulted space. Grey in colour, the floor is dotted with puddles of water. High above, the roof is half-covered with corrugated metal, with large, jagged gaps caused by collapses that allow them to see the blue sky above and glints of sunshine that provided the only natural light in the space.

A closer inspection reveals that this space had a noble past as a beautiful theatre. Crumbling remnants of the stage, box seating and balcony are clearly visible. The space is somewhat shocking and creates dissonance for the students, as it is hard to imagine a globally successful and prestigious performance ensemble working within such an austere environment. Of course, the students grab their cameras alternately framing shots that illustrate the decay and the former glory of this theatre. Many of these photos find their way into our post-trip multimedia journals, providing evidence of their profound sense of dislocation.

Nothing in the American tourist imaginary prepares our students for the experience of learning to dance in the dilapidated and yet beautiful workshop of Raices Profundo. Here they respond to a sense of dislocation that challenges both their sense of other and their preconceived views of American superiority. Rather than posit the decaying state of theatre as evidence of Cuban shortcomings, our students imagine it as a symbol of hope. As one student put it, 'It was beautiful. It was this raw beauty that had been entirely untouched by American capitalism. It was fresh and real, unlike anything I had ever seen before'. The profound sense of wonderment expressed by the student hints at the challenge this place issues to preconceived constructions of otherness. The sheer dystopian beauty of fallen modernity, once perceived as inferior, is transformed into an expression of perseverance and of the authenticity of Cuba. This strong response was shared by many of our students as evidenced by a similar comment that 'the dilapidated theatre that was home to our dance lessons became a metaphor for Cuba itself, as traces remain of a once grand venue that has eroded with time, but perseveres nonetheless'.

Dislocation can have an embodied element as well. One can become acutely aware of his or her body when asked to engage in unfamiliar actions and movements. Many tourists come to Cuba with the express goal of learning social dances like salsa that are designed to facilitate exuberant, sensual, playful and 'festive happenings' in tourist dance clubs (Simoni, 2016, p. 153). However, these tourist-centred activities do little to promote a sense of dislocation as they cater to pre-formulated expectations and desires. Though activities such as salsa lessons may appear exotic to the participants, and likely push many outside of their physical comfort zone, the classes actually reinforce tourist imaginaries that Cubans, much like other imagined 'primitives', are carefree and sensual, and constantly dancing.

Unlike most tourists who voluntarily take salsa dance classes, our students are *required* to take lessons on the religious dance of Afro-Cuban Santeria. The instructors, who live and work outside the tourist bubble, are not paid to smile and make sure that our students are having fun. There is no play involved in the sessions, and individual bodies do not touch except to correct a posture. Unlike salsa, Afro-Cuban ritual movements are highly prescribed, and are intimately connected to the mythology and broader belief systems of their respective religions. These religious dances are difficult, both physically and conceptually, and require the dancer to relate with individual Afro-Cuban deities (called *orishas*) and their metaphysical essence. The goal of exposing students to this dance tradition is not simply to have them learn the dance steps. Instead, we use this exercise as an alternate means of acquiring knowledge, so that the students develop a corporeal understanding of each *orisha*'s personality. That is, through dance we ask the students to embody the essence of the *orishas* and to feel these traits. It gives them a more holistic understanding of the religious tradition.

The sense of dislocation experienced by our students during dance lessons is outwardly projected and clearly observable in their frustrated behaviour. Analysis of journal entries indicates that students experience an acute sense of spatial and social dislocation. They feel incompetent and are unfamiliar with learning to dance for religious purposes rather than for performance or social engagement. Their discomfort can be attributed to the synthesis of a multitude of sensory inputs including an unfamiliar physical setting, intrusion on the norms and expectations for dancing in the Caribbean, being instructed in an unfamiliar language and adapting to a new sonic environment of Afro-Cuban drumming. These sensory inversions combine with the physical exertion that comes from engaging the full body in unfamiliar movements, and the mental exertion of learning about the metaphysical/ritual contexts of the movements. For the duration of the classes the immersion was complete, enveloping their senses, minds and bodies. As one student pointed out:

> As much as I enjoy to dance on my own, the dance class was completely out of my comfort zone. I struggled a lot during this class and found myself getting very overwhelmed and stressed out … the dance was not physically tiring for myself, but it took a lot out of me emotionally.

Ritual can be more fully understood through participation (see Griffith & Marion, 2018; Schieffelin, 1985; Simoni, 2016; Skinner, 2008), as much ritual knowledge can only be apprehended through the body. We argue that the experience of embodied dislocation can also lead to a more thorough understanding of the other by lowering social and cultural barriers in the student psyche. For our students engaged in religious dance lessons, the act of embodying unfamiliar cultural concepts enhanced a sense of 'being there' and provided our students with a means to better integrate themselves within the various Afro-Cuban religious rituals that we attended throughout the trip. One student identified the dance classes as 'some of my favorite hours spent in Cuba because I felt like I was physically feeling what it was like to live in Cuba'. Another student felt that 'the dance lessons acted as the platform to transition our exposure of Afro-Cuban music from thought to action,' and helped to 'experience their spiritual rituals instead of merely watching'. An insider's experience is an embodied experience, and dislocation is amplified by the sensation of being an insider within unfamiliar geographies.

Dislocation can also create shifts in power relations that lead to critical self-reflection about unquestioned assumptions of the other. Like most tourists, our students arrive in Havana primed to observe, to 'gaze' upon Cuba's cultural and physical wonders. As tourists, they are consumers. They imagine that they will see colonial architecture, listen to world-class musicians, eat interesting cuisine, chat with locals and hear interesting views on life, politics and many other things. Mandatory religious dance classes, offered in the middle of a working-class neighbourhood, invert this gaze and cause extreme discomfort for our students.

Arriving by foot, dressed in designer workout clothing, carrying colourful backpacks and water bottles, twenty college-aged Americans inevitably draw the attention of locals. When the dance classes begin, the students enjoy a degree of privacy. But as the morning passes, local residents are drawn to the open entryway of the old theatre. They appear curious, and a bit humoured by the American students who seem to struggle to learn the unfamiliar movements. In their journals, the students note the presence of the observers, and indicate an awareness that they are no longer just consumers of Cuban culture but are increasingly the object of the Cuban gaze. This becomes a powerful instance of displacement for our students because they are aware that they have transformed from edu-tourists who consume a semi-packaged version of Cuban culture into suddenly becoming the subject of the Cuban gaze. The watchers become the watched. The privileged American middle-class student becomes the subject of curiosity and entertainment for Cuban observers. This occurs during their initial dance class on the first morning in Havana and extends throughout the two-week period. This inversion has powerful implications for the students' perception of self and other. It forces some of them to question their privileged status.

Though our students always drew a small crowd when dancing in this theatre, on one occasion the instructor decided to engage the spectators more deliberately and moved the students from the relative safety of the theatre out into the street. Whereas their initial response was one of intense discomfort, the students accepted their new role and relaxed. One in particular shared, 'It didn't matter if I was the worst dancer, ... it's about having fun and sharing an experience'. Though the inversion of gaze had an initial impact of generating anxiety, it also helped transform the students' views of themselves and redefine/displace their relationship to Cubans. One student appreciated that the 'locals seemed to enjoy watching us Americans struggle to learn'. Another demonstrated her awareness of the inversion noting that 'the locals displayed passion that we were trying to learn instead of viewing them [the Cubans] as a show'. Having allowed themselves to become the spectacle, our students began to perceive themselves as pseudo-insiders. One student summed up the experience, 'The dance classes were some of my favorite hours spent in Cuba because I felt like I was physically feeling what it was like to live in Cuba'.

Displacement and Changing Views of Otherness

Displacement, which results from first going through the processes of disidentification and dislocation, is when the individual is confronted with a new reality and is forced to respond in their own psyche (Sharma et al., this volume). Displacement can take the form of an unexpected burst of emotion, or it can trigger psychological mechanisms such as denial, intellectualizing, rationalization or repression. We argue that displacement can also manifest in a breakthrough from entrenched ways of thinking such as suppressed ethnocentrism and racism. When an event causes an individual to suddenly realize that they harbour ethnocentric or racist feelings, it can trigger the individual to explore these unconscious feelings perhaps for the first time and often in a more thorough fashion. This process can cause an emergence (often in sudden and emotional fashion) of a new understanding of both the other and of the self.

Two similar events that occurred in Cuba during our 2019 study abroad trip illustrate displacement leading to radical changes in views of the other. In preface, it is important to note that our pretravel lectures include extensive conversations emphasizing safe travel practices. Students are encouraged to be careful with their personal safety, to walk together in groups especially at night and to be vigilant of their belongings. At the same time, however, we emphasize that Havana, which is one of the most crime-free cities in the world, is also widely viewed as one of the safest places for single female travellers. Students are told that most Cubans are warm, friendly, open and curious about the world. We also tell them to trust the families that run our homestays, and to leave their passports, credit cards and the majority of their spending cash in their rooms. This will greatly mitigate the chance of losing something important and or having it stolen. Pre-exposure to political rhetoric and stereotypes is powerful;

however, our students tend to be somewhat wary of Cubans who they view in racialized ways and perceive as impoverished and potentially desperate. Many students feel it is safer to carry their money and passports with them at all times so that they can personally protect their belongings.

One event that reveals preconceived stereotypes and prejudices occurred during a relaxing day trip to the countryside. When we stopped for an extended lunch, the students spread themselves over a large area to engage in small group discussions. As we ate and talked, a couple of Cuban nationals who were not part of our scheduled programme joined the groups. They were invited to eat lunch and engaged the students in friendly conversation. In this relaxed environment, students were free to come and go, and to explore our natural setting. Feeling at ease in the rural environment and in the company of friendly locals, they became less vigilant about watching their personal belongings. Despite being told to keep their bags together, the students' belongings were strewn all over the lunch area. After several hours in the countryside, we packed up and returned to Havana on the bus.

Later that afternoon, one of our students came to us in a panic and told us his wallet had been stolen from his backpack during the day. All of his money, about $3000 in total, was in the 'stolen' wallet. We asked why he was carrying all of his funds, rather than leaving most of it in his room, and the response was that he felt that it would be safer to carry his money with him (an indication that he did not trust his homestay hosts). The entire group was very upset and angry, and everyone felt that the obvious culprits were the Cubans who had joined us during lunch. There was a palpable feeling amongst the group that we had collectively made a serious misjudgement in trusting these young men. Through the evening and well into the next morning, a dark cloud hung over the group. The next day, by sheer luck, we got onto the exact same bus to travel to another destination. Perhaps ten minutes into the trip, the student discovered his wallet underneath the seat on the floor of the bus. The wallet was intact, and all of his money was there.

The reaction from the group was profound shock, shame and guilt. The group had spent the last twelve hours displacing the blame for the loss of the wallet on friendly Cubans who had innocently and enthusiastically engaged with them in conversation the previous day. When it was presumed the wallet had been stolen, pre-existing stereotypes concerning the desperation and criminal nature of the Cuban other had been confirmed and reaffirmed. Finding the wallet shifted the blame from Cubans, squarely onto the shoulders of the student himself. We found ourselves having conversations about social and ethical norms in Cuba and about how otherness is not something to automatically distrust but is, in fact, generally created by pre-existing stereotypes and prejudice. Narratives in student journals indicate that students underwent displacement in their thinking about Cuba. For example, one student wrote about the event, saying, 'I was able to conclude that Cubans are a deeply ethical people. They live and breathe their beliefs rather than keep their spiritual and daily lives separate, which may be the reason they are such honest and happy people'.

The second event that profoundly impacted our students' imaginaries of otherness occurred while we were touring Havana's Old Town (La Havana Vieja). After several hours of learning about the city's five-hundred-year history, and visiting its museums and historic sites, we all split up into smaller groups to go to lunch. Two hours later, as we regrouped in the central plaza, a Cuban waiter entered the square holding a wallet over his head. He quickly located his target, one of our students who had eaten at his restaurant, and came over and handed him the wallet. The student, who was shocked and dumbfounded, offered the waiter a reward. But the waiter waived him off and quickly retreated. The wallet was intact, and everything in it had been returned to its rightful owner. The restaurant the student had eaten at was a couple of blocks away, indicating that the waiter had spent quite a bit of time and gone far out of his way to find the student and return the wallet.

Everyone was stunned and there was an overwhelming sense of disbelief among the group. The waiter had not only returned the wallet intact, but he had hunted the student down through the streets of Havana to do so. Repressed preconceptions of Cubans as impoverished and desperate were demolished through one simple act of kindness and responsibility. The students relished in telling the story to anyone and everyone who wasn't there to witness the event. Months later in the United States, the student who had left his wallet at the restaurant proclaimed to us: 'I'll never forget that moment for the rest of my life. I tell everyone that story' while shaking his head at the incredulity of the act.

It is likely that these events caused many of our students to fundamentally reorganize their understanding of the Cuban other. Prior to the trip they rationalized that Cubans are desperate based on the fact that, according to government statistics, the average Cuban earns the equivalent of $40 US per month. These wages are so low that our students imagine an essential criminality that does not exist, and justify their fear of the other as rational. They perceive a very real power differential between their own wealth and privilege and that of Cubans, and assume that Cubans, as a result of poverty, will take any opportunity to take advantage of tourists. These assumptions are further strengthened by racialized views of Cubans and the perception of enmity between Americans and Cubans.

Conclusions

Tourists often seek out unfamiliar locations and unfamiliar social and cultural norms in what resembles a 'pilgrimage' towards transcendence of everyday reality (Griffith & Marion, 2018). While the tourist experience often causes discomfort, which has the potential to trigger critical reflection, uncomfortable experiences can also refresh, renew and confirm pre-existing assumptions about the other. Furthermore, ensconced in the tourist bubble, many tourists find themselves surrounded by smiling service personnel ready to provide all of the comforts of home. Such experiences are not likely to cause transformations in perspectives about otherness.

Using the DLN as an analytical framework (Sharma et al., this volume), we have argued that short-term study abroad programmes which intentionally and unintentionally challenge a student's comfort zone are more likely to create critical self-reflection and transformation of perspectives about the other. Our programme, which is spatially outside the tourist district, fosters intellectual and cultural discomfort. The activities we use to engage students with the host community challenge them physically, create authentic interactions with local peoples and lead to inversions of power relations. Immersion in local activities outside of the tourist zone provides opportunity for coincidental encounters that lead to unanticipated outcomes and new perspectives that challenge images of essentialized others.

Cuba is a mysterious place for Americans. The long history of colonial and neocolonial relations between these two countries sets the stage for powerful tourist imaginaries of Cuba. Most Americans imagine that Cubans will hold this history against the American people. Lingering cultural longings for a simpler place, one that has the trappings of 'pristine' tropical beaches and pre-modern peoples is part of the fabric of these imaginaries. The notion that Cuba is frozen in time is also embedded in pre-existing stereotypes and essentialisms. The fact of 'being there', in a working-class community of Cuban people struggling to find security and meaning in everyday life leads to disidentification from these pre-existing student-tourist imaginaries.

Pre-existing essentialisms of Cuban people are tied to a larger racial project of Caribbean fantasies. Music and dance are associated with sensual primitivism and simple pleasures in the tourist imaginary. The spatial and cultural dislocation inherent to a study abroad programme can challenge such imaginaries. We argue that embodied experiences are even more powerful at creating dislocation from familiar ways of being and modes of thought, opening the student to critical reflection of previously held assumptions. Engaging in Afro-Cuban religious dance is so unfamiliar that it leads to transformation in perspectives on the essence of Caribbean dancing. It also allows students to explore Afro-Cuban rituals in more holistic ways. Religious dance also challenges pre-existing power relations between mostly white American students and mostly Black Cubans. The tourist gaze becomes inverted when Cubans watch American students attempting to learn religious dance moves. The dissonance this creates opens the student to new perspectives about these power relationships.

The tourist imaginary, which fundamentally relies on an unequal relationship between the tourist and local peoples, includes an aspect of the fear of the unknown other. Part of this is tied to racial beliefs, and part of it is tied to socio-economic disparity and the concern that the impoverished other is desperate. Unexpected encounters that result from deep immersion in the host community can lead to displacement of preconceived assumptions. In Cuba, we show that distrust for the other can be transformed when stereotypes and prejudices are challenged, leading to a new sense of how powerful essentialism can be, and attempts to overcome ethnocentrism.

The DLN provides a framework for understanding how these pre-existing perspectives are transformed. Through robust engagement with different cultures, students experience discomfort and dissonance. This provides new opportunities for growth and learning. Thus, such experiences can transform essentialized notions of otherness. Such transformations are not inherent to the tourist experience, we argue, but come from the deep immersion, authentic interactions, and discussion and critical reflection of embodied experiences.

4

Disruptive Learning Narratives: Canada to Kenya Returns

Hermia Anthony and Njoki Wane

Education in Canada, a colonized, settler country, is skewed towards the Western European world view (Pete et al., 2013; Syed, 2010; Tetty & Putlampu, 2005; Wane, 2009). White settler colonialism has functioned in part by deploying institutions of Western education to achieve cultural assimilation (Alfred, 2005; Smith, 2012; Tuck & Yang, 2012; Wane & Simmons, 2011). The system reproduces graduates who have been 'marinated in Eurocentrism' (Battiste, 2013), and whose success in educational institutions prepare them for roles as teachers, administrators and policymakers to sustain the system. Canada's *Truth and Reconciliation Commission Report* (2015) acknowledges the traumatic impact on Indigenous population, as well as the historical biases, exclusionary, and violent practices that devalue Indigenous knowledges and learning systems, and recommends that educational institutions implement corrective measures. How do we respond to the strident calls for this kind of change to realign relations of power that dislodge the hierarchy of knowledges, which are the source of global coloniality of power and de-pathologize relations of knowledges in Canadian education? Is educational transformation possible?

Transformative education disrupts hegemonic discourses, institutional practices and systemic structures that perpetuate dominant knowledge forms. Educators who recognize teaching and learning as political acts are challenged to disrupt conventional pedagogies and knowledges that perpetuate social inequity and injustice. Indigenous scholars (e.g. Alfred, 2009; Codjoe, 2005; Tuck et al., 2014; Waziyatawin & Yellow Bird, 2012; Wildcat et al., 2014) have advanced the decolonization of education as a pathway to transformation.

This chapter foregrounds the narratives of graduate students pursuing studies in Social Justice Education in a Canadian institution and a professor who organizes educational visits to Kenya. The participants are of African ancestry. Their subjective positions as students of Social Justice in Education disclose the significance of their attention to issues of race and anti-racism in order to decolonize knowledge forms and flows. Njoki, who is Kenyan, initiated the group visits and her narrative anchors the stories of three students, Ashfa, Yanika and Ebony, who dialogue reflectively as scholars of Social Justice Education, on the moments that they committed to memory of their first visit to Kenya. This chapter highlights their stories as they dialogue reflectively about their experiences.

We pay particular attention to how the Disruptive Learning Narrative (DLN) framework (Sharma et al., this volume) interpolates with theories of decolonization to better understand how students who pursue studies in equity studies in a Canadian institution make sense of their educational visit to Kenya. In what follows, we review perspectives on decolonization. We bring to the forefront the current preoccupation with Indigenous knowledge in educational scholarship as a social justice education imperative and how race has been used in Western thought and ideas to promote the essentialist view that Africans and African societies are a monolith of poverty and depravity, with lacks and deficits that ascribe greater value to Western European thought that is conceived in the Global North. Finally, we concretize these theoretical concepts with research we carried out with graduate students from the Department of Social Justice Education. Our empirical research demonstrates an effort to highlight certain aspects and gaps in educators' learning that, if corrected, could contribute to the preparation of educators for transformative roles and in effecting pedagogical changes to develop a consciousness of being in a majority country with a racialized population in educational institutions.

This chapter emerged in the context of the findings of a similar study that analyses Canadian teacher candidates' experiences in Tanzania. Sharma et al. (this volume) utilized vignettes based on their observations of participants' intense, disruptive and uncomfortable moments to develop the DLN framework. The DLN contemplates a three-stage adjustment phase, which begins with disidentification through dislocation, and finally displacement. The 'stagist' construct that the researchers noted requires deconstruction and furthermore attention when considering such international experiences.

Njoki's Story: Longing for Both Worlds, and Belonging to None

In 2004, I travelled to Kenya with four colleagues from a large Canadian University. The trip marked the beginning of many such ventures to the continent. These trips became my way of showing off my Kenya, my continent, my culture and everything about me. Little did I know that I cannot claim Kenya, Africa or its culture as mine. The continent, or any part of the African continent, does not belong to any one of us, and as Cheikh Anta Diop said, the continent lives in us. Colonization has claimed almost the whole of the African land mass. In addition to this, the colonial project has convinced many people of the African continent that it is not a place to live or there is nothing good that can be found in that continent. The African land mass has been referred to as the 'Dark Continent'. Its habitants have been called all kinds of names: primitive, backward, uncivilized and lazy. As the first term in the DLN framework indicates, I intend to *disrupt* this narrative. This disruption is supported by my ongoing research on the continent's wealth of knowledge on every subject. Also, the narrative is supported by my research among rural women in Kenya, in addition to my eagerness to share what I have learnt with Canadians who are willing to join me on my yearly trips to Africa.

Moments of Dislocation

In 1987 I travelled to Canada to pursue a master's degree in education. Despite the fact that I had a master's degree from a university in Kenya, I was willing to put that aside and go to the West and enrol in another graduate programme. I wanted to fulfil my dream of being part of the Western mosaic, being as close as possible to whiteness. During my colonial education in Kenya, I learnt so much about the West and in particular about Canada: the Great Lakes, lumbering, wheat growing in the prairies, the Rocky Mountains. In my own imaginary world, Canadian streets were paved in gold and money could be collected everywhere. Growing up in Africa, the nursery rhymes were about princesses who had blue eyes and skin that was as white as snow. I had never seen snow. In my own imagination, I could not visualize someone whose colour was white and whose eyes were the colour of the sky or where one could easily be a princess. I was in for a shock when there was an announcement from the captain that we were close to St. John, Newfoundland, and we should look out through the window. All that I saw was marshland spotted by lakes.

What is that? I remember asking myself. I thought I would see the prairies and dense forest. I remember checking my ticket and flight information to ensure that I was indeed going to Canada and that the first stopover was St. John. I can still remember coming out the plane and looking around for the skyscrapers and not finding any. I consoled myself because Fredericton, New Brunswick, was my final destination. I could not contain myself. The three-hour stopover felt like a lifetime.

My new hometown, Fredericton, brought me face to face with the reality soon enough. I had no words to describe my disappointment in what I saw. The city was quite small with a population of less than thirty thousand people. I had come from Nairobi that had more than 3 million people in it. I honestly felt like I was dreaming and that, at any moment, I would wake up from my dream. Let me pause and talk to you a little bit about Kenya, my country of birth.

Kenya is a land of diversity – from the mountains where my village is to the arid areas of the North Eastern province, the white sandy beaches of the Coastal province or the tea farms in the Rift Valley. I always breathe deeply while travelling through these areas, taking in the contrast of the landscape as I travel across Kenya. Kenya's history is fascinating. However, the fascination depends on who tells the story. My initial dislocation from the original Kenyan story was when my parents sent me to a colonial boarding school. I learnt nothing about the African culture; everything was Eurocentric and nothing like Dad's stories of the great African societies, which later I learned was the African cultural wealth of knowledge that the Europeans wanted us to forget about. I have always argued that attending the colonial boarding school marked the end of my traditional African education and the beginning of a world full of contradictions and tension. More importantly, it interrupted my peaceful village life – the beautiful evening when mother would be making dinner and telling us stories, or the morning or evening prayers to our Creator (Ngai) when either my dad or mum would give thanks for the rising or setting sun, for the day ahead of us or the day we had just spent. They would give thanks for everything, including our food and our neighbours (Wane and Simmons, 2011).

The colonial school marked the end of my traditional teachings and the beginning of my inculcation to a foreign way of living, spiritual practices and education, different culture and morning rituals. What was unfortunate for me was that my parents did not know that my traditional teachings were not going to be taken up in the colonial school. They trusted the European Sisters to whole-heartedly prepare their daughter to be who she wanted to be. My parents did not know that the Sisters' teaching, their way of life, had no space for ours and could not even compete with the new life I was going to be introduced to. My African teachings would then be squashed and pushed to a distant memory, creating a sense of disidentification, one of the elements of the DLN framework, with what I once knew but had not completely disowned. I say this with pride because, many years later, I picked up the threads that I had dropped at the entrance of my primary education and started on a quest to research, teach and write on African Indigenous knowledges.

My dislocation and discomfort pushed me to create a central place in my psyche for African knowledge. Over the years, I have privileged my Africanness over other ways of knowing. It was my wanting to show off Africa that made me start organizing trips to Africa for Canadians. I wanted to dispel the myth about Africa. I wanted to disrupt the narrative of poverty, backwardness, of the primitive and uncivilized savage. One thing that my research has enabled me to assert is this: I come from a great people. My words are affirmed by what other people have written about people of African ancestry.

For instance, *Black Inventors: From Africa to America* by Gibbs (1995) provides detailed accounts of innovation and invention that first began in prehistoric Africa. The book also shows what is happening today in Africa. It describes the current achievements that can rescue Europe and America from the woes of over-industrialization. Africa has numerous physicians and technicians working with the World Health Organization, whose contribution to the depredation of smallpox or river blindness have gone unreported in the West (Gibbs, 1995). Ali Mazrui quoted by Gibbs states:

> The old images of the African in the western romantic thought are now realizing a new meaning for the western civilization itself. The African has indeed often conceded a nearness to nature. But in the context of modern problems ... the African continent, partly through ancient Egypt, helped to release the forces of rationality by contributing to the Greek intellectual miracle. Out of that Greek rationality there gradually evolved a Western rationalism ... and finally a sense of anomie at the heart of western civilization. ... Sub-Sahara traditions of fusion between ideals and materialism ... between the individual and society, could ... put Africa once again in the mainstream of relevant civilized values. (Gibbs, 1995, p. 228)

My own research has reaffirmed Mazrui's words. African Indigenous ways of knowing included the total person, society and integrated into science and technology. It is important to note that African Indigenous education was not compartmentalized into disciplines, rather it was highly integrated (Omolewa,

2007). For instance, Odora (1994) demonstrates what used to happen when children would be taught how to build houses. They would simultaneously learn about the soil types, different forms of wood that would be resistant to degradation due to rain or ants. The Indigenous education was almost wiped out by colonization, but not completely as my research has shown. Kwame Ture and Charles Hamilton demonstrated in their book, *Black Power: The Politics of Liberation in America* (1992), that we, people of African ancestry, have to tell our story. We are the ones to correct the miseducation and misinformation about ourselves. No one will do it. Different people will choose different methods of correcting the misinformation. I have chosen two paths, research and writing and taking people to the continent to see for themselves her reality, her rhythms and her beauty. My hope is to create a collective memory that is cohesive and coherent. However, my writing will have different interpretations for those who read it. The visitors who visit Africa with me may wear coloured, colonial glasses and see what they have been taught about Africa. That is also fine. The important aspect of this work is to create a narrative that is disruptive.

My passion for Africanness is also articulated by Thabo Mbeki who laid claim to his heritage during his speech in 1996. He affirmed the fundamental truth that he was born of a people who are heroes and heroines. He was proud to state, 'I am an African'. In that speech, he called for an African Renaissance and challenged outside perceptions about the continent and her people. Mbeki's argument resonates with scholars and activists such as W. E. B. Du Bois, Cheikh Anta Diop, Maulana Karenga, Molefi Asante, Ama Mazama, C. Tsehloane Keto, Marcus Garvey, Kwame Nkrumah, Ngũgĩ wa Thio'ngo, Malcolm X and many others. Their call for renaissance continues in the tradition that rejects the myth that Africa has no civilization or history – nothing. A scholar such as John Henrik Clarke (1991) indicated that the struggle to centre the African system that was disrupted by colonization began with a revolution soon after the First and Second World Wars. The African revolution, characterized by a resurgence in pan-Africanism, determination to achieve political independence and the appreciation of African culture, was to challenge colonialism and white hegemony that made people dislocate from their traditions, values and directions. Molefi Asante (2007) calls on the African people to pursue, in the most determined way, the rebirth of their culture, philosophy and systems of thought in the form of a renaissance, and redemption, perhaps, from feelings of dislocation from Africa.

The vision of African Renaissance is best echoed by Amy Jacques Garvey (1968) who stated:

It is my sincere hope and desire that this small volume will help to disseminate among the members of my race everywhere the true knowledge of their past history, the struggles and strivings of the present leadership, and the glorious future of national independence in a free and redeemed Africa, achieved through organized purpose and organized action. (p. viii)

Ngũgĩ wa Thio'ngo in his book, *Something Torn and New: An African Renaissance* (2009), points to the significance of naming in subjugation and liberation – because the colonizer acquired the right to name African people, in his attempt to take the land and her subjects. Ngugi wa Thiong'o (2009) also asserts that 'the quest for wholeness' has been an enduring struggle for Africans 'since the Atlantic slave trade' (p. 35), and identifies Garveyism as 'the grandest secular visions for reconnecting the dismembered' (p. 35). Vision and practice re-membering have had their most visible results in the gains of Black civil rights in America, the independence of the Caribbean territories, the independence of Africa, the rise of the Organization of African Unity (OAU) and, more recently, the African Union (p. 37). The process of dismemberment and re-membering, memory elimination, amnesia, recovery and reclamation as part of the African Renaissance project is similarly explored as a central concern by Carter G. Woodson, John Henrik Clarke and Saidiya Hartman to cite a few examples, and is central to Afrocentricity and Kawaida (Asante, 2007; Karenga, 2008). Also, wa Thiong'o (2009) lays emphasis on the importance of language when he states that

> to starve or kill a language is to starve and kill a people's memory bank. It is equally true that to impose a language is to impose the weight of experience it carries and its conception of self and otherness – indeed, the weight of its memory, which includes religion and education. (p. 20)

These thoughts constitute the feelings of disidentification and dislocation felt but resisted by leaning on the yearning to reconnect via research projects and revisiting Africa.

Fresh Eyes Longing to Return

Ashfa's Story: A Somalian Canadian Perspective

I have visited Somalia, that is where my parents are from. They were both professionals. They came to Canada and virtually had to start over as though they had no education or work experience. Anyway, I expected Kenya to be similar to Somalia since they share a border. The difference I saw in Kenya is that people are more welcoming, they wanted to share their culture, they wanted to share tradition and experiences and they didn't want to know what is happening in North America; they wanted to know what is happening to you as a person. They wanted to know what I knew about Africa, what I knew about Kenya; so when I said things like mandaasi or mohamri and mentioned various foods, they were surprised because they wanted to know how I knew about these foods and how I knew how to make it. The experience in this travel was that the locals had these preconceived notions about us, but we also have preconceived notions about them.

When I returned home, I experienced what is known in Somalia as 'boofis'. It's a sort of mental illness that you go through, like a depression, when you come back from somewhere that you really enjoyed. So, for months I was telling everybody I want to go back, I want to do something there, I don't want to live here in Canada anymore. These feelings and desires were emerging, perhaps due to my disidentification with local Canadians. In my mind, I think [I am] still in the process. I would go to work and talk about my experiences, people would not understand because they haven't experienced [things] like: being at one with the land, seeing the red sand, seeing the natural beauty, seeing the animals, living among the people. I stayed back an extra ten days, so I lived with my family, so I experienced the food, I experienced the people, and now that I am here, [in Canada], you can see the difference because there is not that communal kind of connection. Here you are actually forced to live in individual kinds of systems. There in Kenya, it's how you engage. So I was donating a lot of my clothes, donating money. In giving your clothes, money, you feel like you are doing something worthwhile. Here you don't feel like you are giving back. There you actually see your product or items used by people, and so that's what I enjoyed.

I have been thinking a lot about this and it is not only about the multiculturalism, but what we need as human beings is to be human. There is that emptiness, I see as a crisis worker. Parents are constantly calling me and saying 'my kid is addicted to heroin, my kid is addicted to cocaine, marijuana and I am asking myself why are these children addicted at the age of 12, 13, 14? And I said to myself, there is some sort of emptiness inside of them that they are trying to fill with these drugs, because drugs give them a temporary satisfaction, a temporary euphoric sense. And so what I've noticed is that if you are culturally connected, traditionally connected, which is part of my research, then you feel like a whole person but like here I see you being dehumanized as human beings, stripped of your personhood. We are not encouraged to connect as human beings, we are encouraged to outsource how we feel, using things like food, shopping, so things become an addiction, rather than a way of life where you are connecting with people, like in the Masai village where I observed people congregating in circles. I wondered why there were so many circles. I remember taking a lot of pictures of them and acknowledging that these circles are made out of no process. They are part of our tradition like coming in and accepting these traditions. In the village we see a lot of people congregating in circles and smiling. I took a lot of pictures and looking at them, I wondered why are they smiling, why are young babies in these circles, why are they not sleeping somewhere, why is the older generation [there], who can't even walk, why are they still standing in these circles, why are the people of Kenya still standing in circles. There must be a reason, there must be a human component that is associated with that, that's when I saw it, the whole of process of living in Canada actually dehumanizes us as human beings and over there it's like you are rehumanized. These memories and reflections echo what Sharma et al. (this volume) theorized as disidentification and dislocation, which have led to a deep displacement in my psyche.

So, whether it's connection through conflict or connection through happiness, or through a memorable experience, it is still connection, and when you can relate to a person, conflict cannot change that relationship, and that's what Kenya is for me (Ashfa, Interview, 10 October 2018).

Yanika's Story: An African American Perspective

I grew up on a naval base in Denmark and Germany and I remember the concepts of Africa from the history books in a very negative connotation. I also was educated by my parents about the actual history of our people and history of where I come from and I think that they did that to prepare me for my entry into school in a predominantly white culture, being Germany and Denmark, a North American setting with very few Blacks and I think they did this to give me some tools so I could hopefully navigate that society and be rooted in my history. My parents made concerted efforts to send me to Nova Scotia and to Virginia and my family talked about it, they took me to the museum … going to Sierra Leone and documenting our history, how rich our culture is, and how I come from a noble culture and how that has been twisted and how that's not what I'm seeing at home. So often when I would come home with assignments, growing up you know the notions we have of Blacks running around huts and half naked, I would see and say to my parents, 'What is this? What's going on here?' They would definitely challenge that and explain to me. I had a very different perception, of a rich heritage of a rich culture that I'm going to see of the start of humanity. Humanity started in Kenya and so I was really looking forward to it even though I'm from Sierra Leone. I was really looking forward to seeing and being there and witnessing my history and my culture as a Black person, so I was excited. So, no negative preconceived notions but notions of a rich, diverse culture.

The lessons I think that I learned lie in the daily lies that I have grown up with in my contemporary education in Canada, North America, and also in Europe. A sense of the lies, how much they intertwine with all of this narration of deficiency and of negative connotations about Black people. Misgivings about Black people, the brunt of the historical conversations so far for me looking at those, and how systemically they've done this through racism, through political, through economics, through the colonial project, through the imperial project; looking at how they pitted us against each other, looking at the complexity of that and learning the lessons of how they've done that and look at my behaviour and my process of decolonizing myself was very important. Looking at the way I interact and looking at people in Kenya and wanting to know how they can help me to decolonize and do that for themselves as well.

The impact was felt when I went in 2016 after I had completed the Masters in 2014 and I was really thinking about the PhD and I thought to myself, at my age do I really want to do that? I had come back to do activism, in the United States and I was living in New York City doing activism about people voting, people having a voice, particularly Black people in New York City. I was doing a lot of workshops on financial literacy also. Those two areas in activism around political and economic power got me thinking about social justice issues and connecting with Africans globally, and writing. Our history is so vast and has so much wealth and depth that we really have to undo all of these misconceptions and I need to make sure my scholarship addresses that. As a Black woman, it was a call for me to do that and so even at my age, I applied and I am here and it's an honour for me to be here to do the work of engaging the conversation about Black women and their experience in North America. I'm doing something in corporate America, corporate Canada, actually, because our stories are not told and we have been … unfortunately we haven't been the ones who have written the stories about us. It has always been the 'victor' [gestured quotation marks] that has written about us, although I think it is very important for us to have that opportunity and take that as a very heavy opportunity to write the story of our people.

It was the first time in my entire life that I was in a place (Kenya) where I was the majority, when I say I, Black people, were the majority. It really was so fantastic to see. For the first day, I was kind of like in a dream, everywhere I looked I saw Black, Black brilliance, I saw culture, Black society, Black people doing, going, coming, doing things from the time I got to the airport, just everywhere, everything ... visually I was seeing the richness of the culture of the land, of the people, the food, the culture and I was like ... I was like in a dream for the first day or so. And then looking at you, because you are a dominant body, race was taken up very differently, like they're the majority, they have a certain power even though they have a colonial history and there's a lot of things about Kenya and it was very colonized particularly around religion.

The notion of race and difference was very different; it was more attuned to shades of blackness and kinship. I think because Blacks were the majority, you know when I talked about discrimination or if I talked about whites, I think I talked to a couple of elders because I wanted to get their idea of what their experience was with whites and for so long they have had Black leadership. One of the things they did say to me was, the whites control the wealth, they control the higher policies, on the ground; there are Blacks, but the whites are pulling the strings. So, their view of race is quite different from my experience being African Canadian and African American. From the African Canadian side, my mother's community, Africville was destroyed by whites, state-sponsored destruction, burnt to the ground in the mid-1960s. My mom went to a segregated school in Nova Scotia; the last segregated school was closed in 1984 in Nova Scotia. My father, same situation, slavery, industrial slavery, seeing that being manufactured by white, that whole production of slavery and what it brought, it was very different but their experience with race and their connection with whites. I can say this much, the colonial power has done a very good job at colonizing the mind of a lot of Kenyans. They might not have put them in an industrial slave complex that they did in the United States, but in some ways they did, and in some ways they didn't, because they shipped people off instead of having slavery there. I feel like that is the issue with Kenyans, it's the decolonization of the mind, of the culture of the society to really inform their own ways of knowing and being and I think in some ways that has to happen. I'm not sure how that will happen, but I think that is one of the things that has remained with me.

I saw the impact of the colonizer, and my experience with the colonizer, them looking at race and the colourism, also the 'shadism'. Although I do have to say in the United States and even in Canada they would say I'm light, but for what? I'd say you know I'm just this colour because my ancestors were raped, right?

Is this something I should be proud about? Why do you think I look like this? Why do you think I have eyes like that? Or hair this texture? Why do you think that is? This is not a thing to have a beauty notion that this is something great. It comes from something so evil and horrific that to think this is something I should be proud about is to me a little confusing. I knew this history, my mother and father always talked about it in that way. The slave master taking a girl and violating her. So, I knew that at a very young age, race for me was taken up very differently, the shadism here is problematic, in Kenya I didn't see that, however people said, oh the men would like you because you're light skin. They'd like to have a woman like you, and I say really? And so, there was that kind of preference for a lighter skin woman and that I saw similar to the lighter shade forming preference in the United States and Canada. I saw some parallels there, I didn't see … and I saw some parallels in positions of persons in higher roles in terms of their complexion. Not in all things, but I did see that (Yanika, Interview, 10 October 2018).

Ebony's Story: A Jamaican Canadian Perspective

I went to Kenya to attend a conference on decolonizing education. It was my first time travelling to the continent and it was my first academic conference. My presentation was about the empowerment of Black women gathering and how we can disrupt spaces just through the energies of our histories being in one collective space. And because I knew that we were going to be in Kenya for some time, and that the conference was the latter part of the journey, I was a little nervous about maybe my own preconceived notions about how I would fit in as a Jamaican woman in the continent, how I would be welcomed. Also, I personally thought about the food and what kind of foods would I be eating, and I didn't want to insult anyone by not or refusing to eat something offered to me. I was very unfamiliar about customs and food so I was just a little nervous about how my day-to-day would go and the initial welcoming of me there. One could argue that these feelings of nervousness were rooted in some sense of disidentification with the local context.

I think the most important thing for my own growth and learning that I got from going to Kenya was that we are one. I still tell the stories of how welcoming every person was that I met. So, if I was meeting anyone for the first time, the first thing they would say to me is, welcome home. I think the biggest learning was the idea of the continent as my home, it's now indelibly etched in my brain, my consciousness, my being, that even more so, it felt like a homecoming than when I go to Jamaica. I think I need time to process the experience of so many Kenyans whom I have never met or communicated with, welcoming me to a space that is unknown to me and encouraging me to look at it as home. I think that it's new knowledge for me because it now informs the way I interact with other Black people here in Canada and at home in Jamaica.

The experience contrasts with the dislocation and disconnectedness that I experience in Canada. My return to Canada from Africa was far more traumatic than my arrival in Kenya. For two weeks in Kenya I had forgotten the burden of race as it is experienced in Canada. On my return I developed a new consciousness how dislocation is experienced and I began to understand how it operated to create distrust and division among Blacks in the diaspora. Prior to the trip, I didn't realize how consciously I was participating in the project of divisive politics among Blacks. The new awareness has been central to what I offer as a process of disidentification in Canada as a consequence of my experience as a Black person in Kenya. I now have this urgency and engage in activism to ensure that I don't continue to participate in that project of separation; so in my walking, in my talking, in my Canadian classrooms, when I encounter other Black people, I try my best to look at them as an extension of me in a different body. I see us as a people who have been dislocated from the same home base and think of the continent of Africa as a space of home and healing, and of a place where I cannot wait to go back to because I now understand the spiritual and cosmological connection with Africa.

I've always felt some level of spiritual connection to the continent, so I knew that one of the first things I wanted to do when I got there was take off my shoes and put my feet in the dirt. I needed to feel my ancestors in that level of connection from body to spirit and that came through in my feet in the dirt. I just envisioned in my mind that my ancestors walked on that dirt, that dirt was there during slavery and before enslavement. That dirt has that history and that spiritual history and I just wanted to feel part of it. I definitely felt the spiritual connection when I was there.

I have a daughter, so all of my teachings, all of my learning, all of my experiences that I gain outside of being a mother here in Toronto as a Black person, I try to include and share with her. The most important learning, which I gathered from being in Kenya that I have brought back to her, is just the spiritual thread that connects us all as Black people, here in Toronto and on the continent of Africa. The level and depth of spiritual connection that was needed for our ancestors to survive enslavement, the level of spiritual connection and importance of it that we now can use to survive and surmount the mental slavery that we, as Black people in this project of colonialism, are still experiencing. It's become more important to me to connect to and maintain those levels of spiritual connection to my ancestry, to the roots that were born in Africa. I would like to be able to share that depth of spiritual connection to all those I encounter in my sphere of influence. The spiritual connection starts in the continent that transcended through enslavement that brought us, and my direct ancestry, to Jamaica that then, brought us over here to Toronto. To me, I automatically see a thread carrying us all through all of that, and I think it's our responsibility to continue to connect in this manner.

I've become more connected to my own spirituality and that gives me strength, but it also makes me wonder of the origins of Africa and how as a people in Africa, how they manifested there, how they used that spiritual connection. So, as someone who is very sensitive to spirit and emotion, that's how I feel I got so connected. I'm just generally a very sensitive, emotionally spiritual person. This trip to Kenya helped build a strong spiritual connection for me. I feel a connection to the continent now, that wasn't there before.

Since the beginning of my reflection, I believe that there is this colonial project that successfully has separated us and divided us. And so, any ties to what would be conceived as home have been severed or are fraying. Thus, I believe what the trip to Kenya did for me was to re-establish those ties to the continent, to home and to spirit. So that's what I mean I feel tied, in a very good way.

I think that every Black person needs to go back home. I think every Black person, it bodes repeating, needs to visit; take off their shoes, put their feet in the dirt of our ancestors and be back home because it is transformative. It changes you in ways that you don't even know immediately, perhaps a way of reidentifying ourselves that was not present upon entering into Kenya. There are times when I just feel overwhelmed with the memories of being there because it has changed me, which can speak to displacement, but in a good way allowing me to reconnect to my spiritual and land roots. I deeply believe that we all need that level of reconnection and I also think it's strengthening. Because this Black experience is hard, it's hard. The business of being Black in a white institution, in this white country, is hard. Thus, anything that will allow us to strengthen ourselves and each other, I'm a strong proponent of. And for me, I think it was very timely, moving into my second year of my PhD to get that level of grounding.

I just feel like because I was so changed by the experience, like I am the biggest advocate of telling other people you need to go, you need to go. Thus, when a trip comes up, I'm like, you need to find a way to get there. Because I will be going back on the next trip, I have to! I feel like it, the first trip, was like a taste. Now I can have a better understanding of what I'm going for. I'm more prepared [for] the overwhelming experience of feeling a sense of disidentification and now I am willing to be in it more to gain a deeper understanding of my identity. When I go a second time around, I want to really be in it. I want to experience it differently than I did the first time as more of an observer, the second time I want to be a participant. I think that again, I can only stress that it is just so important for our connectedness to each other and to the roots of Black culture for every single Black person to make a trek to Africa (Ebony, Interview, 11 September 2018).

Reflections and Afterword

Our intention was to apply the DLN framework to the stories, but as you read through the narratives, you can see that the visit to the African continent had a different impact on Black students than it did on non-racialized people, which did not fit directly with how the DLN framework is explained in Chapter 1 of this book. Given that, the four participants' narratives show that there were feelings of disidentification only at the beginning of their physical entry into Kenya but not a feeling of disidentification throughout the whole trip, and it had nothing to do with feeling racially different, as that was not applicable. We see this disidentification through the lens of participants experiencing a proclivity towards assimilation in their early adjustment phase. This tendency contrasts with the axiomatic 'code-switching', 'passing' and hypersensitivity which echoes Lorde's (2007) sentiments of learning to live with our racially scarred and oppressed selves in a white, settler society. And as for race not being a disidentifying factor, some of our participants mentioned the term 'melanated' that they coined to describe a feeling that validated their embodied Blackness in Kenya. This embodied Blackness evokes feelings of belonging and seamless entry into the Kenyan society, which preclude a context requiring a great deal of disidentification. Colourism or shadism, phenotypical concepts of difference that manifest as a source of tension among racialized, Black majority populations, communities and societies in the African diaspora emerged as consistent in Kenya, and thus in that sense it can be seen as an opportunity to unify Black people due to their race, rather than as a moment of disruption.

As for the dislocation, again the four stories don't share in the power dynamic concerns that would be applicable to white people from Canada going to Africa, but rather in some stories, like the last one, it is clear there was a level of dislocation in readjusting to Canada, with a deeper understanding of self-identity and spiritual connection amongst Black people. Upon return from Kenya, racialized students identified the prevalence of colonized institutions, language and practices as sources of disquiet. This unease is consistent with Asante's (2002) definition of intellectual dislocation, which purports a disjuncture between how African society is conceptualized in scholarship and what is real. The representations of an exoticized Africa, uncontaminated by colonization, that is documented as primitive and uncivilized by some or an untouched, Indigenous preserve by others, are ideals. Scholars of decolonization hold a more realistic perspective designed to dislodge the effects of colonization on changing African societies and to encourage transformation guided by Africa-centred principles, such as Ubuntu and sancofa. These principles ground the resilience of Indigenous cultures and the pedagogical implications of international educational initiatives involving African countries. Thus, the dislocation was understood not in Kenya but in the ways culture, knowledge and richness were dislocated with respect to the lack of power and acknowledgement these received in Toronto, Canada.

In conclusion, a reading of the stories suggests that the students' experiences reflect notions of return, relocation and reconnection, which disrupts the Eurocentric notion of a first visit to a country. It offers scope to develop a framework of analysis for students of African ancestry, who experience their first physical contact with the African continent, to explore conceptually notions of cosmological connections and spirituality as relevant to understanding the absence of intense disruptive experiences or shock, as is often associated with the first physical contact and to unpack the inequity embedded in terms such as 'less developed' peoples and cultures. Additionally, these stories disrupt the negative troupes and narratives that form and inform mainstream Canadian ideology about how to understand Africa. They counter the opportunity for displacement as an inevitable outcome for students who engage in learning tours to Kenya and similarly disparaged countries. Consequently, the stories offer a critical perspective for readers and researchers as they interpret relations between students and their experiences on tour learning practices and practicums as they engage with the narratives shared in this chapter.

Thus, we cannot conclude that the narratives and the analysis of them fit neatly into the conceptual framework or comply with the stages in the order proposed – disidentification, dislocation and displacement – but rather that the findings demonstrate a mix of the elements in the DLN framework in the varying degrees of impact felt by our racialized participants in an untraditional manner. What is most interesting from these narratives shared is that it is apparent that the racialized students and their racialized professor experience a flipped sense of disidentification, physical dislocation and displacement in its full force in their daily routine as members of racialized populations in Canada.

It is anticipated that the stories will open up constructive dialogue towards change about how we impart education, how educational initiatives that are intentionally meant for good can reinforce stereotypes of people and countries whose knowledges have been marginalized, appropriated or pathologized. It is hoped that this research offers insights that educators and academics would find helpful as they develop culturally sensitive pedagogy and curricula for educators and for all members of Canadian society. Real-world experiences that broaden the vision of educators who integrate the experiences into their pedagogical practices should provide inspiration for policymakers.

5

Linguistic Discomposure: Disruptive Learning Narratives and Lacan in a Short Study Abroad Programme

Michelle Parkinson

Introduction

Studies on distress in international study abroad programmes tend to fall into two large categories. First, many detect a self-authoring process by which an individual faced with a situation of cognitive dissonance may choose a more active role in self-formation by consciously deciding to 'author' their own fate, while still cognizant of real-world limitations (Pizzolato, 2005). This first approach seems related to and is perhaps an outgrowth of Markus and Nurius's (1986) theory and study of what they call 'possible selves'. Here, they discuss past conceptions of self, present conceptions of the self and future ideas about the self as they affect people's behaviours. These selves seem like a less self-directed version of Pizzolato's more self-determining, self-authoring model. The second kind of description centres around the traditional definition of cognitive dissonance and – much like the first – sees the moment of disorienting or challenging experiences as an opportunity for personal growth on the part of the individual. That is, the dissonance created in an encounter with ideas that challenge the self as previously conceived is processed and resolved into personal change and growth that integrates the new idea or circumstance (Trilokekar & Kukar, 2011).

In a five-week study abroad programme called 'The Catalyst', run out of a consortium of Midwestern universities, I was observing something much more like a disturbance of the wholeness of the imaginary register by the symbolic experiences of cognitive dissonance and its subsequent resolution. This was especially true since many of the experiences were centred around language, or a lack thereof. Lacan saw the psyche as being structured like a language. As I observed students studying in London and Paris, I began to think about their distress. I wondered whether I could see their disturbances through the lens of Lacan. Specifically, Lacan posits the imago being confronted and disrupted by the linguistic register of the *symbolic*, and sometimes even the *real*. In the process of considering Disruptive Learning Narratives (DLNs) as a lens for viewing these experiences, I wanted to know if there was a way to understand this process as a psychological and a linguistic phenomenon that parallels the theoretical framework of DLN (Sharma et al., this volume). This hypothesis might prove even more interesting in light of the language differences students would be facing in three of their four weeks of direct instruction.

Literature Review

Trilokekar and Kukar (2011) discuss pre-service teacher candidates studying abroad and their experiences with 'disorienting experiences' (p. 1141). They argue that some of these students' experiences led to 'critical self-reflection' but that this requires 'greater awareness of one's frame of reference' (p. 1141). Their article focused largely on students' status as Canadian citizens with varying racial appearances and self-identifications and how their own claims about 'where they were from' were sometimes disbelieved by people they encountered in, for example, China. Nadine Dolby (2004) also discusses national identity in terms of encounters with others. Her article, 'Encountering an American Self: Study Abroad and National Identity' discusses a group of students from the United States studying in Australia for a more extended amount of time. For her, the salient issue is students' sense of nationality. Particularly interesting is that the post-trip interviews were conducted in the wake of 9/11, and while it was unclear to Dolby how this affected the responses, it seems reasonable to assume that it had some bearing. Primarily, however, Dolby's focus was on difficulties students from the United States experienced amongst Australians, particularly when it came to (some) Australians' critiques of US historical and contemporary actions on the world stage. Her argument was that students had to negotiate information that clashed with their former view of themselves as 'Americans' and of the United States being unproblematically 'good', and that this often led to more nuanced ways of understanding themselves.

Scholars more interested in the subject of conflict as an opportunity for 'self-authorship' such as Pizzolato (2005), Baxter Magolda (2008) and Marginson

(2014), similarly make a case for conflict between self and environment creating a need for adjustment or decision. In situations resulting in 'self-authorship', one sees the need to take the reins of one's life, to *decide* one's identity and to act within conscious, rather than habitual, parameters that are newly informed by a chosen identity trajectory. While only Marginson (2014) addresses study abroad explicitly, arguing for 'new forms of hybrid identity' issuing from the subject-conflict situation (p. 6), all use a model of subjectivity or selfhood that posits a relatively coherent subject formation with a kind of ontological status which can be revised, but perhaps only to a finite degree, and always with at least some order and coherence. Even more stable was the presentation of 'possible selves' in Markus and Nurius's formulation (1986), which, while it acknowledged some pliability in one's 'now self', focused more on notions of possible future and already-established past selves, and especially how the affect attached to given future selves could be impacted by situations faced by subjects in the present (p. 959). While seeing traumatic events as influential on subjects' ideas about what they could become, they also noted that those with fairly stable positive self-esteem appeared to maintain positive forecasts for their lives in spite of major negative life events such as illness, death or separation from a partner.

These latter articles addressing self-authorship could inform how students think about changes in themselves as a result of studying abroad. Specifically, students *decide* to do these studies in efforts to change. In recruitment, study abroad educators often emphasize the impact of the programme on personal growth. Students therefore are primed before leaving to conceive of studying abroad as a personally transformative experience. The ways in which students negotiate displacement may depend in part on this positive framing and priming before the experience itself. Further, in their discussions of study abroad, it is virtually axiomatic to hear students refer to how the conscious decision to engage in the experience changed them positively.

Introduction to Study

Several opportunities to engage DLN and Lacan as related principles present themselves in the study abroad experience. I will discuss them here. In regard to disidentification, a strong parallel can be drawn with Lacan's understanding of language *itself* as an identificatory disruption. Disidentification, dealing as it does with identity markers that (1) are linguistic, and (2) can be alienating, since they are by their nature classifications, dovetails with Lacanian linguistic theory about a world cut up, apportioned, by language (Sharma et al., this volume). Among many identity markers that would fall into the category of alienating language are ethnic and racial markers, as well as those of nationality and culture. That one might experience disidentification in the face of another language, another set of cultural and social norms, and be forced to revise one's own relationship to one's home culture and language in new and alien surroundings is prefigured by Lacan in his notion of the shattering of the imago. This shattering by language in the symbolic register and by the register of 'the real', which he insists is not 'reality' but rather a mysterious concept, sometimes pointed at by references to trauma, hunger or the extreme grotesque. We might say, therefore, that what occurs in visiting a foreign country for the first time is simply more radical than the everyday ruptures of the imago by the symbolic, and sometimes the real, that Lacan posits. Whilst my students did not express outwardly experiences tied to ethnicity and race that DLN emphasizes, they did anecdotally discuss their sense of being unnerved by no longer being in the majority culture, by having their identities as US nationals no longer be an automatic privilege but in some cases, a liability. DLN helps show that it may be doubly alienating to be a cultural outsider who does not know the dialect, or even the language.

Dislocation similarly works with Lacanian frameworks. While our ideal psychic locus for Lacan is in the register of the imaginary, where Lacan places the imago, where we experience briefly a kind of original wholeness, a sense of completion and contentment where we desire nothing, this is broken by language. Dislocation describes at a macro level the unveiling of this state, as a fiction. It describes how the symbolic invades in a particular situation – that of being thrust into another nation, culture and set of linguistic codes in which one loses linguistic and cultural power. Operating alongside this, but not in precisely the same way, language – in the symbolic register – will disturb the imaginary's wholeness again and again, shattering the imaginary figure of the self. If we presuppose Lacan's theory to hold, then dislocation must be an extension of the symbolic that, rather than simply disturbing the imago, shuffles the symbolic keys by which we refer to it by, for example, changing our location within a group or geographically. Changes in the normative might even introduce elements of the real to the psychic experience, becoming so alienating that they constitute quasi- or real trauma, and requiring the kinds of repairs the symbolic allows us to make through references back again to the imago, the imaginary register. This might be seen as a parallel to the loss of privilege or shifts in privilege accompanying international learning experiences.

The loss of privilege I refer to here regarded primarily how being a US citizen simply *means* differently when one is abroad. Students expressing varying degrees of discomposure over nationality illustrates this (see below, and appendix). There were also shifts towards more power, a greater sense of wholeness in the imaginary, but which also constituted dislocation. Things like race, for example, became *less* salient in contexts where racial diversity was much greater – in Paris and London – and students of colour may have been more comfortable in their racial categories than they were at home, where the populations were majority white. Unfortunately, these observations are only anecdotal, as race/ethnicity was not part of the survey tool I used here, but conversations with students of colour bore it out.

Finally, if we see displacement as the place where disidentification and dislocation intersect, and where, in Freudian terms, a subject might integrate a substitute for her real target of aggression or unacceptable emotion – something that for Lacan has always already happened between the imaginary and its shattering by the symbolic system as substitution for the imago – then we see again that the two sets of concepts dovetail well. For Lacan, a constant task, driven by basic symbolic desire for the ultimate signified (God, The Father, The Mother, the wholeness of prelinguistic existence), is the search for a signified we will never reach within language, but will continue to seek. For Lacan, this is ongoing; displacement, on the other hand could be viewed as a moment in which this seeking only becomes more consciously salient to the subject, but will later be resolved. We could, consequently, see displacement as a more intense, but less permanent, version of the will to find that ultimate signified. Further linking these theories, displacement is built into the very process Lacan describes, because substitution is always the name of the game. Moreover, although Lacan's theory describes the object of desire and how it is displaced by lesser objects, there lies a strong parallel between this and the idea of displacement of one target for another through a Freudian defence mechanism that kicks in because of the unacceptability or unavailability of the desired target.

The changes thus described through Lacan and DLNs are difficult to measure quantitatively, but through qualitative textual analyses of student narratives about study abroad we might better understand them. Because they are constructed in narrative, and therefore linguistic forms, these narratives imperfectly struggle to re-establish the imaginary fullness that must be profoundly fragmented by contact with new languages, cultures and lifeways. While something will always be lost in translation, the gestures of the symbolic nonetheless can indicate something about the nature of the struggle in the imaginary. In that way, they are gestural; they point in the direction of the imaginary. So, when students describe moments of discomposure in the course of their travels, they may be describing what Lacan would describe as an intense degree of 'shattering' of the relationship between imaginary and symbolic occurring in a more dramatic way than would occur routinely. This experience might even flirt with the register of the real. These events require recovery through strong 'ego defences' and the rebuilding of the imaginary fortress of the self-image, or imago (Lacan, 1966/2006, p. 78). Understanding this process as it occurs in these dramatic ways might assist study abroad programmers in creating optimal conditions for successful student development through Lacan and DLN. DLN might be most useful for framing the unique situation of international study and what it does at the macro level of power, privilege, race, ethnicity and identity, whilst Lacan can work alongside DLN to illuminate at the micro level the linguistic changes and struggles that DLN entails.

Background

While participating in 2016 and 2018 as an English professor in a programme, The Catalyst, that took place in London, Paris, Berlin and Prague, respectively, over the course of a five-week sojourn, I wanted to understand what was different about this programme from programmes with other formats. For example, I had also taught in a programme that took place in Scotland with a group of students from the United States, where they lived and studied in one location, over the course of an ordinary fifteen-week semester. Though these students took short trips away from their 'home location', they remained mostly in a small village outside of Edinburgh, and so made social connections there, and with one another. While I clearly saw the benefit of the latter programme, especially for students new to travel and in need of a little more stability, something about the effect of the shorter, more intense programme seemed to be more influential on students, and this influence was usually perceived in a good way.

I taught in the first 'unit' of the programme, which took place in London and Paris, while the students went, first, on their own one-week journey, which they planned and executed themselves, and then onto the second unit in the other two cities with other teachers and classes. While there, I noticed that in this particular model of teaching, the city locales were the teaching foci or provided the central course material. In addition to course readings, for students to analyze, which then essentially set them loose in Europe, this teaching approach seemed remarkably impactful. I had been to both cities and I had led students on short trips in London before, but something different was happening, and I wanted to better understand what that something was. Since so much of what students experienced became the basis of their conversations when they were not in class, I thought it might have to do with language.

I also thought it was related to the fast pace of the programme in which students changed cities weekly and were almost constantly on a timetable. We brought students into Heathrow and they found their myriad ways to their hostels and subsequently to the first whole-group meeting place in a nearby park. Classes began the next day. Classes always began on time and lateness was not tolerated. The class always went somewhere, to some site – a museum, a monument, an archaeological site – and often began at that site and then progressed onwards; so being late usually meant missing the entire class day. Consequently, students arrived on time and ready to go. The effect this created was immediate, full immersion in London, its streets and alleys, and its transport system. There was no way that a student could avoid riding the tube, negotiating a tube map or getting lost at least once.

Almost as soon as students had their feet under them in London, we had them at the train station preparing to cross under the English Channel to Gare du Nord in Paris. So, from London, where, while the customs differed, at least most people spoke English, students landed in an enormous train station and heard a cacophony consisting of French. The same approximate routine was followed in Paris as in London with students finding their hostel, meeting with the large group and beginning classes straightaway at designated meeting places. Sometimes the meeting places were very near their hostel, and sometimes, for the sake of time, we met across town, requiring students to make one or two metro changes to reach the destination. With many service people speaking at least some English in Paris, students never found themselves completely unable to communicate, but depending on their own skills in French, there was at least some language barrier.

This barrier, I believe, contributed to, rather than diminished, their engagement with the programme and the change that resulted. In addition to being distanced from the cultural norms in England, students found themselves linguistically alienated in France. Since Lacan's linguistic model provides an idea of how language always already results in dislocation and disidentification away from the imago, as discussed above, new sets of customs and a different language would certainly intensify that experience by providing one more step of removal from the imaginary register. In France, it is likely that students even experienced the real, which Lacan defines as the ultimate kind of displacement, an experience of mute alienation at the level experienced during trauma and other psychic breaks. Rather than leaving students in a state of trauma the resulting restoration of psychic wholeness, accomplished through the mastery of the skills and some of the language required to navigate difficult new situations, resulted in growth.

Method

Participation

Online surveys (see appendix) were distributed to student participants in the programme, most of whom had been on the 2016 or 2017 programmes. Students came from a demographic range, which was not tracked, but all were enrolled college students from universities throughout the Midwest at the time of their study abroad experience. Many knew one another before the experience, and many formed close friendships over its five weeks. The surveys were strictly voluntary, with no incentive to participate or disincentive not to, unless a few students felt that they 'should' do it to help me out, and perhaps for students who might have me as a professor for future courses. None of the participating students were visibly, to my view, non-white, though students were not asked to self-identify regarding race, ethnicity, gender or social class in the survey. While such information would have been useful to this study, it did not occur to me to include these until later, after surveys had been distributed. Future studies would benefit from their inclusion. Two respondents, whom I knew, had participated earlier or later than 2016 or 2017, but by no more than four years. A total of six students completed all questions on the survey.

Procedures

Surveys distributed electronically through Qualtrics gathered what was primarily qualitative data from six respondents (see appendix). Questions centred around students' perceived levels of and corresponding narratives about distressing or stressful situations in their experiences as well as their experiences of personal change. Questions also elicited information about students' previous experiences (if any) abroad and asked for length of time spent in each country, with the idea that more experienced travellers might find this experience less disruptive to their senses of self. A few examples of questions asked included, 'How were you feeling before departing for Catalyst in the hours leading up to going to the airport?' Two questions asked to what degree students felt 'welcomed' in London and Paris and asked for explanations, and another question asked whether they felt they had experienced 'culture shock', which then elicited a narrative if the student replied in the affirmative. The final question asked students the degree to which they felt they had changed in the course of the sojourn. Again, I designed questions to detect, but as much as possible not to manufacture, a link between distress and change. I took this approach, because I found the impact level of this programme in anecdotal comments from students to be particularly striking and had begun to think that something about the encounters with distressing situations actually provoked positive growth. This hypothesis came about through observing my own states of mind as the programme unfolded each time. I noted that *I* had frequently felt fairly high levels of stress and even distress over negotiating unfamiliar things – I had not taught abroad 'on the go', I had not been abroad in a few years, I did not know London and Paris extremely well, and I was getting to know new colleagues and students – but I also noted a sense of change as a result. I wondered if this, in addition to being a source of discomposure, was also a source of renegotiation of self, if the source of discomposure was how the change was taking place.

In interpreting results, themes brought up by students in written responses were the primary guide for gauging those reactions. If themes came up more frequently and in more student responses, they were assumed to have more salience and to merit more analytical weight. More specifically, I grouped the use of certain topics into clusters, which I then interpreted; these are itemized by headings below. The numerical data, since the sample was too small to be significant, were seen simply as corresponding qualitatively to written responses rather than as meaningful on their own. Since I was working through a framework of DLN with underpinnings of Lacanian psychology, this framework informed the organizing principles for my final analysis of the data.

Results and Analysis

Excited and Anxious

Three of the six respondents reported having spent some time abroad (see appendix). Their experiences ranged from a lot of time in many countries – one student reported fifteen weeks spent in eight different countries – to less time – three weeks, but spent in a single country. One student reported spending a week in Canada every few years to visit family. In a way which appeared to correlate with their previous experiences outside the United States, students' level of anxiety before leaving varied, but most students reported this anxiety as coterminous with excitement. One student, who had never left the United States, reported feeling

> equal parts excited and anxious. I was sad to be leaving my family and dog for so long, but at the same time, it was something I had only ever dreamed of doing and never thought would be possible, so I was just … so excited to go.

Another, who had travelled outside the United States before, reported feeling 'extremely emotional and my emotions ranged from anxiety to elation'. Four of the six answers were very similar to this, combining the terms 'excited' and 'anxious' or very close synonyms of them together into phrases or sentences – that is, combining negative and positive terms for psychological arousal. Those students who did not combine these terms used one or the other. Perhaps not surprisingly, the student who reported feeling 'very anxious' had never been abroad, and the student who reported being 'pretty excited to go back to Europe' had the most extensive experience travelling outside the United States.

It is no very great revelation that young adults going overseas would feel anxiety and excitement, but can we see these emotions through a lens more interesting than to simply say that they are anticipating being in a 'new place'? I think we can. For one, they appear to be anticipating the process of dislocation and disidentification with which DLN concerns itself. Thinking ahead, they would at least have known that international travel might threaten their secure sense of primacy as US citizens and English speakers. Moreover, I agree with Lacan (1966/2006) that it is exactly at the point where speech becomes so simple as to '[verge] on the ineffable'– at the point, for example, where a child learns from its parent the foundations of language – that 'would seem to require examination more than ever' (p. 202). If we pay attention to these students' words of apprehension as they describe their feelings pre-travel, almost all of them betraying what might be called 'upset' or even 'frustration' over a lack of a way to fully understand what they are about to undertake, we might detect the typical Lacanian ego which, rather than being '[defined] by its capacity to bear frustration, is frustration in its very essence' (p. 208). Another way to put this might be to say that it is right at this moment, readying to untie oneself from almost every intersubjective and cultural mooring one knows, in the face, perhaps, of symbolic death, that the subject is both the most terrified and the most *excited*. She contemplates this nearly complete loss and creates the 'I am' statement in attachment with an adjective about feeling unmoored, in order to force a new symbolic self into the threatened register of the imaginary, the about-to-be-exploded imago.

These are the words of students facing disidentification even as they contemplate their future surroundings. They have already begun recasting and reframing themselves *as selves* in relation to the disruption they are preparing to face. They look forward to the challenge, but they may also fear what will be the dislocation of their usual subjective certainties as experienced in their home countries – places where they know the language, how to get around, how to interact without offending. They may even imagine themselves anticipating the loss of their relative cultural dominance in the United States to a different status as 'mere foreigners' or tourists who lack understanding of English or French customs and language. As the trip got underway, their anticipated loss became an actuality.

I am suggesting that, unconsciously, students had an awareness of approximately what kind of loss they were about to face, the form of which they could not foresee, and which therefore, at the imaginary level anyway, was complete. What would this 'reality that is estranged', this disidentification as referenced in the DLN, *do* to them? What aspects of their shaped selves would remain? Would logos, words, ferry them through and over this river? Could they, if they fell in, negotiate its currents without losing themselves completely?

This analysis might not be convincing to every psychologist or educator, especially those dismissive of Lacan. However, looking again at participants' comments on how they reported feeling pre-departure, we might find more evidence, or at least suggestions, of Lacan's and DLN's usefulness here. While one student, sitting at an airport gate alone, worried over the trip, 'unsure of what anything on my trip would be like', s/he 'got a reassuring text from my father telling me how proud he was of me for going on this big adventure' (see appendix, Q6). In the simplest terms, this student was anxious, and was reassured by a doting father. However, the worry over 'what anything on my trip would be like' could translate as worry over 'what I would be like on my trip'. That is, would the subject hold? Would identity remain intact or be disrupted? The textual reassurance, symbolic shoring up of the imaginary essence of the self, worked. It even brought tears to this person later. We might posit that this text had such an impact because the Father, source of the symbolic, of the law, stability and of social norms, approved of, even praised, this departure from the familiar. Symbolically, this traveller had received the ultimate symbolic sustenance to the imago, the father's approval, and the illusory comfort that came with it.

Planes, Trains and Automobiles

While one usually thinks more about what one will see and do when travelling to new places than transportation and its vicissitudes, the latter does tend to elicit at least some anxiety in even very experienced travellers. This came through in many of the answers on the survey as well. For example, for a question regarding students' overall experience of the Catalyst, the first 'written' answer that was asked for, one student wrote that for 'the first week and a half [s/he] was very stressed whenever there was traveling[,] be it walking to a hostel or riding the subway [sic]' (see appendix, Q3). In Question 9, where students were asked: 'Describe a specific incident that you feel characterizes your answer above' to a question about how welcomed they felt in London, four of six students mentioned transportation. While the question was about their sense of feeling welcomed by the inhabitants of a new city, transportation featured in many of the illustrative stories. One student discussed leaving a phone on the shuttle bus at Heathrow. Another discussed having an overall impression of 'traveling with a large backpack, on the tube, specifically through busier areas [, which] attracted more unwelcome stares and looks. Really only if my luggage was falling all over the place and taking up more room than it needed, though' (see appendix). Moving from place to place, taking up (new) space, trying to keep oneself and one's things together, these formed the bases of some of the most vivid descriptions provided by students.

Further illustrating the importance of means of transport for these subjects, in response to question nine, one respondent, to illustrate that 'people were kind to me' reported that someone had given 'me directions in the airport'. This same person noted, though, that a 'taxi driver was rude and made me feel stupid'. While it is difficult to gauge why one set of people might be more helpful and kind than another based only on these responses, the salience of (lack of) ease in transportation comes through clearly. Another student, generalizing about the programme in another question, noted no longer being afraid 'to venture out on my own, I see everything as an adventure, and even got the courage to move across the country [sic]' (see appendix, Q3). Remarkably, two answers to Question 17 about the degree to which students felt 'changed' by their experience also mentioned modes of travel: 'I was a very different person upon arriving home than I was sitting at my tiny gate in my hometown's airport.

I felt empowered by all I had accomplished on my own without my family or friends present, and I felt new motivation for my life and my future career'. Another noted that it was 'the first time I had planned my own trip in a foreign country, and I think that was very important in growing as a person'. While this respondent did not elaborate on what they meant by 'growing as a person', one might speculate that they felt a sense of empowerment and motivation similar to the previously referenced response.

One of the most alien aspects of a new place is the transportation system, even down to how to hail and pay for taxis. It is enough to put anyone on the back foot. However, it emerged in the written answers almost as a subtheme, despite the fact that none of the questions asked specifically about it. So, what about modes of movement from place to place is salient here? Lacan's idea, part of which he builds on Derrida's theories, that the psyche, being in the form of a language, experiences a space or a cut in the sign between the signified and the signifier (the idea and the word), and that this space remains regardless of the efforts to reconnect the sign's parts with other signs, may be instructive here. This ties directly to disidentification, dislocation and displacement, and the DLN framework in that all three of these main concepts can be characterized as ruptures. The 'dis' prefix denotes this. When Lacan describes this motion to close or connect the 'signifying chain', an endless series of signs that point again and again to the next in the series, he uses the phrase: 'Where it was just now, where it was for a short while, between an extinction that is still glowing and an opening up that stumbles, *I* can [peut] come into being by *dis*appearing from my statement [dit]' (p. 802, translator's brackets, my emphasis). Lacan almost appears to describe students' discomposure in the face of exactly the kind of displacement involved in physical movement. In particular, the 'extinction that is still glowing and an opening up that stumbles' feels like a description of the loss and momentary sense of reacquisition that one sometimes feels when displaced in physical space, or when attempting to capture an idea with words. Finally, the student who began seeing movement – moving across the country – as adventure seems to have found a way to enjoy the 'opening up that stumbles', that has every possibility of being a fall, but that is just as likely to become where *I* am.

This 'where I am' could be seen as the displacement at the intersection of disidentification and dislocation. The space the subject now inhabits is new, and brought on by both movement and the questioning of identity. The new place, the displacement, becomes, perhaps, the newly grown person, the person now able to move to yet more new places with greater ease. This new person has had to negotiate a DLN to come to this new sense of place and this new sense of self.

Speaking a Little French

As referenced earlier, two questions asked respondents how 'welcomed' they felt in London and Paris, respectively, with follow-up questions asking for explanations. In neither city did students report feeling unwelcomed 'most of the time' or 'all of the time'; however in Paris students appear to have felt less welcomed than they did in London, with three (n = 8) reporting '[s]ometimes I felt welcome; sometimes unwelcome' in Paris, and only one (n = 8) reporting the same for London. The written responses reflected these responses. Three students reported strangers being exceptionally kind or helpful to them as they navigated the enormous city of London. In Paris, some students reported positive interactions with Parisians, especially when the students themselves made an effort to speak French to them. Other students reported feeling either ignored or having people who heard them speaking English refuse to talk to them at all (see appendix, Q11). One student's experience with a Parisian couple was particularly interesting:

> A friend and I had met a couple who lived right down the street from the hostel. They invited us to dinner one night and were so eager to talk to us, but only one of them spoke English, and we didn't know very much French. One of them also invited their mom, brother, and a family friend. None of them knew much English, but were so eager to talk to us through the one that did speak English. We felt embarrassed for not knowing much French, although we had a fun evening. (see appendix, Q11)

This student, in describing a linguistic impasse, only made slightly less distressing by 'the one that did speak English', identifies feeling embarrassed about lacking knowledge of the alien language, expressing both the DLN elements of disidentification and dislocation. Lacan describes in *Écrits* (1996/2006) how the analyst's job is to bring the subject to this point of incoherence:

> With the mythical manipulations of our doctrine, we bring him yet another opportunity to become alienated, in the decomposed trinity of the ego, the superego, and the id, for example.
>
> Here it is a wall of language that blocks speech, and the precautions against verbalism that are a theme of the discourse of 'normal' men in our culture merely serve to increase its thickness. (p. 233)

I should clarify that I do not intend any kind of diagnosis in this analysis, but simply highlight what seems to me the kind of impasse that Lacan wants to foreground as therapeutic. Being drawn back into the imago, the outline of the self that, according to Lacan was formed at the mirror stage, however, appears to be made possible precisely when one loses speech, the inability to articulate what one feels or sees or experiences and when asking for the salt becomes impossible or difficult. At the point of dislocation in the DLN framework, the possibility for growth exists.

What is more, the mirroring required to shore up this self, at least at the level of speech, which is dragging it into symbolic loss, cannot occur here smoothly or even appear to occur smoothly. One translator in a family attempting to bridge a gap between English speakers and his or her family members perhaps only emphasizes discursive failure by momentarily succeeding. Lacan's '*Non*' of the symbolic, then, really does become a 'no', a divider, through which one might nonetheless briefly glimpse those others across the table as subjective beings.

Me but Not Me

The final question on the survey addressed change. It said, 'Sometimes people's self-conception – their idea of who they are – changes when they go abroad for any length of time. How different do you think you are as a person than when you left for [the programme]?' Designed with the notion of the DLN's element of displacement in mind, this question set out to measure whether respondents did in fact experience change in their self-concepts. One of eight respondents reported being only 'a little' different, while the remaining seven reported being at least 'somewhat' changed. The other seven respondents were almost perfectly evenly distributed with two reporting being 'somewhat' different; two reporting being 'different'; and three reporting being 'very different' from when they left (see appendix, Q14). Citing positive experiences, increased self-efficacy and an increased sense of clarity about personal goals in their explanations, these students appear to have returned from their five weeks abroad feeling like important things had shifted in their self-concepts (see appendix, Q17).

Specifically, one student said, 'It [is] not like I feel like I'm not me. I just feel so much more blessed having been on the trip? [sic] Like, it is my single most favourite experience of my life, and what stands out to me when I try to think of the experience as a whole is the beauty I got to experience' (see appendix, Q17). This might be interpreted as a significant change in this student's self-concept. The double negative 'not … not me' introduces strongly the interpretation that the post-travel 'me' differs from the one who this student imagines as the pretravel 'me'. Lacan's ideas about the statement, now more common than 'it is I', now more usually expressed as 'it's me', are that this latter expression makes the subject less likely to regress to the state of the mirror, and more likely to engage in normative, functioning life. This expression, paradoxically, is separated from the very imago – this student's 'not ... not me'– by which it is constituted. For Lacan, the imago must be misrecognized because it is imaginary.

Discussion

Limitations

At first glance, a limitation of this survey is its sample size; I found, however, that in the qualitative analysis I engaged in, I had more than enough data to work with. I certainly could make no general claim about there being a positive correlation between disturbance level and the individuals' experience of personal change or sense of growth, but I could understand on a basic level how the self, according to the individuals themselves, experienced the programme through a Lacanian and DLN lens. Still, I wonder whether a more effective way to measure the phenomena I sought to measure might have been personal interviews. I suspect that some students grew impatient with typing the written answers, and it was precisely those that were the most important sources of information for this study. Since I was interested in linguistic phenomena, interviews would have allowed for me to record more of them than requiring participants to type it all out; so it is regrettable that these were not included. The study also would have benefitted from an ability to ask follow-up questions requesting elaborations or clarifying the original question.

Further, one question on the survey asked very squarely about culture shock, simply saying: 'Most people who leave their home country experience "culture shock" – which usually involves some distress. Were you ever very distressed while on [the programme]?' Four students answered 'yes'; three answered 'maybe' and three answered 'no'. When the questionnaire went on to ask respondents to describe their most distressed moment, their replies demonstrated that only one of them, and only partially, understood a definition of 'culture shock' that would reflect the literature on it. Other students replied by describing endangering incidents, or incidents that felt endangering or otherwise 'scary', rather than the more ambient sense of disorientation of being in an alien culture, which is the more conventional understanding of the concept. This question would have benefitted from a thorough definition of the term. Its results, while they can provide some insight, did not provide a measure of a shared definition of culture shock per se.

Finally, the study has the weakness of being the work of a single researcher from an unusual point of view. Psychological lenses seem common in this type of study, but not psychoanalytic lenses. This may throw the entire study into question for some audience members.

Possibilities for Further Study

The follow-up questions in interview form that I mentioned earlier in this section also present a possibility for further research. Had I included them, they would have allowed me to capture some of the comments I hear from students about the experience several years on, as well as some of the conversations I engaged in and overheard from those students when we were on the Catalyst. For example, the number of times I heard students say, 'I felt so stupid', in casual conversation when we were abroad, was significant. There were a smattering of cases of disidentification and dislocation spread throughout the entire experience. The conversations I had with our younger guides, who had themselves already been on the programme and had come back to assist us with logistics, also had content that I would like to have used. Many times, one of these young folks would talk about their 'Catalyst experience' and lapse into a kind of reverie in which they described how their lives changed forever, which almost always included discussions of intense disidentification and dislocation, and almost never described an easy or smooth experience. As these were some of the conversations that led me to write this essay, I imagine future studies in which a survey is distributed three times rather than just once: before the trip, during the trip and after the trip. I would follow this up with interviews in order to get richer detail and depth, and perhaps to get more explicit understanding about whether students saw a link between the difficulties of the trip and its rewards.

DLN has the virtue of defining almost perfectly what I observed as a study abroad educator, and Lacan worked well in conjunction with it to extend its interest in terms of language. This essay may have interest for educators working abroad and domestically, who elicit personal narratives from students as a way to help the students process their own writing and psychic experiences. Making the theory directly available to students, particularly psychology students or students studying creative writing or literature, could be both beneficial and therapeutic to students and their facilitating faculty. It may also have value in training student faculty preparing to work abroad.

Conclusion

Despite some design flaws, this study did provide some provocative qualitative data that may call for more study. In particular, a quantitative study on disturbance and its relationship to self-image and personal change in study abroad would either firm up or undermine this speculative connection. Should this connection prove to be positively correlative, a follow-up question would be what the most optimal level of disturbance actually is. How can students be introduced to experiences that are destabilizing without endangering them psychologically? And are some students simply not psychologically equipped to handle the stress that a study abroad programme will introduce? On the other end of the spectrum, are some students already well-travelled enough that such experiences would have little impact on them? One response to the survey seemed to suggest this, with the most 'travelled' student saying that s/he had not 'gain[ed] any insight', in turn suggesting that not much changed for this student as a person.

Appendix: Report Your Study Abroad Experience

Q1 – What year were you on Catalyst?

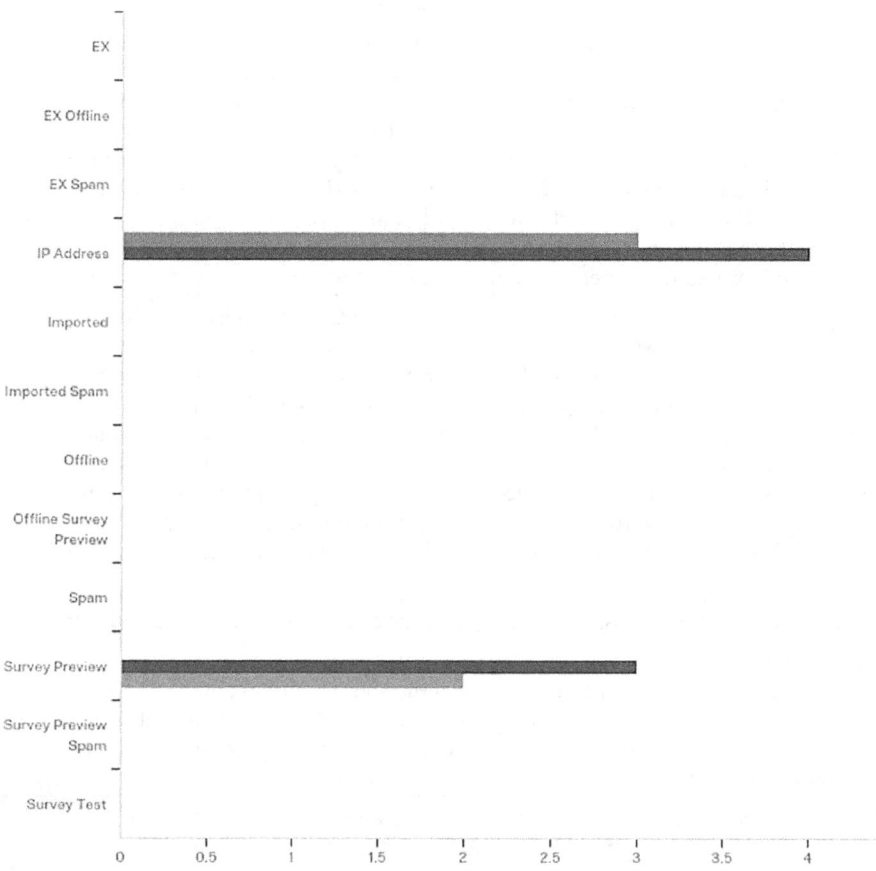

Q2 – Overall, how was your experience?

#	Question	Total
1	Extremely positive	5
2	Very positive	2
3	About half and half	0
4	Very negative	0
5	Extremely negative	0

Q3 – Please briefly explain your answer to question 2

Please briefly explain your answer to question 2.
Although there were many hiccups and not great communication of information, overall the experience was more positive than negative.
My experience with the Catalyst was my first time abroad and my first time travelling by myself as an adult. I was immersed in new experiences, and everything from the seemingly unremarkable stays in hostels to the remarkable tours of landmarks, museums, and course-related field trips was an experience I will never forget. The faculty were passionate and enthusiastic and encouraged every student to explore as much as possible and soak up all we could in each city we visited. The learning opportunities I had in my psychology and communication courses have helped me shape my future plans in a career in psychology and I am proud and excited to tell people about my Catalyst whenever I have the chance.
I knew from attending the International Travelling Classroom in 2014 that the style of teaching was different than anything I had previously experienced. Taking the lessons into the field allowed for me to connect to the material in ways I couldn't in a traditional classroom setting. I gained insight into how the history impacted modern-day society in each city we visited. I got to meet individuals outside the programme who were also visiting, as well as people who lived in each city we visited. Meeting new people abroad was an important takeaway for me. Meeting new people with outside perspectives on the world provided me with a wider scope of how the world operates, and strengthened my identity as a global citizen.
I really enjoyed the atmosphere, along with the classes that coordinated with the programme.
Going on the Catalyst completely changed me and my outlook on life. I am no longer nervous to venture out on my own, I see everything as an adventure, and even got the courage to move across the country. I can't begin to explain how grateful I am for the changes that the Catalyst made possible.
Didn't get along with some other students, had an emotional breakdown after week one and for the first week and a half was very stressed whenever there was travelling, be it walking to a hostel or riding the subway. But most of my experiences were positive and I learned how to deal with the stress well by week three.

Q4 – Before going on Catalyst, had you ever been out of the United States before?

#	Question	Total
1	Yes	3
2	No	4

Q5 – Where else had you been abroad before Catalyst; please list countries and approximate length of stay: for example, 'Switzerland, 3 weeks'.

Canada, 1 week every few years to visit family.
Costa Rica, 1 week. Scotland, 2 weeks. England, 2 weeks. France, 2 weeks. The Netherlands, 2 weeks. Germany, 2 weeks. Austria, 2 weeks. Italy, 2 weeks.
Germany, 2 weeks. Belize, 1 week. Costa Rica, 2 weeks. Nicaragua, 1 week. Canada, 1 week.

Q6 – How were you feeling before departing for Catalyst in the hours leading up to going to the airport?

Equal parts excited and anxious. I was sad to be leaving my family and dog for so long, but at the same time, it was something I had only ever dreamed of doing and never thought would be possible, so I was just … so excited to go.
I was extremely emotional and my emotions ranged from anxiety to elation. I was finally ready for the experience I had spent months preparing for. I remember sitting at my gate all by myself, unsure of what anything on my trip would be like, when I got a reassuring text from my father telling me how proud he was of me for going on this big adventure. I will always feel happily tearful when I think of that moment.

Excited. Anxious, I had flown abroad before, but with ITC the initial flight was made as a group. Catalyst was more independent travelling. My anxiety translated into ensuring I had committed to memory the proper trains to take from the airport in London to the stop nearest to the hostel we would be staying as a group. Running over those plans, again, and then again.
I was pretty excited to go back to Europe, especially because I had a direct flight into London and had never been there before.
I was very excited but also very nervous – I had never left the country before and I had never travelled anywhere on my own.
Very anxious. I had some other Catalyst students on my flight with me, so it helped calm me down.

Q8 – When you arrived in London, what was your perception of how you were perceived by Londoners – that is, those who were not your peers?

#	Question	Total
1	I felt welcome	3
2	Most of the time I felt welcome	4
3	Sometimes I felt welcome; sometimes unwelcome	0
4	Most of the time I felt unwelcome	0
5	I felt unwelcome	0

Q9 – Describe a specific incident that you feel characterizes your answer above.

Once outside of St Pauls, I told a lady I was from America and she had a lovely conversation with me about American politics. She was very polite, and hated Trump as much as I do.

When I arrived at Heathrow airport, I took a shuttle bus to my gate. I left my phone on the bus, of all things that could have gone wrong! When I realized this, I was already inside the airport again. I was frantic and panicking, and I ran up to an information kiosk that was clearly marked to help travellers. The attendant immediately sensed my panic, and started trying to help me right away. He contacted all of the shuttle drivers and found the shuttle I had been on based on the route I had gone since I, of course, had not taken note of the number. Miraculously my phone was still in my seat untouched! After that experience, I felt welcome and grateful. I can't imagine what would have happened if I hadn't been helped by the attendant or someone had picked up my phone.
I can only remember a set of generalized experiences, rather than one specific incident. Usually travelling with a large backpack, on the tube, specifically through busier areas, attracted more unwelcome stares and looks. Really only if my luggage was falling all over the place and taking up more room than it needed, though.
People were usually pretty nice. If you were around loud people though, or loud yourself, you were seen as a nuisance.
When I first arrived, people were kind to me and gave me directions in the airport. However, the taxi driver was rude and made me feel stupid – but he was my only negative Londoner.
Had an older couple help me get to a metro station when my phone's battery ran out.

#	Question		Total
1	I felt welcome	0	3
2	Most of the time I felt welcome	0	1
3	Sometimes I felt welcome; sometimes unwelcome	0	3
4	Most of the time I felt unwelcome	0	0
5	I felt unwelcome	0	0

Q11 – Describe a specific incident that you feel characterizes your answer above.

Right when we got to our hostel, the first thing I did was find the nearest boulangerie, and the baker there was very kind and asked all kinds of questions when I said I was from Minnesota!! He was very happy to see foreigners and was very kind to talk to.

Many Parisians were not outwardly unfriendly, but there were times when some would hear our accents and refuse to speak English to us. That was frustrating and a little nerve-wracking. Also, one of my fellow students was the victim of an attempted robbery while we were in Paris.
I remember a few unique experiences while in Paris. A friend and I had met a couple who lived right down the street from the hostel. They invited us to dinner one night and were so eager to talk to us, but only one of them spoke English, and we didn't know very much French. One of them also invited their mom, brother, and a family friend. None of them knew much English, but were so eager to talk to us through the one that did speak English. We felt embarrassed for not knowing much French, although we all had a fun evening.
I felt like having a little background knowledge of basic French phrases helped here.
The people of Paris were amazing. I don't speak much French, but they always seemed to be grateful that I tried and would usually switch to English to accommodate me. They were amazing.
Nothing specific. Most Parisians either ignored me or were strictly professional.

Q12 – Most people who leave their home country experience 'culture shock' – which usually involves some distress. Were you ever very distressed while on Catalyst?

#	Question		Total
1	Yes	0	2
2	Maybe	0	3
3	No	0	2

Q13 – Please describe the incident in which you felt most distressed on Catalyst in as much detail as possible. Include circumstances, interactions and your feelings.

Upon arriving in Santorini, Greece, while on our break around 6am, this man came up to me and a friend and grabbed her hand, telling her he would take us to our hotel. That was a bit alarming, but other than that, things went quite smoothly.

I came very close to being stranded over the Acceleration week, because I couldn't get a train and a flight was too expensive. I had to call home to find someone to loan me the money for a plane ticket. I also came close to running out of money at the end of the trip because my student loan disbursement hadn't come in, but it thankfully all worked out in the end.
The day we left London to go to Paris, I woke up and accidentally scrapped a recent tattoo I had gotten off. There was blood and it would definitely be infected. Heard later about the attack at the Ariana Grande concert. Started feeling a cold coming. Also, the hostel only had like one outlet and wasn't working with my adaptor. I cried a lot and found a place to buy a new adaptor. That was the roughest day.

Q14 – Sometimes people's self-conception – their idea of who they are – changes when they go abroad for any length of time. How different do you think you are as a person than when you left for the Catalyst?

#	Question		Total
1	Not at all	0	0
2	A little	0	1
3	Somewhat	0	2
4	Different	0	1
5	Very different	0	3

Q17 – Please briefly explain your answer to the previous question.

Its not like I feel like I'm not me, I just feel so much more blessed having been on the trip? Like, it is my single most favourite experience of my life, and what stands out to me when I try and think of the experience as a whole is the beauty I got to experience. The beauty of the art, architecture, people, food, sights, sounds, and experiences.

Even though my experience abroad was over two years ago, I was a very different person upon arriving home than I was sitting at my tiny gate in my hometown's airport. I felt empowered by all I had accomplished on my own without my family or friends present, and I felt new motivation for my life and my future career. I felt so lucky just to have had the support that got me abroad in the first place, and to have seen the rare sights and met the people I had the good fortune to meet. I had more thrilling experiences on my trip of only five weeks than I have ever had.
I had many positive experiences in Paris that changed the way I thought of myself. During the Catalyst programme I gained confidence and self-esteem, from meeting new people I saw my self-worth positively altered. I meant something to people on the other side of the world, as something more than just the ideas that the United States projects into the world. I experienced that in Berlin, talking politics with some of the locals, and especially to a great friend I had made who was visiting Berlin, from Denmark.
I feel like travelling to new places, and returning to old places, changed me a bit, but I think my previous travels also prepared me for this time. However, the Catalyst break was the first time I planned my own trip in a foreign country, and I think that was very important in growing as a person.
I am a changed person. I look at all aspects of my life differently. I became confident enough to move across the country, I no longer fear doing things on my own, and I am able to speak to strangers more effectively. I am more adventurous in all aspects of my life.
I'm already very liberal minded so I didn't gain any insight into the plight of immigrants in my country, I already was very sympathetic towards them. Mostly I realized that, when I travel, I like to be independent and a leader which I am not usually.

6

Navigating the Discomfort of International Teaching Placements: Resistance or Flexibility?

Leva Rouhani and Ruth Kane

Introduction

Classrooms within Canada and elsewhere are becoming increasingly culturally diverse, and educators are recognizing this diversity – and its correlated educational needs – more acutely than in years past (Briscoe & Pollock, 2017). The increase in classroom diversity has led to the critical need for teachers who possess the skills and understandings to work across cultures (Smolcic & Katunich, 2017). Consequently, many teacher education programmes now include alternative teaching and international service learning opportunities as part of their Bachelor of Education degrees (Larsen & Searle, 2017). International service learning placements are opportunities that combine academic instruction and community-based service in an international context (Crabtree, 2008). In Bachelor of Education programmes, international service learning placements are generally short-term and outside of the traditional classroom context. As such, the demand and popularity of international service learning placements have increased rapidly over the past decade (Larsen & Searle, 2017). While the popularity for these programmes has increased throughout the world, so has the complexity of the power dynamics, 'including the impact of one's own involvement' (Langdon & Agyeyomah, 2014, p. 54), that govern the experiences of both teacher candidates and host communities. Questions have been asked by some researchers as to what degree host communities benefit from international service learning placements and the degree to which access to such placements is itself a product of the white power and privilege in academia (Thomas & Chandrasekera, 2014). Indeed, service learning programmes contribute to the realization of cultural senses of superiority – where participants from the Global North feel they have the right to go to locations in the Global South and 'help' residents live better, thus reproducing their power and privilege and deepening the North-South divide.

Much of the literature on international service learning programmes has documented the benefits that accrue for students who participate (e.g. Batey & Lupi, 2012; Cushner & Mahon, 2002; Hurtado et al., 2013). However, limited research exists that explores how teacher candidates navigate the internal and external tensions that arise when international service learning placements are not coherent with the standards and structures teacher candidates are familiar with in Canada.

Using the Disruptive Learning Narrative (DLN) framework (Sharma et al., this volume), this chapter will consider the various ways teacher candidates, participating in an international service learning programme offered by a large Canadian university, resist conforming to local teaching contexts of the host community and the implications of pursing their own pedagogy for the host communities. This chapter is organized into four sections. First, we review the literature associated with both the benefits and costs that frame international service learning placements. We outline our conceptual framework, followed by the context of our case study. The final section consists of our findings, which are analyzed using the DLN framework to determine the degree to which teacher candidates in international service learning placements resist adapting and conforming to diverse teaching contexts and the impact of such resistance on host communities. Using the case study of teacher candidates participating in an international service learning practicum in a rural village in Uganda, we argue that while international service learning placements can help teacher candidates build their competencies to support diverse classrooms, one of the challenges when building these competencies is that the short duration of the placements do not allow teacher candidates to break through power dynamics that govern their relationships with local schools and teachers. In addition, teacher candidates need to be provided with opportunities prior to, during and following the international practicum experience, to critically consider their own motivations and expectations of the practicum (Langdon & Agyeyomah, 2014; Thomas & Chandrasekera, 2014).

International Service Learning Placement: The Benefits and Costs

The significance of international service learning, as an important tool for linking theory and practice, is well articulated among the expanding literature (Larsen & Searle, 2017; Tiessen, 2014; Smith et al., 2014). In this literature, international service learning has been framed as an educational methodology that combines community service with (1) clear learning objectives, (2) preparation for community work and (3) critical reflection (Gelmon et al., 2001). Framed as a pedagogical tool, international service learning combines learning in community contexts with academic knowledge. Hurd (2008) argues that as pedagogy, international service learning seeks to combine service and academic learning to promote increased understanding of course content, while also supporting students to develop knowledge, skills and cognitive capacities to deal effectively with complex social issues.

As the literature surrounding the importance of international service learning placements continues to expand, so has the literature on the benefits of these placements for teacher candidates (e.g. Batey & Lupi, 2012; Cushner & Mahon, 2002; Hurtado et al., 2013). A number of studies link international service learning placements with providing valuable insight and awareness among students by widening their understanding of economic, political and social welfare systems, by enhancing their cross-cultural knowledge (learning about the history, values, family systems of the groups they serve) and by providing new knowledge in broader structural issues of social justice, equity and rights (Drolet, 2014; Maynes et al., 2013; Sarri, 1997). Similarly, Hurd (2008) contends that courses with an international service learning component provide a deeper understanding of course content because the international experience provides a space where students can bridge the theory taught in class with the practice experienced through service learning. For teacher candidates, Coles (1993) argues that international service learning can enhance their respect for diversity, can raise their awareness of societal issues and can develop their moral and ethical sense.

Given that the majority of teacher candidates will teach in culturally diverse classrooms, Butin (2003) suggests that the experience of engaging with communities different from their own (through international service learning) will allow teacher candidates to come to better understand, respect and engage with the cultural plurality of diverse societies. Specifically, Larsen and Searle (2017) argue that research on international service learning demonstrates that through international placements, teacher candidates come to realize the importance of culturally responsive teaching and positive perceptions of their own abilities to teach students of diverse cultural and linguistic backgrounds (e.g. Grierson & Denton, 2013; Mwebi & Brigham, 2009). Therefore, for teacher candidates, international service learning can be used to foster 'key curricular concepts about culture, multi-culturalism, pluralism, and multi-racism, while supporting their life-long commitment to understanding themselves as global influences on children' (Maynes et al., 2013, p. 161).

While the range of benefits for teacher candidates is extensive, so are the possibilities for negative consequences in host communities. Indeed, international service learning can provide grounds for ethical challenges as it can create new inequities, exacerbate old ones and further expand the North-South divide. For example, Langdon and Agyeyomah (2014) suggest that communities that host volunteer placements and international practicums have become laboratories where individuals test their academic and career choices. Positioned as a means to enrich the learning experience of teacher candidates, international service learning placements can reinforce and reproduce the historical hegemonic power dynamics between the North and the South (Langdon & Agyeyomah, 2014). The reproduction of power dynamics was also observed in Chapman's (2018) article where she argues that students are often not qualified to run the programmes or conduct the activities they are tasked to do. As such, they are often taking away job opportunities from local communities. In fact, Chapman (2018) argues that rarely do international service learning placements question whether the physical jobs that students do would otherwise be paid employment for a local resident.

While research outlines that one of the benefits of international service learning is to raise cross-cultural awareness, Scheyvens and Leslie (2000) suggest that international service learning placements might expose host communities to great risk because they have become sites for trial and error, and for theories to be practiced. Tiessen's (2014) research on volunteer abroad programmes confirms that many volunteers have difficulties adapting to local cultural practices and norms, especially in cases where volunteers create a 'foreigner bubble' and stick to one another, rather than engaging with local staff and culture. This foreigner isolationism can have detrimental effects on host communities as it can reinforce the 'us' and 'them' divide (Tiessen, 2014). Above all, the research demonstrates that in their goal to 'help' host communities, volunteers in international service learning placements have the potential to recreate a neocolonialist environment, where volunteers feel entitled to go to the Global South to 'help' communities (Drolet, 2014; Langdon & Agyeyomah, 2014; Thomas & Chandrasekera, 2014). As such, the preparation course we used prior to departure for the international service learning practicum sought to redress these possible costs. The course content involved focus on issues of power, privilege, motivations, global citizenship and ethical challenge (see appendix A for syllabus). Overall, the research is clear: participating in international service learning has the potential to not only enhance teacher candidates' competencies as educators but also the potential to cause harm to host communities and reinforce inequalities. However, questions exploring how teacher candidates navigate power dynamics within host communities and how they navigate the discomfort of unfamiliar teaching contexts to make sense of their changing identity as future educators are largely missing in the existing literature. Using the DLN framework (Sharma et al., this volume), we will analyze how one group of teacher candidates resist immersing themselves in contexts that induce great discomfort and, as such, reduce their potential to develop their teaching competencies.

Disruptive Learning Narrative Framework

The DLN framework (Sharma et al., this volume) has been developed as a tool to examine how teacher candidates, engaging in international service learning placements, navigate both the internal and external discomfort that emerges as they immerse themselves in cross-cultural experiences. The DLN framework comprises three intersectional elements: (1) disidentification, (2) dislocation and (3) displacement, which have been elucidated in earlier sections of this volume. These three elements help inform how the teacher candidates, at the focus of this study, (re)create their identities when immersed in international service learning.

Contextualizing the International Placement

The increasing interest in international service learning placements among teacher candidates, and her own work with a not-for-profit situated in Uganda, led Dr. Kane to create an alternative practicum option for teacher candidates who desire to gain experience outside of the Canadian classroom context. Building on her volunteer work for a Canada-based organization that supports vulnerable children's education and health care in Uganda, Dr. Kane established an international service learning placement in 2015 for second-year graduating teacher candidates. This practicum is open to second-year teacher candidates with a view to equip them with the practical teaching competencies that will assist in their transition into becoming teachers. It is not offered to first-year teacher candidates as their annual calendar of practicum placement does not align with the school term in Uganda. In addition, it was considered that first-year teacher candidates would not have had the opportunity to complete the sociology-based courses within their programme that challenge them to think about their privilege and how different social constructions of privilege might play out in school classrooms. This alternative practicum placement consists of teacher candidates spending the academic year developing programming for their eventual placement and then travelling to Uganda for three weeks at the beginning of April when final coursework requirements have been completed. During their placement, teacher candidates teach in local primary schools during the day (with classroom sizes ranging from thirty-five to eighty-five students), and run an after-school programme at a community centre in the early evenings (with approximately sixty community children attending).

Every year, Dr. Kane, along with the founder of the organization (himself a Ugandan from the host community but now living in Canada), and teacher graduates who have completed the international practicum in the previous years, provide information sessions for incoming second-year teacher candidates who are interested in registering for the international alternative practicum. These information sessions provide details on the importance of cross-cultural competencies for teachers, the benefits of international service learning practicums, the context of the host community, while also outlining the expectations for teacher candidates. In addition, the sessions provide explicit information about the costs (airfare plus $1500 project fee for three-week placement, which covers transfers from airport, accommodation in a modern guest house and all meals).

Once they have registered, teacher candidates spend their second year organizing fundraising events, gathering donations of resources for children and developing programming for both teaching and the after-school programme. Of the funds raised, half contribute to the teacher candidate's costs, and half are donated to fund school fees and educational resources for the children and youth in the host community. The money fundraised by the teacher candidates is split to help support the projects that build local capacity in the Boys and Girls Club (BGC) in Uganda. This has been an ongoing issue in the operation of the international practicum placements. It is important that the teacher candidates recognize that one of the key goals of the BGC in Uganda and that of the home committee in Canada is ensuring the education and well-being of 135 vulnerable children and youth in the host community. This entails large fundraising activities each year to ensure that the capacity to fund the school fees of the children and youth is maintained. From our perspectives, as those responsible for the placement and supervision of teacher candidates, it is inappropriate for Canadian teacher candidates to use the life stories of vulnerable children in Uganda to raise funds solely to facilitate their own airfares and costs – to fund their international experience. Thus, from the outset of speaking about the international placement, we are explicit about the teacher candidates making a financial contribution to the local host community. It is also important to note that both the project lead (Dr. Kane) and the researcher (Leva Rouhani) pay the same fees.

Details of Teacher Candidates' Activities in Their Placement in Uganda

Since 2015, Dr. Kane has taken four groups, ranging in size from three to ten teacher candidates, to Uganda for an immersive teaching experience. In 2018, fifteen teacher candidates registered for the international service learning placement. While no official screening mechanism was in place for the selection of teacher candidates, tensions that arose in 2017 led us to incorporate a mandatory preparation course for all those registered for the international service learning placement in 2018. The course ran for six weeks and sought to prepare teacher candidates for critical reflection and analysis of their international practicum. The underlying goal of the course was to provide teacher candidates with an overview of the ethical dilemmas that are associated with international service learning placements and the impacts of internationalization. The assigned readings were informed by Dr. Rebecca Tiessen and Dr. Robert Huish's edited book *Globetrotting or Global Citizenship? Perils and Potential of International Experiential Learning* (2014) and the modules of the course were informed by Dr. Tiessen's online course on global citizenship.[1] The course seeks to engage the teacher candidates in critical reflection to facilitate understanding of the challenges and opportunities of global engagement in a world of inequality. The original fifteen students registered for the international practicum were informed of the requirements of the six-week course at our initial group meeting. As a consequence, five people chose to withdraw their interest (citing excess workload and them not being aware of this 'training' requirement), and the course proceeded with the ten participants who subsequently completed their international practicum in Uganda. The five students who withdrew from the placement at this point demonstrated a sense of entitlement that was somewhat unexpected by us as project leads. There were immediate responses such as 'I was not expecting there to be a course component', 'I am spending almost the cost of tuition to go, why do I have to also do a course', 'I do not understand why we need to do a separate course' and 'other placements do not have to have additional coursework'. Such responses signalled that these students did not see any value or need for pre-placement preparation for teaching in a significantly different cultural and geographical context of Uganda.

The 2018 international placement comprised ten teacher candidates (participants self-identified as eight white females, one racialized female and one white male) who arrived in Uganda at the beginning of April and spent three weeks in the host village. The village, located 60 kilometres south of the capital Kampala on the main highway between Uganda and Tanzania, has expanded over the years in a north-south direction along either side of the highway and east towards Lake Victoria. Within the village itself there are seven primary schools (two managed by the Catholic church, four government schools and one Muslim school), and two high schools (one Catholic and one government). Teacher candidates are accommodated in a guesthouse owned by the founder of the organization and are hosted by youth who have been supported through their primary, secondary and, for some, post-secondary education, and who now manage small-scale local enterprises and oversee the activities of the community centre. The host community is accustomed to receiving international volunteers from Canada on medical and education projects. They are generally supportive of visitors as they bring health care, educational support and employment to the village, albeit for short durations. It is typical for villagers to greet volunteers with a warm welcome and for those who return repeatedly, such as Dr. Kane, relationships are grounded in respect and care for each other.

The schools with which we have a partnership in Uganda are typical of the Ugandan rural education system. Schools have no electricity, generally no glass within windows and have tin roofs. When it rains heavily as it often does in Uganda, the noise of the rain falling on the tin roof is so loud that students and teachers alike put their heads on their desks and rest – there is no chance of any teacher or student speaking above the noise of the rain. The children sit on rough wooden benches, typically four or five to a bench and classes can include up to eighty children. Resources are scarce and pencils and notebooks are treasured possessions. The teacher teaches from the one and only textbook and work is generally written on the blackboard with chalk and the children spend time copying what the teacher has written and reciting the content aloud. The children, teachers and principal are very welcoming and take the opportunity of having Canadian teacher candidates to catch up on meetings with parents and other planning and marking tasks. Our teacher candidates are assigned classes in consultation with the principal and generally are asked to teach specific units of work from the approved textbook.

Given the large number of teacher candidates, we grouped the teacher candidates into teaching teams. As a teaching team, they were responsible for teaching two to three subjects a day. The teaching schedule varied for each teaching team, with some teaching subjects in the morning, while others were responsible for teaching in the afternoon. Teacher candidates were responsible for preparing the lesson plans for their teaching subjects as well as for the after-school programme at the community centre, which was modelled on the Boys and Girls Clubs of Canada. In 2018, we incorporated a mandatory debrief session after dinner where the authors engaged with the teacher candidates to reflect and discuss the events of the day: if there were any challenges, any questions and stories they wanted to share. The debrief session provided a space for critical reflection and to help teacher candidates navigate any issues that may have come about during the day. Teacher candidates were also encouraged to record their thoughts and questions in a daily reflective journal. Data for this paper are taken from semi-structured interviews conducted by the first author with the teacher candidate participants, with youth members of the host community and from evening debriefing sessions (Appendix B).

The following discussion considers the data through the lens of the DLN framework and is organized according to the three elements: (1) disidentification, (2) dislocation and (3) displacement. We use excerpts from interviews and our own observations and debriefing notes to consider how the teacher candidates at the focus of this study (re)create their identities when immersed in international service learning.

Element One (Disidentification): Resistance Leading to Increasing Allegiance to Canadian Identity

While all ten teacher candidates enthusiastically embraced the opportunity to teach in local schools and facilitate after-school activities for the children from across the community, there was evidence of resistance by some to immersing themselves within the ebbs, flows and expectations of the local context. A key element of the 2018 international service learning placement was the resistance of some teacher candidates to engage flexibly with the nature of their surroundings and to respond to the changing context they found themselves immersed in. The literature on international service learning argues that international placements enhance teacher candidates' competency to be flexible in diverse situations (e.g. Batey & Lupi, 2012; Cushner & Mahon, 2002; Hurtado et al., 2013); however, what we found was that some teacher candidates could not dissociate themselves from their familiar identities and ways of knowing and being in Canada. This was demonstrated on numerous occasions. For example, upon arriving in our host community, teacher candidates were introduced to Samuel as the education project coordinator and a teacher in Uganda with over five years of experience. Samuel, a young man in his mid-twenties who has a baccalaureate degree from a Kampala university and teaches part-time at a private high school in Kampala, is one of the youth leaders within the community centre. Samuel organized the teaching schedules and assigned two teachers per classroom with grades ranging from grade two to grade eight. Once teaching schedules were assigned, Samuel accompanied the teacher candidates to the two local schools where they would teach, and introduced them to the students and the teachers. Although Samuel had experience working as an educator in both urban and rural environments and the private and public education system, some teacher candidates could not disidentify from their Canadian identity and their hidden power laden with being a white foreigner on a volunteer placement in the Ugandan context. As such, some teacher candidates held on to the power that was associated with being a foreigner and constantly resisted Samuel's authority, challenged his decisions and disregarded his instructions. This was in stark contrast to how they would work with an associate teacher or school liaison teacher in Canada. In other words, the Canadian teacher candidates disidentified with their role as students and learners (which is the case in Canada) and rather identified with the role of being experts and professionals, claiming higher positions of power in their new roles in Uganda.

The teacher candidates who taught the lower-level grades were shocked at how difficult it was to teach in a class where students had limited proficiency in the English language. On numerous occasions four of the teacher candidates brought it to our attention that they could not teach in their classroom because they did not have an interpreter in the class, even though this was never the intended practice. These teacher candidates, working in pairs, had had Samuel or another of the local youth with them during their first week of teaching to ease their introduction into the classrooms and came to rely on the interpretation offered. In contrast, the other teacher candidates who were in their classrooms without a local youth member, developed strategies to ensure they were understood by students in the absence of an interpreter. The discomfort of not having an interpreter in the classroom to support their teaching, and not expecting to have sixty to seventy students in their class, resulted in the teacher candidates either not teaching or singing songs to pass the hour. While we, as researchers, thought teacher candidates would use these difficult situations to develop their teaching competencies (such as using various resources to enhance their adaptability and flexibility), a critical analysis demonstrates that in fact some teacher candidates were reluctant to immerse themselves in contexts that caused them linguistic discomfort. This raises questions as to how these teacher candidates might meet the needs of linguistically diverse students in Ontario classrooms where interpreters are not provided.

In addition to teaching within the schools, teacher candidates were responsible for organizing a programme for the sixty to seventy children who attended the community centre after-school programme. To manage the large group of children, the teacher candidates decided to divide the space in the community centre into ten different stations, each led by one teacher candidate, and to have the children rotate between the stations (activities ranged from doing puzzles, colour images, playing basketball, skipping rope) every fifteen minutes – a mechanism that tends to work well in Canada. At the stations the children could work individually, in pairs, or in small groups to complete puzzles, word tasks, reading or more physical activities like skipping, basketball and other team games. The teacher candidates quickly realized this format would not work because the children arrived at different times, were too excited with all of the stations and were constantly jumping from one station to the next, or were keen to linger at one station (e.g. puzzles) so that they could complete a task they had begun. The tension arose when the teachers persevered with the stations constantly reprimanding the children to stay at the station they were designated to and to only change stations when the timer went off.

This example is not presented to suggest that daily life is unstructured in Uganda – far from it. Children are very used to tasks and chores they must complete before school, and most have responsibilities to complete chores after school and before coming to the community centre. What appeared to the teacher candidates as unstructured, however, is when children came to the centre, they wandered in as they have finished whatever chores they might have had to complete at home. Thus, children arrived as they can, usually over a period of an hour, and even though we said activities begin at 4 pm, children do not have watches and so they were welcome to arrive and to join in whenever they were able to.

During the debrief session that night, the teacher candidates mentioned how frustrated they were that the evening programme did not follow the structure they had planned and how their coordination did not run smoothly. They could not understand why children wandered in at any time, even though the children knew that the centre opens for activities from 4 pm. The frustration this caused one member is evident in the following quotation. In this case children had arrived at the centre before 4 pm and so one of the local senior youth committee members had asked the teacher candidates to begin programming early.

> The children were there for a while already and it was not 4:00 PM but [Senior BGC youth member] asked us to begin the activities. But this was not what we planned, so why are we expected to change just because [Senior BGC youth member] asks us. We had planned to begin at 4:00 PM so that is what should happen.

It was clear that the above teacher candidate held fast to the structured routines that govern Canadian norms and had difficulty adapting and responding flexibly to the local context. Indeed, one teacher candidate during a one-on-one interview mentioned how she struggled internally with the tension of her 'Type A' personality needing a clear structure to function, and the reality of the local community centre flourishing without the structure she was accustomed to. Rather than adapt and respond to what they observed as local contextual norms, some teacher candidates chose to resist and their allegiance to their planned ways of operating became increasingly important. This was a missed opportunity for us to reflect on our need for the afternoon centre activities rolling out as planned rather than us developing the capacity to respond to the context presented to us.

Element Two (Dislocation): Resistance to Authority Resulting in Dislocation

A key finding that was apparent during the 2018 international service learning placement was the subtle ways in which power relations shifted among the teacher candidates from their position in Canada to their position in Uganda. In Canada, teacher candidates usually assume a subordinate position in their practicum classroom and school environment in relation to their associate teacher (Beck & Kosnick, 2000). Indeed, during practicum placements, there tends to be power relations that govern the social interactions between the associate teacher and the teacher candidate. Within this environment, the associate teacher is positioned to have power due to their years of experience and the mentorship role they assume, while the teacher candidate is positioned to have less power and to learn from the associate teacher's experience and in situ guidance (Dillon & O'Connor, 2010). However, this was not the case when the teacher candidates dislocated from Canada to Uganda. Rather, the physical dislocation from Canada to Uganda also resulted in the subtle dislocation of power relations among the Canadian teacher candidates and the Uganda educators who hosted them. For example, upon arriving in Kammengo, the 2018 cohort were given their teaching schedules, with subjects split between two schools. Upon realizing that they would be teaching some subjects at one school and others at a second school, six of the teacher candidates immediately resisted this decision and argued that they did not want to travel between two schools. Similarly, some of the teacher candidates took it upon themselves to count how many subjects each teacher was teaching and those with more subjects challenged the education project coordinator's decision to give them more to teach and others less. Some teacher candidates dismissed classroom instructions given by the project coordinator and in some cases claimed that he 'does not know what he is talking about'. This careful scrutiny of their teaching responsibilities in comparison to others within the team was very disappointing. As project leads, we asked if they would complain in the same way if they were on a practicum in Canada, where, given the teacher candidates were close to graduation, they could be teaching for full days within their assigned classrooms. In response, some teacher candidates offered to take on more classes in an effort to ensure a peaceful group environment, and those who complained were gratified that they could do less.

The paternalistic attitude of some Canadian volunteers was also reported by the Ugandan youth who work at the community centre and who took responsibility for hosting the international visitors from Canada. One of the host volunteers mentioned in a one-on-one interview that 'natives are treated like they know nothing and that [international] volunteers know everything' (Victor, April 2018). In essence, teacher candidates used the 'white' privilege associated with them being from the West to create a shift from positioning themselves as teacher candidates learning from their associate teachers in the Canadian context to being a group leader making decisions and informing the host community on how things should happen in Uganda. This shift in power relations can be associated to some degree with the constant praise teacher candidates receive when they volunteer in the host community. One of the teacher candidates also observed this and in a one-on-one interview mentioned that they received undue praise from the host community for the very little work they did and it made her feel at times uncomfortable as she knew she had done minimal work but was receiving excessive gratitude (Patricia, Ottawa, July 2018). This constant praise from the community, itself a cultural way of showing respect to visitors, reinforces the privileged positioning of the teacher candidates and potentially supports the shift in power relations that allowed the teacher candidates to resist the local authority of some of our hosts, including people of authority such as Samuel.

Element Three (Displacement): Resistance to Privilege

While most of the teacher candidates immersed themselves in the international practicum as an opportunity for learning and for developing their own ways of being a teacher, there was evidence that on some occasions, during the three weeks, some of the teacher candidates sought refuge and security in their privileged positions. Bear in mind, these are teacher candidates who have recently completed degree requirements in the week preceding the practicum. While they have met all requirements of graduating with a baccalaureate of education, the convocation ceremony was scheduled for June, two months hence. Leading up to the travel to Uganda we took many opportunities to consider white privilege and this might play into their interactions when in Uganda. In completing the course based on Dr. Rebecca Tiessen and Dr. Robert Huish's (2014) edited book *Globetrotting or Global Citizenship? Perils and Potential of International Experiential Learning*, we examined case studies of young medical students being called upon to make medical decisions and perform medical work while on international practicum well beyond what they would be trusted to do in Canada. We linked this to the power and privilege of skin colour and engaged in quite robust discussions around how this might also be experienced within education and schools.

In this international practicum, for some teacher candidates the placement enhanced the privilege of the teacher candidates. It reinforced the authority and power of skin colour as the teacher candidates positioned themselves as authorities on teaching and pedagogy ahead of Samuel, a qualified teacher and indeed, in some cases, ahead of the other teachers within their schools. Poverty, lack of school resources and linguistic differences were interpreted as representing lower competence, experience and knowledge. These teacher candidates took on an authority of experience even though they had no previous experience within this educational or cultural context. They assumed authority based on their Western education and their confidence that they knew how to be a teacher.

Concluding Reflections and Imperatives Moving Forward

The aforementioned findings raise serious questions for us moving forward with offering further international service learning practicum opportunities within our teacher education programme. As the person responsible for organizing the international practicum, Dr. Kane takes responsibility for the ways in which teacher candidates are prepared (or not) for the experiences that await them in Uganda. While the benefits to students from international service learning is well documented in literature (e.g. valuable insight for teacher candidates on new knowledge, personal growth, etc.), the negative and unintended consequences of such programming on the local host communities, particularly student populations (e.g. ethical challenges and inequalities), is less understood. For example, Langdon and Agyeyomah (2014) suggest that communities that host volunteer placements and international practicums have become laboratories where individuals test their academic and career choices. We are now considering whether the annual international placement for teacher candidates is contributing to such unintended consequences within our partner host community. How can we support our teacher candidates to recognize our host community as knowledgeable and experienced partners from whom we can learn a great deal? How can we help teacher candidates to offer reciprocal respect and gratitude, in equal measure to what they receive, to our volunteer youth who host our visits?

The responses of some of the teacher candidates as documented above have given us cause to wonder if, in these cases, the international service learning practicum served to reinforce power and difference rather than work towards breaking down such barriers. There is, in these tentative initial findings, enough to cause concern as to the way in which we prepare teacher candidates for the international placement and how we select teacher candidates to participate.

Due to the significant consequences of these unintended outcomes on local host communities, it is important that those of us studying such programmes be open to noticing the unintended programme outcomes, in addition to those outcomes promoted in the goals of the programme. In this three-week practicum within a small village in Uganda, teacher candidates did have an immersive cultural experience that they could not have achieved through a practicum in their local Ontario school. Their curriculum vitae is no doubt enhanced by this notation and most did report that they would be more aware of children and youth, within their classrooms, who come from different cultures and who might be learning English as a second language:

> I am sure that this experience will help us with teaching ESL students back in Canada for sure. I think I will be more aware of thinking about examples I use – using more relevant examples to their lives, culture, etc.

This chapter sought to consider the experiences of the ten teacher candidates through the DLN framework. However, it has become apparent that unlike the experiences reported by teacher candidates in Tanzania (Sharma et al., this volume), some of the teacher candidates at the focus of this study did have intense uncomfortable experiences, but rather than these leading to disidentification, dislocation and displacement, some teacher candidates drew on their discomfort to reinforce their allegiance to Canadian norms and values. This chapter focuses on these teacher candidates who 'doubled down' and resisted the possibilities of deep learning that can come from tensions and uncomfortable situations. The fault of this lies not in the teacher candidates themselves, but in how they were prepared and how we managed the tensions in Uganda.

On reflection, there were missed opportunities for rich learning through potentially uncomfortable conversations, each evening. As the teacher educator, Dr. Kane missed the chance with these young teachers to have courageous conversations about their own resistance to embracing the different and seemingly difficult Ugandan classroom contexts. We are encouraged looking ahead through consulting the work of Langdon and Agyeyoman (2014), who speak to the process of deep reflection on power relations and the need to continually examine the personal versus project goals of international placements.

Given the importance of these opportunities, and their potential for scaffolding deep reflective learning that questions global/local power relations and one's own role in these relations, it is important for all of us engaged in building the experiential elements of Development Studies programmes to ask critical, reflective questions about them on an ongoing basis.

Appendix A: Practicum Syllabus

Course Syllabus

Required Textbook

Globetrotting or Global Citizenship: Perils and Potential of International Experiential Learning

Course Objectives

To prepare you for critical reflection and analysis of your international practicum. The purpose of critical reflection is to facilitate understanding of the challenges and opportunities of global engagement in a world of inequality.

This course aims to provide students with an overview of the ethical dilemmas that come with international experiential learning and the impacts of internationalization. The readings and modules of the course will reflect the concerns of international experiential learning programmes that nurture paternalistic attitudes, experiences that reinforce stereotyping, and projects that merely view host communities as extensions of classroom space.

Students in the course will be guided into processes of reflexivity, whereby students are encouraged to consider the origins of their knowledge and to deconstruct their motivations for participation. Such reflexivity also leads to better understanding of how participants' privilege informs their interpretation of host realities, and raises awareness of the limitations of their ability to comprehend local contexts.

Weekly Schedule – Fall Session

20 September 2017 – Module One: Introduction to Global Citizenship

Required Reading

In *Globetrotting or Global Citizenship? Perils and Potential of International Experiential Learning* edited by Rebecca Tiessen and Robert Huish, 2014, University of Toronto Press.

- Chapter 1 by Tiessen and Huish – 'International experiential learning and global citizenship'
- Chapter 2 by Cameron – 'Grounding experiential learning in "thick" conceptions of global citizenship' (short video of author speaking provided below)

27 September 2017 – Fundraiser Planning
4 October 2017 - Module Two: Understanding Motivations for Participation in International Experiential Learning

Required Reading

In *Globetrotting or Global Citizenship? Perils and Potential of International Experiential Learning* edited by Rebecca Tiessen and Robert Huish, 2014, University of Toronto Press.

- Chapter 4 by Tiessen – Career Aspirations and Experiential Learning Abroad: Perspectives from Canadian Youth on Short-term Placements
- Tiessen, R. (2012). Motivations for learn/volunteer abroad programmes: *Research with Canadian youth. Journal of Global Citizenship and Equity Education, 2*(1), 1–21.

11 October 2017 – Module Three: Critical Reflections

Required Reading

In *Globetrotting or Global Citizenship? Perils and Potential of International Experiential Learning* edited by Rebecca Tiessen and Robert Huish, 2014, University of Toronto Press.

- Chapter 3 by Langdon and Agyeyomah – 'Critical hyper-reflexivity and challenging power: Pushing past the dichotomy of employability and good global citizenship in development studies experiential learning contexts.'
- Chapter 5 by Thomas and Chandrasekera – 'Uncovering what lies beneath: And examination of power, privilege, and racialization in international social work.'

18 October 2017 – Fundraiser Planning
1 November 2017 – Module 4: Images and Discourse Surrounding Learning Abroad

Required Reading

In *Globetrotting or Global Citizenship? Perils and Potential of International Experiential Learning* edited by Rebecca Tiessen and Robert Huish, 2014, University of Toronto Press.

- Chapter 11 by MacDonald – '(De)colonizing pedagogies: An exploration of learning with students volunteering abroad.'
- Chapter12 by Clost – 'Visual representation and Canadian government-funded volunteer abroad programmes: Picturing the Canadian global citizen.'

8 November 2017 – Module 5: Ethical Challenges

Required Reading

In *Globetrotting or Global Citizenship? Perils and Potential of International Experiential Learning* edited by Rebecca Tiessen and Robert Huish, 2014, University of Toronto Press.

- Chapter 7 by Desrosiers and Thomson – Experiential learning in challenging settings: Lessons from post-genocide Rwanda.
- Chapter 8 by Huish – 'Would Flexner close the door on this?' The ethical dilemmas of international health electives in medical education.

15 November 2017 – Fundraiser Planning

22 November 2017 – Module 6: Getting the Most Out of and Making Sense of International Experiential Learning for Global Citizenship Education

Required Reading

In *Globetrotting or Global Citizenship? Perils and Potential of International Experiential Learning* edited by Rebecca Tiessen and Robert Huish, 2014, University of Toronto Press.

- Chapter 9 by Drolet – Getting prepared for international experiential learning: An ethical imperative.
- Chapter 10 by Travers – Getting the most out of studying abroad: Ways to maximize learning in short-term study trips.
- Chapter 13 by Roddick – Youth volunteer stories about international development: Challenges of public engagement campaigns.
- Chapter 14 by Huish and Tiessen – Afterword: There should be nothing experimental about experiential learning: From globetrotting to global citizenship.

Weekly Schedule – Winter Session

29 January – Practicum Planning
5 February – Fundraiser Planning
12 February – Practicum Planning
19 February – Fundraiser Planning
26 February – Practicum Planning
5 March – Fundraiser Planning
19 March – Practicum Planning
26 March – Fundraiser Planning
2 April – Practicum Planning

Course Requirements

Students are expected to attend classes, read the weekly readings, and participate in class discussions and activities. The Fall session will focus on exploring the ethical dilemmas of international experiential learning and planning fundraisers. The Winter session will focus on preparing lesson plans for the practicum and planning more fundraisers.

Appendix B

Sample Interview Questions with Host Community

1. How, if at all, do you feel the teacher candidates on the international service learning practicum benefitted the school and/or BGC?
2. Do you feel that the teacher candidates were prepared for their international practicum?
3. Do you feel there were negative effects associated with their placement?
4. How, if at all, could the international service learning practicums improve to meet the needs of your school or BGC?

Sample Interview Questions with Teacher Candidates Post-Practicum

1. What did you gain from this international practicum experience?
2. How, if at all, do you feel you have become a better teacher through this experience?
3. Were there any barriers/challenges during the international practicum?
4. How, if at all, do you feel the preparation you received prior to going on placement helped you address any barriers or challenges?
5. Have you given any thought to the possible impact on the organization and the community that hosted you?
6. What do you think the impact of your placement was on your host organization?
7. Do you think your counterparts see value in this kind of cross-cultural learning opportunity?
8. Are you concerned that there may have been 'costs' or negative effects associated with your placement for both the host organization and the broader community? If so, what would these be?

7

Helping Future Teachers Negotiate the Paroxysms of Patriotism at Home and Abroad: A Parallax View

Stephen Parliament and Geoffrey Scheurman

As teacher educators, we increasingly ask our teacher candidates to step outside the safety zone of their college environment to experience teaching in a different culture. The potential psychological consequences of such an experience are amply described as a 'Disruptive Learning Narrative' (DLN) in Chapter 1 of this volume, which proposes that the resulting disruption to our teacher candidates 'would provide a greater opportunity for growth and learning'. We expand on that discussion and on the nature of 'growth' itself by offering a 'parallax' view where personal growth is dependent on dialogue between incommensurable perspectives (Žižek, 2009). We also provide a reflection on what we call 'patriotic paroxysms'– sudden explosions or expressions of emotion aroused by one's sense of national identity – experienced while living and teaching in foreign cultures ourselves (Scheurman & Parliament, 2018). The result is a reciprocal reward that comes from crossing divides where no bridge seems to exist.

Theoretical Background

We would like to propose a metaphor for the theoretical elaboration of the Disruptive Learning Narrative (DLN) framework as described by Sharma et al. in Chapter 1 of this volume. As teacher candidates move from their formal academic training to a new environment in a foreign country, they will be looking at the world differently. They will be experiencing a 'parallax view' of teaching, the elements of which are aptly described in this book as the dislocation caused by their physical change in location to another country and through an alteration in their power relations among their new colleagues and students. We further expect that they will be less identified or 'disidentified' with their customary social and cultural norms. These elements – *dislocation* and *disidentification* – result in the psychological transference of the candidates' original expectation from a conventional field placement experience to the substitution of a totally new target, the third element in the DLN framework: *displacement*.

As disruption to their psyche occurs, the object of their interest changes. Making an application based on the work of dialectical theorist and contemporary philosopher, Slavoj Žižek, we find that the teaching contexts for which candidates have been prepared, and the new reality of teaching in a different culture, become contradictory. The candidate is faced with 'the illusion of being able to use the same language for phenomena which are mutually untranslatable and can be grasped only in a kind of *parallax view*, constantly shifting perspective between two points between which no synthesis or mediation is possible' (Žižek, 2009, p. 4, our emphasis).

We shall explore this phenomenon in detail, beginning, as Žižek does, with two seemingly comparable stories. The objects of our inquiry are the experiences of candidates teaching in the United States and in a foreign country: in our case studies, China and Ecuador.

Case Studies of Profound Disruption from International Encounters

Each of our undergraduate candidates are self-confident and enthusiastic young women who received glowing evaluations with no concerns – academic, developmental or emotional – from professors and cooperating teachers during intensive block field experiences prior to student teaching. We selected them as contrasting cases for two reasons. First, despite their credentials, as their respective experiences unfolded in new locales, we found that each candidate faced a situation overseas that was severe enough to warrant a modification of assignment in order to lessen the burdens of disidentification and dislocation. As their domestic supervisors, we encouraged each candidate to absorb challenges into their normative expectations, to adjust to revised power relationships among their peers and, in each case respectively, to change living arrangements or modify school assignments.

Second, we recognized significant differences as each synthesized and summarized their experience upon return. Each of these candidates travelled overseas as part of our Consortium of Overseas Student Teaching programme (COST). COST allows candidates to complete half the semester during their student teaching experience at home and the other half (nine weeks) in a foreign country. So the idea of 'displacement' is built into the experience for both candidates through post-placement reflection and analysis. It is our belief that there is no final synthetic resolution of the conflicts generated by the parallax view of the world that our candidates experience. We could call this component of the overseas experience an adjustment to a substitute target or the acceptance of the parallax view. Here are details of our candidates' stories:

Participant One

Rebecca, an elementary education major placed in China, was delighted to learn that part of her assignment included no-cost housing with a Chinese family. She soon discovered that the free rent came with an expectation of English tutoring for the family's single child, an assignment Rebecca was – naively as it turned out – happy to accept. Part way into her assignment, the intensity of the expectation grew to uncomfortable proportions. The candidate learned that she was expected to report home immediately after school nearly every day for tutoring lessons, compromising her ability to champion an English language club and take part in other extracurricular activities at her school. The family tension became so intense that once she was sent to her room in tears after the father of the house confronted her sternly, in Chinese, about what Rebecca concluded were her failed obligations to the family. After trying to mediate the situation from afar and interacting with local supervisors, a local Chinese coordinator eventually made a new family placement and Rebecca completed her assignment in good standing.

Participant Two

Mary, also majoring in elementary education, was placed at a national school in Ecuador. She was also presented with a challenging and near debilitating situation, although hers involved a relationship with a cooperating teacher. Mary described her condition as 'floundering in a mis-matched classroom'. She felt as if the first-grade children did not 'connect' with the cooperating teacher and, despite trying strategy after strategy, Mary felt as though she always came up short in pleasing her mentor, feelings exacerbated by a language barrier that prevented her from processing her feelings with the veteran teacher as well as from connecting with the children herself. Refusing to blame the teacher and calling it a 'bad fit', Mary still had to deal with her misery and feelings of inefficacy. Coincidentally, an American faculty member who happened to be in Quito sensed the emotional crisis right away. In Mary's words, 'she did what I was not brave enough to do – she asked for something to be done so that my experience wasn't sour'. Mary was relocated to a fourth-grade classroom and also completed the placement in good standing.

Each of these candidates participated in debriefing sessions after they returned home. Rebecca submitted a reflective statement with photos for a COST newsletter and was part of an intensive meeting with the programme coordinator, and Mary took part in a pilot project where she and twelve other overseas student teachers participated in pre-departure assignments and seminars, check-in correspondence during the experience, and a post-practicum survey and group debriefing dinner and celebration.

Preliminary Analysis While Debriefing Our Candidates' Experience

The question posited in this chapter is whether teacher candidates like Rebecca and Mary experience an apparent emergency of 'unrepresentable' experiences because of a 'gap or inner distance' between the anticipated context for which they were prepared and the one they faced (Jameson, 2006, p. 8).

As our candidates tried to make sense of their experiences, the result was a disadaptation or maladaptation of the subject to his or her environs, which we shall incorporate into the doctrine of DLNs. The reader will judge from the case studies in this volume whether parallax theory has been fruitful.

In the first scenario, Rebecca was never able to acknowledge the value of the disidentification and dislocation she experienced. In other words, she was unable to move fruitfully within the parallax. In Žižek's (2009) terms, Rebecca could have used the experience as a catalyst for the emergence of Self, which derives from social interaction (p. 245). Sharma et al. pose the question as to what the act of teaching does to the teacher? Or, what does the parallax experience of field placement do to the candidate? Žižek looks at social interaction as an opportunity for inner dialogue between yourself and reproaches of others resulting in the formation of self-image. This inner dialogue is not easy, and Rebecca did not take advantage of the opportunity.

This does not mean her experience overall was unproductive. She reported a very positive and enriching experience in the elementary school, with considerable evidence to support her report. She received top-shelf evaluations from her cooperating teachers, had lovely stories about, and shared artefacts by, the children she taught and even figured out how to make an after-school language club work in spite of the challenges with her host family. Nevertheless, she clung tenaciously to the judgement that the tension in her Chinese 'home' constituted a detriment to the experience and should never have happened. Her supervisor counselled and provided feedback about the lessons of overcoming adversity and the value of growth that happens when routines are disrupted, and cultural expectations are confronted. As mentors, we talked about how this is the very reason for choosing to student teach overseas in the first place and how her experience resulted in the identification of dispositions and acquisition of skills she may not have experienced had she stayed within her comfort zone. In other words, we tried to coax her into accepting a parallax perspective. Nevertheless, Rebecca (and her mother) remained fixated on the negative aspects of the experience.

Rebecca's debriefing reminded us of the unavoidable and intrinsic nature of national representation that is attached to every student, traveller, wanderer, vagabond or anthropologist who we set loose on the world with a US passport. How differently are we viewed from what we intend or what we surmise? Let us consider how different Mary's debriefing was from Rebecca's. By the end of her experience, Mary was able to provide a concrete list of lessons learned, which, 'if I hadn't had the difficult time, I did for the first month of my stay, I would not have learned these things about myself'. Her somewhat naive post-practicum responses demonstrated a nascent understanding of the difference between 'being miserable and having one bad day' while reiterating how the change in placement served as a kind of salvation from her misery. Still, she offered this conclusion with confidence during her culminating assignment:

> So, as always, the arduous, spirit-straining, faith-testing times have brought about positive change, far more joy, and have strengthened me. … My confidence is increasing, as is my grace for myself as a teacher. … There's always another day, a new day. I can always grow from those mistakes. (Scheurman, 2017)

Even more striking was how Mary spoke at our culminating dinner and debriefing session. She was given over to emotions while describing the challenge of processing American news in Quito, especially of a police officer's acquittal after shooting a young African American in Ferguson, Missouri. She described her desire to be proud of her country and yet having to admit feelings of shame as she tried to explain the division and destruction that our brand of democracy had unveiled. Mary's ambivalence corroborated initial findings from a cumulative study we have begun wherein candidates returning from overseas experiences fill out a survey on their conceptions of democracy (Scheurman, 2018). Early returns indicate students often feel apologetic for American policies and events, while simultaneously expressing pride in being an American. This leaves us wondering if these results are contradictory or understandable for American students in what is most likely their first engaging experience in another country. What will take longer is to fully understand to what extent students recast or reframed those norms to make them more compatible with the culture in which they were working.

Most interesting about Mary's reflections is how she was able to understand her paroxysms in terms of cultural mores and ideological perspectives. On one hand, feelings aroused by perplexing news about potential police brutality in the United States forced Mary to confront an unconscious patriotic belief that things in the United States are always defensible. On the other hand, the way she and some of her colleagues wrote about a 'paradox of freedom' and the 'reclaimed value of choice' helped her to affirm a belief in herself as an agent in the American educational system. Her reflections after returning from Ecuador reveal a maturity beyond what we typically expect from teacher candidates, wherein she even frames her perspectives about teaching standards in terms of an ideological conundrum:

> Although there were still standards to be met, I could go about meeting those standards in a myriad of ways; almost any way that I wanted to. … I had more freedom to differentiate, though I did have fewer resources than in the [United] States. If anything, this challenge excited me more than ever. Odd; coming from the 'Land of the Free', I encountered a freer education implementation in Ecuador than in the United States. This re-ignited all my passions for what I love about education. (Scheurman, 2017)

As seasoned international travellers, we resonate with the pangs of growth we witnessed because of this candidate's seminal overseas experience. We realize that when our own norms have been challenged, we too have felt paroxysms of uncertainty in our preparation as well as in our sense of patriotism, all of which brings our own disidentification into question.

In the case of our young charges, one candidate seemed to embrace the dislocating encounter she had in Ecuador when she was able to confront her cooperating teacher and request a different location assignment, while the other could not seem to get past her disgruntlement with a dislocating experience in China. The experience of both candidates can be captured by Foucault's (1986) frame for what he calls heterotopias or 'unreal' spaces brought about by the challenges of experience well outside the individual's realm of cultural experience. Introduced by the editors in Chapter 1 to this volume, Foucault's concept helps explain the difference between our two candidates' reactions. It also helps illuminate our own conception of patriotic paroxysm, since the candidate in Quito, Ecuador, discovered her own utopian image of America being shattered, while the candidate in Hangzhou, China, had her utopian image of the American family and social norms strengthened because of her idealized expectation of her host country being destroyed. These explorations lead us to contemplate what qualities we might cultivate in them if they are to have a healthy engagement with disruptive intercultural experiences and eventually pay those experiences forward while working with their own future charges.

Disidentification: Incommensurabilities While Looking Outside of One's Perspective

We would like to interject our personal narrative here to illustrate the power that experiences in a foreign country can have in dramatically increasing our identification with social and cultural norms with which we are familiar. This is important because it runs contrary to the expectation that working and teaching outside our customary environment will automatically reduce our identification with the familiar. As instructors, we need to be aware of the influence that nationalistic or ethnocentric pride – not necessarily negative feelings in and of themselves – can have on ourselves and potentially on our teacher candidates. We, therefore, offer the following narratives from both of us authors, which we share with the reader in hopes of providing insights into our growth and reflection during international experiences. Geoffrey Scheurman is the narrator of the European narratives and Stephen Parliament is the narrator of the American (Early Childhood class) and Mexico narratives.

European Narratives: Geoffrey Scheurman

Professor Scheurman once missed a connection with an ex-student host whom he was supposed to meet at the train station in Vienna. After wandering around the city in search of a telephone, he approached the front door of a luxurious hotel when someone obviously from his native country appeared at the entrance. As he approached this swaggering, mustached and cowboy-booted American, he noticed a large button prominently attached to his leather vest. It read, 'I am an American and I hate Bush, too!' Despite Scheurman's own less than enthusiastic support for President Bush at that time, and his passionate support for freedom of expression, he became so incensed at this public display of disrespect for the 'face of my country' that he walked on by, choosing to go it alone rather than taking the risk of a confrontation.

Feelings of patriotic pride are often intensified in a foreign country, although they aren't always 'negative', as Professor Scheurman learned while leading a workshop in Mosjøen, Norway. He was the Fulbright Roving Scholar in American Studies and dozens of teenagers were assembled in a gymnasium to explore 'The Tapestry of American Music'. He was sharing an example of what happens to the style and meaning of a song – in this case, Bob Dylan's *Like a Rolling Stone* – when it ends up in the hands of an artist from a different genre, in this case, Jimi Hendrix. Scheurman has no special affinity for Hendrix – his previous reactions might even be characterized as patronizing at best and reprehensible at worst. But when he pulled up a rare video clip of Hendrix doing *Rolling Stone* at Monterey, he suddenly found himself with tears on his cheeks, absorbed in a previously undiscovered thought, namely, 'that's one my people'.

Are such moments a visitation of a patriotic spirit that one really can't choose or control? Does patriotism choose us more than we choose it? In cognitive psychology, we explore the nature of conceptual understanding, specifically how we come to 'know' what something is by contrasting it with what the thing is not. In Norway, Scheurman would often begin a workshop on the rights of students with a discrepant event inquiry involving the case of a teenage boy who gets suspended for wearing a 'straight pride' t-shirt. The shirt was a response to his observation that peers clothed in 'gay pride' regalia had commandeered so-called 'safe spaces' in the school as their private domain and, claiming no malicious intent and supported by his parents, he simply wanted to make a statement.

Generally speaking, most Norwegian students were dumbfounded by the entire ordeal. Rights are rights, they would argue, and kids have rights to wear what they want, for whatever reason, period. Furthermore, a principal has the right to intervene, but why would she? And the student has a right to disagree with the intervention, but why would he? Their default answer was always that it was the other person's right, something they thought that America championed above all else. Despite a considerable background in constitutional law, Scheurman found himself groping at an explanation for why such a scenario would occur in the United States. He tried to explain the nuances of 'balancing test' language from the US Supreme Court and the difference between rights for some groups but not for others, depending on circumstances like history and cultural context. At every turn, however, he usually ended up stumbling towards an answer that culminated with some form of 'because in America, that's what we do'.

After many similar responses to issues in schools all across Scandinavia, he came to refer to the phenomenon he was observing as the 'frame theory of democracy'. He concluded that many Norwegians frame their democratic perceptions in terms of participation in inclusive dialogue, but with carefully prescribed parameters. At some point in a debate, an answer to a question is declared and everyone walks away thankful for the privilege of having had their voice heard. To our Nordic friends, individual rights are inviolable but contained, and the Straight Pride case should never have ended up in such an ambiguous rabbit hole.

The takeaway is that defending a commitment to national principles that one really considered or articulated during all his years as an American social studies teacher was the product of a disorienting confrontation. As a teacher in a foreign land, Scheurman was forced to formulate an explanation, which was never before considered, for how democracy works in the United States of America.

A Concluding Note on the Norwegian Story

From America's rambunctious and violent beginning until today, many Americans deem it patriotic to embrace what our Supreme Court has described as a kind of 'hazardous freedom' that encourages such provocative controversy to arise. In Norway, students told us consistently that while they possess a right to protest, their support of country demands acceptance of a decision once deliberated and they almost never challenge the process by which such decisions are made.

In the end, our Norwegian students found these two idealized conceptions of democracy incommensurable with one another. The real revelation is this: *so did we*. This is Zizek's parallax view in practice, even if we couldn't articulate it as such at the time.

American and Mexican Narratives: Stephen Parliament

Another story from the perspective of Stephen Parliament raises questions of loyalty, faith and obedience that lurk in the backdrop as any student teacher seeks to carry out his or her responsibilities. We offer this story to demonstrate how the confrontations with a parallax perspective can occur at home as much as they can occur overseas.

Challenges at Home and Abroad

This time a student in a class on diversity in early childhood was teaching at a private religious elementary school while pursuing the final few credits for a license. A nearby school district was recently confronted with demands from the parents of a young child who was presenting feelings of gender confusion. The child was taunted, ridiculed and bullied. The parents asked the school and the district to institute a policy and practice of understanding and acceptance for the child's feelings.

The classroom teacher was perplexed. She identified strongly with her personal social norms and was being asked to accept and understand that which was not consistent with her beliefs. This disidentification was causing a severe psychic event in which her values were being displaced with a substitute target. The displacement was serious and intense, causing her to question her professional commitments. She held strong personal religious beliefs. How could she investigate gender and sexual identity questions in her classroom as a patriotic teacher who is supposed to support the freedom of expression when she personally believes that such exploration or inquiry is a violation of her faith?

'I teach in a private religiously affiliated school that makes its beliefs clear. Why should I have to introduce something into my classroom in which I do not believe?' she argued.

'You can believe what you want,' Parliament explained, 'and your beliefs are protected by the Constitution, but you are seeking to be a licensed agent of the state and therefore owe your allegiance to a broader frame of patriotism,' which, though not stated so explicitly, is the implication of a class on diversity in early childhood education.

A Concluding Comment on This Story

We never came to a definitive agreement, conceptually or politically, but in the discourse between seemingly incommensurable alternatives, we were both able to move forward in our respective professional roles.

Synthetic Resolution and Parallax View of Patriotic Teaching

Returning to the original question posed by Sharma et al. in this volume, what happens to teacher candidates when they are exposed to the displacement of their psyche through geographic and mental displacement? One possibility is that candidates can attain higher levels of cognitive ability through the synthesis of conflicting points of view. Another is that points of view do not always need to be synthesized, but rather embraced in a kind of parallax tension suspended between disparate experiences.

Each of the candidates in our stories represents the different kinds of experiences and responses typical of student teachers based on their individual psychological make-up. Even though for some candidates (see the debriefing notes above regarding Rebecca compared to Mary's experiences), disidentification cannot be resolved, this does not mean that meaningful growth has not occurred when translated through a parallax lens. Our stories affirm the observation that 'the DLN framework helps us shed light on healthy tensions and dissonances that sometimes are left unanswered but touch a deep part of us that forever becomes transformed' (Sharma et al., this volume). Regardless of the power of our mental capacities, we should not always expect a creative resolution arising from analysis and synthesis. This result is Žižek's (2009) description of the parallax function in its purest form, in which he explains that 'the gap between two versions [of reality] is irreducible, it is the "truth" of both of them, the traumatic core around which they circulate; there is no way to resolve the tension, to find a "proper" solution' (p. 19). It becomes the job of the instructor to help candidates apply the reflective tools of DLN framework to bring them to a 'better understanding of their own experiences in the practicum' (Sharma et al., this volume). When faced with inconsistencies or contradictions, we should 'renounce all attempts to reduce one aspect [of the parallax view] to the other' (Zizek, 2009, p. 19) through a dialectic synthesis of opposites. 'On the contrary,' as Žižek maintains, 'we should assert antinomy as irreducible' (p. 20), in reference to Immanuel Kant from Karatani (2003) 'to see things neither from his own viewpoint, nor from the viewpoint of others, but to face the reality that is exposed through difference (parallax)' (p. 3).[1]

What happens to our candidates, then, is the acceptance of a parallax view of irreconcilable opposites into an enigmatic paradox in which tension and the incommensurability of psychic displacement are recognized and accepted. The foundation of constructivist pedagogy is to inquire into antinomy or anomaly (the reader may think of Jerome Bruner (1960) and Thomas Kuhn (1962)) without an expectation of resolution. From this mental perspective, we prepare our candidates to fulfil a teacher's sense of patriotism by saying that we remain both loyal to our country's principles of free expression, and simultaneously question the authority that gives our democratic system its legitimacy.

When the civil libertarian Henry David Thoreau spoke at the funeral of John Brown, he returned to the theme, in *Civil Disobedience* (1866), of the life and death of conscience. John Brown's body may be mouldering in his grave, but his appeal to the soul of America goes on. W. E. B. Du Bois asked about Brown: 'Was John Brown simply an episode or was he an eternal truth?' (as cited in Carton, 2006, p. 1). The eternal truth of John Brown's challenge to the idea of patriotism continues to percolate, simmer and explode in classrooms daily, especially in our current age of ignorance and manufactured fear. Radical patriotism is emerging in wildly different manifestations from extreme nationalistic xenophobia to urgent appeals for multicultural internationalism. To be constructivist teachers, we must look at the idea of America with a parallax view: as we walk around it and view it from different angles, our understanding of the teaching experience in different cultural settings will be full of inconsistencies and contradictions.

Conclusion: Including Explicit Focus on Disruptive Learning Elements

As Sharma et al. explain in this monograph, and the case studies and personal testimonies in this chapter exemplify, tensions that are revealed through international experience might well be understood by comparison with domestic experience in terms of a DLN framework. We agree and believe their observations are pertinent to the following extension of the argument. Namely, teacher candidates could be well served in identifying their own struggles with disidentification, dislocation and displacement. In doing so, they might come to understand how a critical constructivist approach in teacher education draws learning from tensions, conflicts and contradictions that arise when learning to teach. For example, it would be valuable to compare and contrast both international and domestic placements in Canada or the United States and apply the DLN framework to see if candidates can unearth issues of power, privilege and marginality that go ignored or unnoticed in pre-service teacher placements at home and abroad.

Furthermore, we are heartened by a vision for a future of teachers who expect to be surprised by all students, who work to demystify the conservatism inherent in teaching the same lesson and in telling the same story over and over even as the context and student population changes, whether subtly or dramatically. Explicit attention to the three elements of the DLN framework encourages teacher candidates to reflect and analyze their own stories from different perspectives, which bring forth new understandings to old stories. It is our suggestion that by using the DLN framework, a teacher candidate is just as likely to be exposed to disruptive learning experiences in Canada or the United States as they would through placement overseas. Buttressed by anecdotal evidence of our own experiences with disidentification, dislocation and displacement, we conclude that it is not until teacher educators use the DLN framework to analyze their own intense and uncomfortable experiences that they are able to trek on the path of uncovering disruptive learning that lies beneath teacher candidates' international vignettes.

Prospective teachers definitely benefit from overseas teaching experiences. However, they benefit more from teacher educators who encourage them to reflect on their own psychological, social and cultural disruptions. The stories and anecdotes we offer certainly support the opportunities that departments of teacher education offer to their students for international work. Our final conclusion, however, is that a parallax view of teaching is the philosophical basis of inquiry which is critical for a constructivist approach to learning, whether overseas or in one's own backyard. Confronted with the reality that students in Norway, candidates in China, Ecuador and Wisconsin, teachers in Mexico, and seasoned American educators encountering the world, all see things like democracy differently, what is the takeaway in terms of guiding the next generation of young teachers? We believe the answer is in accepting the displacement of our psyche through the absorption of the parallax dilemma, which in turn requires a transformative and revolutionary view on the part of the teacher.

Paulo Freire (1997, 1998a, 1998b), the Brazilian educator who dedicated his life's work to educating students about, and encouraging resistance to, the authority of the state, argues that the teacher is a cultural worker who must engage students through dialogue. If teaching and patriotism are caught in a parallax view of reality, then the only synthesis available is Freire's dialogical approach of changing schools and society so that inquiry becomes part of patriotism, in which the two become intersubjective with one another, and where the observer or teacher becomes part of the object of democratic society. This lesson is relevant no matter the age or epistemological maturity of the people involved in the paroxysms of international teaching and learning. As such, teacher educators and teacher candidates become instrumental guides for one another as they negotiate the respective parallax of their disruptive learning networks.

If the essence of teaching is inquiry, Freire might say that we are encouraging our future teachers to endlessly question authority but, as the perpetual optimist, to ultimately transform society itself into an equitable and just organism. Žižek, however, might say that the concept of 'growth', which the editors of this volume are seeking, is ephemeral. He would restate the Kantian solution of the 'transcendental turn' that 'rejects ontological closure: it recognizes a certain fundamental and irreducible limitation ("finitude") of the human condition' (Žižek, 2009, p. 21). Nothing is reconciled. There is no synthesis. The inquiry goes on as does the pursuit of knowledge. We shall leave it to our readers as to the fruitfulness of our elaboration on the parallax perspective as it applies to teacher education, and to teaching itself.

8

International Experiences in the Bahamas: A Tropical Restoration Experience

Kevyn J. Juneau

The British economist E. F. Schumacher (1973) stated in one of the more influential books on economics,[1] *Small Is Beautiful*, that "the best aid to give is intellectual aid, a gift of useful knowledge. A gift of knowledge is infinitely preferable to a gift of material things."

In the section of the text in which this quote is derived, Schumacher discusses the fallacy of providing aid in monetary or material form to poor communities. The crux of the matter, Schumacher (1973) argues, is bridging 'the gulf between rich and poor; the gulf between educated and uneducated; and the gulf between city-men and country-folk' (p. 140). As part of a class, we travel to Andros Island, a family island in the Bahamas, to help restore degraded ecological habitats. When I developed a study abroad course to bring students to The Bahamas for the University of Wisconsin–River Falls, I knew that as a white man taking a class of relatively privileged, primarily white college students to a country where 93 per cent of the population identifies as being of African ancestry, where many of the residents suffer from extreme poverty and a lack of education, especially in the 'family islands' and where the population had only recently gained their independence from the United Kingdom in 1973, I had to be cognizant of the racial and colonial tensions I may come across in the country (see Saunders, 2016).

The indigenous history of the Bahamian archipelago was quickly erased and replaced with a typical colonial history after Columbus made landfall on Guanahani (renamed San Salvador by Columbus) in 1492. The original Bahamian inhabitants, the Lucayans, quickly died off (reportedly within twenty years after Columbus's arrival) due to the newly introduced diseases brought to the islands from Europe and the hardships of being taken from the islands and forced into slavery. The Bahamas were essentially uninhabited for approximately 130 years once the Lucayans were extirpated. The Bahamas then became a British colony in 1648, and it was around this time that English Puritans along with slaves and former slaves from Bermuda settled in the colony; these events shaped the present state of the country. The Bahamas, especially Nassau, was an important trade port over the next two centuries. The soil was not conducive for growing produce, so plantation slavery was not as common in the Bahamas as was on other islands or in the United Colonies (name of the United States of America before it became independent), but the Bahamas, as a British colony, did have significant connections to slavery.

I was speaking with a native Bahamian, and she told me the story of how the settlement of Fresh Creek on Andros Island was named. Fresh Creek is a tidal estuary that has salty oceanic water, not fresh water; therefore, it is not the water it was named after. She told me that the port was a place where slave trade ships would stop after the trans-Atlantic crossing to resupply, and it was here the West Africans in the holds of the ship were disembarked and then washed or 'freshened' in the estuary before they were then sent to the Carolinas to be placed into the slave trade. She also told me Africans that 'didn't make the cut for slavery', as she put it, were abandoned on Andros Island. The current population of The Bahamas is now a combination of British loyalist descendants and expatriates from the United States; however, the country, the family islands in particular, primarily consists of descendants of the slaves who immigrated with British loyalists from the United States during the United States War of Independence, 'liberated' slaves (Africans taken from Spanish slave ships by the British and placed into indentured servitude when slavery was banned and later abolished by the British in the early 1800s) and 'freed' slaves (slaves abandoned when, in the 1830s, sisal[2] and cotton plantation owners left the family islands for Nassau) (Howard, 1999).

Given the history of the Bahamas, I had two primary concerns when creating this course: I wanted to develop an ecological restoration course in a tropical or subtropical biome, but I did not want to approach the restoration with a 'white saviour' mentality or take a colonial approach to environmental issues. The Bahamas has done extraordinary work towards sustainability and environmental conservation and, as often the mentality is with the 'white savior industrial complex', a term coined by Teju Cole (2012), we, in this course, do not need to 'save them because they can't save themselves' (n.p.). I also did not want this course to fall under the pedagogical 'tourist model'. By tourist model, I mean, I did not want to view or interact with the local people from either figurative or literal distances. I wanted the students in this course to be immersed in the community as we learned about environmental issues the Bahamians face while helping them rehabilitate degraded ecosystems. My aim was to give my students a gift of knowledge pertaining to ecological restoration, but I also wanted my students to provide intellectual aid, as Schumacher (1973) suggested, to the residents as we collaborated on a variety of restoration projects. The transfer of intellectual aid, I find, occurs in the field when the students, who have taken formal classes in ecology and biology, share their knowledge and comprehension of ecosystem processes and how ecological theories are applied during restoration to the community. Hopefully, through their conversations, the locals would develop a fuller understanding of the process and continue with the restoration efforts after we left the island.

Demographics of the Student Population

The University of Wisconsin–River Falls is a four-year, public comprehensive university located in the Upper Midwest of the United States of America. According to 2017–18 Enrollment Reports, the University has an enrolment of approximately six thousand undergraduates and four hundred graduate students (University of Wisconsin–River Falls, Enrollment report Fall 2017, n.d.). The University was formed as a Normal School – schools and colleges that prepare students for teaching careers – and then later grew and incorporated more programming across the liberal arts after the Second World War. The heritage as a normal school remains strong, and teacher education, specifically elementary education, is one of the largest programmes on campus, only behind animal science (the largest major) and business. The largest graduate programme at the University is the Master of Science in Education. The University's only doctoral programme is the Doctor of Education in Montessori Studies.

According to the Enrollment Reports for the 2017–18 academic year, the population of the University students is approximately 87 per cent white American and 11 per cent American students of colour (University of Wisconsin–River Falls, Campus Data Reports, n.d.). The remainder are international students. Of the 11 per cent students of colour, 2 per cent identify as African American, 3.5 per cent as Latinx, 3 per cent Asian American and the remainder identify as several other groups including Middle Eastern, South Asian, Indigenous or a combination of ethnicities. Approximately two-thirds of the students identify as female and one-third identify as male (it should be noted that at the time these data were collected, there was no option for non-binary gender identity).

Most of the students who are enrolled at the University are from either rural Wisconsin or Minnesota – although, being close to the cities of St Paul and Minneapolis, Minnesota, there are many students who come from those urban and suburban areas. Approximately 45 per cent of the students at the University of Wisconsin–River Falls are first generation, meaning their parents or guardians do not have an academic degree from a four-year higher education institution (University of Wisconsin–River Falls, Quick Facts, n.d.). Of the six thousand students enrolled, 27 per cent receive Pell Grants. The Pell Grant is a US federal assistance programme that provides people with demonstrated financial needs the money to help pay for college. Pell Grants are awarded to students who come from households that have a yearly income of less than $50,000 (USD); however, most Pell Grant awardees come from households that receive less than $20,000 (USD) per year. Seventy-five per cent of the undergraduate students enrolled at the University receive some form of financial aid, mostly loans, and 51 per cent have some non-Pell federal grant (University of Wisconsin System Education Reports and Statistics, Student Financial Aid, n.d.). Most of the students at the University work during the academic year. The University has been referred to as a 'suitcase college', referring to the number of students who leave the campus to go home on the weekends. This suggests that most of the students live within a close travel distance to the University. Specifically, in the College of Agriculture, Food and Environmental Science, one of the four colleges at the University and the college in which this course is housed, most of the students have some form of agricultural background and may be or feel obligated to return home to help on the farm or have a need to work a job for income in their hometowns over the weekend.

History and Development of the Course: ESM 242 – Tropical Restoration Experience

In a recent survey of graduating seniors, 32 per cent of the responders stated they had participated in a formal study abroad course during their time at the University (National Survey of Student Engagement [NSSE], 2018, p. 29); however, many of the students in the College of Agriculture, Food and Environmental Science do not participate in these programmes. This is suspected to be either due to the prohibitive costs of these experiences or the lack of courses specific to the degrees offered. It can be argued, and it should be, that all study abroad experiences are relevant for student development as a high-impact practice, but the issue is that many of the study abroad experiences do not count towards degree completion and are taken as free electives or are in addition to the curricula required for the degrees. Many students cannot fit these experiences into their already heavy curriculum requirements. One of the University's core values is global engagement, and the University aims to 'engage with ideas, people, cultures, and places beyond our campus' to develop a 'global perspective' (University of Wisconsin–River Falls, About us, n.d.). This value is met through study abroad experiences; so there is an initiative to increase the opportunities for students to study abroad.

I developed the Tropical Restoration Experience so that students at the University in the College of Agriculture, Food, and Environmental Science, especially those in the Conservation, Environmental Planning, and Environmental Science programmes, could participate in a study abroad programme that fit their schedules while also gaining experience restoring tropical and subtropical habitats, which are unlike those in the Upper Midwest and Great Lakes States of the United States. There are no prerequisites for the course, so students in any major can take the course with no coursework restrictions. This course does count towards degree completion for those in the Conservation, Environmental Planning, and Environmental Science programmes. The course is also part of the Sustainable Justice minor.

Schumacher (1973) stated that 'the power of [non-marginalized] people, who today tend to feel utterly powerless, does not lie in starting new lines of action, but in placing their sympathy and support with minority groups which have already started'. Heeding this, I initially made plans to take a group of students to Kumasi, Ghana, to work with colleagues at the Forestry Research Institute of Ghana where we would learn about and experience first-hand the restoration of Ghanaian tropical forests by participating in current projects. My hope was to make the course so that it was not cost-prohibitive and I aimed to actively recruit low-income, first-generation students with limited experience travelling internationally for the course. Although the budget for a course in Ghana was within the range of costs for these types of study abroad experiences the University currently offers, it was at the upper end, and I felt it was cost-prohibitive for the students I was looking to recruit.

Around this time, I was speaking with a friend from graduate school, and she mentioned that she was the newly hired executive director of a programme that operated a field station in The Bahamas. She invited me to explore the idea of taking a group of students there. After discussing my objectives and our options, she contacted the Government of the Bahamas Ministry of the Environment and Housing-Forestry Unit where she was able to set up a meeting for all of us to further discuss this course.

The Forestry Unit, formally established in 2010, has a mission: 'Guided by prudent policy and the provisions of the Forestry Act 2010 and Regulations, the forest resources of the Bahamas will be sustainably managed as a viable renewable natural resource for the benefit of The Bahamas' (Government of the Bahamas, 2011, Forestry Unit: About us section). The Forestry Act of 2010 provides the country with a legal framework for the sustainable management and conservation of the Bahamian forests.

The forests in the Bahamas, especially on the four 'Pine Islands'– Abaco, Grand Bahama, New Providence and Andros – have been degraded over time due to poor management and overharvesting, with much of the degradation occurring when the country was gaining its independence from the UK in the early 1970s. During this time, a division of the glass-making corporation, Owens-Illinois, was harvesting trees on these islands for pulpwood to make paper and cardboard packaging, and on Andros Island specifically, the forests were liquidated by 1973. After the forests were cleared, Owens-Illinois surrendered its holdings to the then newly independent Bahamian Government. After that cutover, the forests have grown back but not in a manner similar to what they were prior to logging. In addition to the degraded forests, other concerns for Bahamian residents include increasing temperatures, sea-level rise and ocean trash.

The Bahamas are facing the impact of climate change. Stronger hurricanes have led to more destruction on the islands, and the threat of sea-level rise will force people off the islands. Sea levels may rise as much as 2.7 meters (8.9 feet) in the next sixty to eighty years (Sweet et al., 2017). Approximately 80 per cent of The Bahamas lays less than 1 metre above sea level. This area could be flooded within the next fifty years. Many of the wealthier Bahamians have plans to move away from the islands within the next few decades and many have already begun sending their children to schools within the commonwealth, primarily to Canada. The less wealthy residents do not have a plan or there may be very few options for them. While at a bar one evening we were chatting with a Bahamian and she said, 'The thing is, that when you fuck with mother nature, she doesn't fuck *with* you. She fucks you!' My general sense is that most Bahamians are aware of the issue of climate change, but there are not many options for them to deal with it.

The Forestry Unit received a capacity-building grant in 2015 to (1) maintain and restore ecosystem services and integrate ecosystem management approaches with the conservation and management of ecosystems, and (2) strengthen their capacity to realign their environmental programmes to address degradation ecosystem services (Government of the Bahamas, 2011, Forestry Unit: Partnerships/Projects section). This grant focused on the restoration and rehabilitation of forested habitats on the Pine Islands. Because the severely understaffed Forestry Unit was awarded this grant, the help that the students in this study abroad course could provide was welcomed. Together, the Forestry Unit and I put together a curriculum for this reimagined tropical restoration experience.

Learning Objectives of the Course

This course has two categories of learning objectives. The first category pertains to the course as a conservation course in the study abroad programme. Upon completion of this course, students are expected to

- Understand the fundamental concepts of resilience, ecological restoration and why we restore impaired landscapes.
- Understand the ecological attributes that give restored ecosystems wholeness and understand reference systems, models and strategies that inform restoration planning.
- Have an increased knowledge of the geography of Bahamas as well as the natural environment – *Global Self-Awareness*.
- Compare and contrast various aspects of Bahamian culture to their own – *Cultural Diversity Appreciation*.
- Use their knowledge, attitudes and skills to engage with issues that address challenges facing humanity globally – *Personal and Social Responsibility*.

The first three learning objectives were developed in line with the lower tiers of 'Bloom's Taxonomy' (Bloom, 1956), while the final two objectives expect the student to be able to analyze and apply the material gained in this course while we are in the Bahamas and after we return. The italicized text specifically highlights the objectives that address the requirements for study abroad and global perspective courses set by the General Education and University Requirements Committee.

The second category pertains specifically to sustainability and is required for the course's inclusion in the 'Sustainable Justice' minor offered at the University of Wisconsin–River Falls.

- Sustainability ethics: students will gain a grounding in the interrelated nature of social, economic and environmental issues, as related to views of interdependence, resource allocation and environmental justice.
- Sustainability praxis: students will be able to analyze, articulate and envision solutions to problems of sustainability, integrating knowledge data across disciplinary boundaries.
- Global citizenship: students will internalize an understanding of the consequences of their social, economic and environmental choices, and the possibilities for taking action on the personal and public levels.

These objectives were developed by a cohort of faculty and staff to meet the programme's goals of (1) exploring sustainability through an environmental justice lens, (2) introducing students to both the environmental humanities and the environmental sciences, developing a transdisciplinary approach to solving sustainability problems, (3) providing different cultural perspectives on human identity, and the way these views shape our environmental, social and economic relations and (4) encouraging students' awareness of their social, economic and environmental behaviours and how they can promote sustainable justice in their personal and professional lives.

All the objectives laid out in this course are assessed through a series of written reflections, daily observations by the instructor and a final public oral presentation that is delivered to the other students in the course, to the staff at the field station and to any other guests or groups staying at the field station.

A list of prompts is given to the students at the beginning of the course and they are required to journal their reflections each day. The students are also required to read the text *How to Read Nature* by Tristan Gooley (2017) and partake in the activities laid out in the readings. In the book, Gooley (2017) wrote, 'It should be expected that we will find wonder in a vast mountain landscape, but it is a more serious challenge to find wonder in a hill. It is a great achievement to find it in a molehill'. My hope is that students find wonder in the small things while we are in the Bahamas, and I aim to assess that in the activities and assignments the students must complete while we are there. Activities range from simple listening and visual observation exercises to deeper introspective exercises. The final, two-part reflection assignment assesses the students on their response to the following series of questions. The first part of the assignment is due immediately when we return to the United States. These following questions are answered in the journal they hand in at the airport upon our arrival:

1. What are the goals of the restoration organization you participated in? How did the activity you completed help towards achieving that goal? What was the target?
2. What was your impression of the activity? Did you enjoy it? Or not? Was it what you expected as a 'restoration activity'? Were there any 'ah ha!' moments or surprises?
3. What type of landscape were you working with (describe it)? What is your relationship to that particular area or the broader region it belongs to?
4. What aspects of the ecological restoration model[3] were being emphasized or affected?
5. After taking this class, what are some actions that you will personally take to live more sustainably? How do these actions impact people on other parts of the globe, including Bahamians?

The second part of the final reflection is due one week after we return, and I ask the students not to work on it for at least three days, so they can have time to digest the trip and have more time for deeper introspection and reflection. In the final reflection I ask:

1. What were the biggest 'Ah ha!' moments during the trip? Why do you think these moments were big for you and stuck with you?
2. Were there any moments that you initially felt 'uncomfortable', but that uncomfortable moment eventually led to a valuable learning moment? (e.g. being in an unfamiliar social environment, etc.?)
3. What was the biggest lesson or message that you took home with you? How did you arrive at or realize that lesson or message was so important?
4. What was the most important experience you had there?
5. Did this class change how you perceive your role as a citizen of the planet?
6. Has the experience changed the way you may approach things now? (things being, really anything: sustainability, your education, how you interact with people, your perceptions, whatever).

The second part of the final reflection aims not only to assess students' growth and change in perspectives, but it also aims to assess aspects of the three elements of the Disruptive Learning Narrative (DLN) framework: disidentification, dislocation and displacement (Sharma et al., this volume).

Course Content

The course material remains consistent year to year. Throughout the two weeks while in the Bahamas, students are instructed on the ecological theories that serve as the foundation for restoration and taught about forest mensuration and how to collect quality data. Students are subjected to lectures on the natural and cultural history of the Bahamian Islands. The formal lectures typically occur in the evenings in the field station's classroom. If there are other researchers at the field station, often they have given lectures or presentations on their projects to the students in this course. There are also ice-breaking and team-building activities the students complete during the early days of the trip to help improve communication and collaboration between the participants.

The course, however, focuses mostly on the in-the-field, applied restoration projects, which vary based on the needs of the Forestry Unit and those of the local residents. To address my primary concerns with this course, I heeded the advice of Ernesto Sirolli (2012) who said 'Want to help someone? Shut up and listen!' and Teju Cole (2012), whose words greatly resounded, wrote 'If we are going to interfere in the lives of others, a little due diligence is a minimum requirement,' and 'there is the principle of first do no harm. There is the idea that those who are being helped ought to be consulted over the matters that concern them', and listened to what the Forestry Unit needed. Prior to the trip, the Forestry Unit and I work together to determine what help they need that given year and develop goals and objectives for reaching those needs. I do not propose activities, but I listen to what their needs are and determine the feasibility of addressing these needs based on the academic backgrounds of the students, including previous courses taken or experiences with environmental conservation and restoration, and the tools I can realistically bring on the trip. For example, we cannot cut down trees with chainsaws if none of my students have that experience going into the course. Weight and space are other major limitations when flying to the family islands. There are limitations for both, and the airlines impose hefty fines if either limitation is exceeded; therefore, we cannot fly with heavy equipment or tools that take up a lot of space such as chainsaws or shovels. Although difficult to predict, weather also determines the type of activities that we can safely accomplish while there, whether it is too hot and heat exhaustion is a concern, or if there are electrical storms and we cannot work due to the threat of lightning strikes.

Restoration activities take place in four ecosystems: pine forests, coppice forests, mangrove swamps and beach sand dunes. The specific restoration activities have regularly included invasive species removal, trash clean-up and transplanting native plants into degraded areas. A major component of the restoration includes data collection, so that we can determine how the systems are responding to the restoration efforts. Permanent plots have been established in each restoration site and data is collected from them each year. In addition to these activities, we have also implemented a prescribed fire to kill invasive species and rejuvenate the native plants, cleaned culverts to improve tidal flow into the mangrove systems, and planted fruit trees in neighbourhoods for residents to harvest, among other various activities.

Extracurricular Activities

I hesitate to call these activities 'extracurricular', but they are activities that are not included formally in the syllabus; however, they tend to lead to organic learning moments that meet the desired outcomes of the course. While at the field station, students in this class get the opportunity to work on projects with other researchers who are staying at the field station. This has, for example, included working with researchers investigating land crabs, anole lizards and endangered orioles. The students also have the opportunity to explore the community. This often means visiting one of the nearby bars, getting ice cream at the ice cream stand or perusing locals' shops that sell handmade crafts. For each of these activities, the students often have conversations with the Bahamian shop owners or the patrons of these shops. As a group, we attend a workshop with a local basket maker who teaches us how to weave our own baskets. During this workshop, the basket maker often gives the students an oral history of Andros or tells stories about life living in the Bahamas. As a group, we also visit locally owned and operated restaurants where traditional local cuisine is prepared for us and we eat family-style. The meals often include freshly harvested seafood typically including fish, conch or lobster, along with other Afro-Caribbean side-dishes, such as plantains, beans and rice, barbeque or jerk chicken.

Experiences That Capture Disruptive Learning Narratives Specific to This Course

Experience One: Visit to Red Bays

The most substantial experience in which I feel the class is subjected to the DLN framework is our visit to the settlement of Red Bays. Red Bays is a community of decedents of Seminole and escaped slaves that fled Florida during the Seminole Wars in the 1800s. During that time, Andrew Jackson and American Troops displaced and killed thousands of native people in Florida so that the Northerners could move into the area. Prior to the wars, the Seminole people accepted and incorporated escaped slaves into their communities. It was a large group of these peoples that left Florida to find sanctuary in the Bahamas, many landing on Andros Island. Although there have been occasions when they had been visited by colonists, they remained relatively unmolested and isolated until 1968 when Owens-Illinois built logging roads into their settlement. Before the logging roads were built, the residents of Red Bays relied on subsistence farming, fishing and crabbing. Many of the residents still do. The residents of Red Bays are often perceived as suffering from extreme poverty, as Rosalyn Howard (1999) points out in her dissertation, 'Red Bays is often maligned by other Bahamians who generally refer to its residents as poor and "backwards" people' (p. 96). There are few opportunities for making money in Red Bays. At one time, the community depended more heavily on harvesting sea sponges out of the ocean. The sponges were harvested and then exported to Tarpon Springs, Florida, and to Greece, but that industry has dwindled significantly from a million-dollar industry in 2006 to nearly nothing today since the lone proprietor died. The community now relies on tourism for money. There are a few bars and restaurants and a convenience store; however, many residents rely on selling crafts to visitors to earn money. Because of this, the community can be perceived as suffering from extreme poverty and, based on feedback from my class, many students had that perception.

During this course, we visit Red Bays and spend a day walking through the settlement and spend time at the homes of some of the residents. The trip to Red Bays is intentionally scheduled on the last day of the course, and I do not provide many details about the visit or the conditions of the settlement to ensure the experience is organic. The students learn the history of Red Bays while we are there and experience the settlement without any preconceived notions. Many of the homes in which people live are small, one-room shacks that may or may not have running water and electricity. There we hear stories related to the history and traditions of the Red Bay Bahamians. We spend time with the local basket makers and wood carvers who tell us about these crafts. We are also told of some of the hardships the folks in Red Bays face. For instance, one resident told us a story about a person who went out sponging one day with a group, dove into the water and never came back to the surface. In some instances, if a resident does not catch a fish or crab, they go unfed that evening. These hardships are a reality that the students in this course are not subjected to in their home country.

Experience Two: Lack of Luxury

This particular experience is less of a singular experience and more so a general state of being during the trip; however, it is nonetheless important for the learning framework, as it is often noted as being a major 'wake-up call' in the students' final reflections. The field station where we stay was built in the 1960s as a dive resort. It was later acquired by the current owner in the 1970s and, although it is more modern than it was decades ago, the upgrades are limited to the confines of the 1960s designs and the limited resources found on the island. While staying at the field station, luxuries such as air conditioning, Wi-Fi, cellular phone service, television, and even sugary candy and treats are not available or are hard to come by. Cold drinks and ice are also not as readily available as students are used to. This tends to be challenging for students, especially when the temperature range is between 25°C and 35°C while we are there. Power outages are common, and there can be periods of many hours to days without electricity. The staff at the field station, being environmentally conscious, try not to use pesticides to manage the mosquitoes and other biting insects as often as tourist resorts tend to do. The students stay in cabins, each with four to six bunks. Each bunk has a mosquito net because the biting insects readily get into the cabins through the screens or through gaps around the door. The cabins provide shelter and have electricity and running water, but there are no air temperature controls other than ceiling fans and box fans to help with air flow. The conditions are not primitive, but students are certainly surprised that we are not housed in a situation more similar to that of a hotel. This experience does not necessarily directly affect the students' positions of dominance or marginality in society; however, it does place them in a position and in a set of similar circumstances that many residents on Andros Island are challenged with. The students in this course have little control over their own environmental comforts as they are used to. This lack of luxury challenges their core values and often their traditional ways of thinking, in environmental, social and economic contexts.

Unpacking the Disruptive Learning Narrative Framework

The DLN framework applies to many of the experiences the students encounter throughout the course and especially to both of the above scenarios. The first scenario leads to a cultural sense of discomfort and disruption to the students, while the second is an environmental discomfort and disruption of their mental state of well-being. This class, being part of the sustainable justice programme, requires both the cultural and environmental discomfort for the students to grow. Most of the students on the trip come to the table with a basic definition of sustainability as it pertains to the environment (e.g. do not pollute, do not exploit natural resources, etc.). The students often lack the understanding of the social or economic pillars of sustainability, and the disruptive experiences they face on this trip help them define, for themselves, these other components. The students are placed into situations where they see these components first-hand. In the realm of sustainability, members of the Red Bays community may only be achieving the most basic of Maslow's (1943) hierarchy of needs (food, water and shelter); so they may be less immediately concerned with local waste disposal or global environmental issues such as climate change. The students who interact with this community recognize their responsibility and role as global citizens having met needs higher on Maslow's hierarchy. This, I believe, is imparted to the students through the DLN framework. The following analysis is my anecdotal assessment based on teaching this course a number of times and seeing first-hand the students' reactions to their environmental and social conditions as well as the feedback provided in their final reflections. The reflections are due within a week upon our return; so I cannot make assumptions about the lasting effects this course has on the students. There is much overlap between each of the three elements, but here I attempt to tease apart the elements as they relate to the experiences.

Disidentification has been defined as the 'process of becoming either increasingly or dramatically less identified with one's own familiar social and cultural norms' (Sharma et al., this volume). Students experience this from the onset of the course. I have noticed that they initially avoid speaking with Bahamians, including the station staff, early on in the trip, and tend to interact more with the white interns or interact with the Bahamians *through* the white interns. This I think stems from two primary hurdles the students need to overcome. An immediate struggle many students mentioned having was understanding the Creole dialect the Bahamians speak and feeling as if they were coming across as insulting when they would ask Bahamians to repeat what they were saying. It takes a few days before most of the students begin interacting and speaking with the Bahamians directly. Once this happens, I notice the students restructure their perceptions and decide that the locals are 'the most welcoming and friendly people'. Their disidentification becomes most apparent when we visit Red Bays. For many of the students, the visit to Red Bays is their first experience seeing a community that is economically destitute where many truly rely on the natural resources available for sustenance. After spending a day at Red Bays, one of the common comments that the students report is that the residents of Red Bays, and Bahamians in general, are always so welcoming and friendly. Nearly every student mentions this in some fashion in their reflections.

This may be in stark contrast from the perceptions the predominantly white students from the Upper Midwest, who interact perhaps infrequently with people of colour, have of Black Americans, which are based on, or cultivated by, media portrayals and social conditioning – the second hurdle that must be navigated. For example, a study, conducted by Narissra Punyanunt-Carter (2008), examined how Black Americans are perceived on television by undergraduate students. The results suggested that students perceived the stereotypical characteristics of Black Americans, particularly the negative personality characteristics (e.g. disrespectful, immoral, dishonest) as true, whereas the positive characteristics (e.g. helper, giver, virtuous) were believed to be unrealistically represented. These perceptions may be possessed, explicitly and implicitly, by the students who take this course, thus leading to this contrast in expression and disidentification.

In the Bahamas, where most of the residents are melanated – the term Bahamians use to describe people of colour, particularly those who are Black and have higher concentrations of melanin – the students are in a situation where they are forced into these interactions. This experience challenges their preconceived ideas and implicit biases and makes the students more aware of their biases. The sense of 'welcoming and friendly' residents of Red Bays sharply contrasts their implicitly biased perceptions of people of colour so much so that nearly every student comments about it in their reflections. Hopefully, although I have no sense of intention, this reaction is not apparently a patronizing or overcompensating one, but rather a genuine one. One student mentioned that after this experience she is now 'more inclined to talk to new people'. And another suggested that he 'definitely approaches new cultures in a different way and has improved [his] confidence in asking people questions about themselves and their life'.

The lack of luxuries plays a role in disidentification too. Daddy Cool, the field station's security guard, tells everyone who walks by him to 'Keep it cool, baby!' However, few take this figurative and literal advice. The lack of luxuries to which students are accustomed leads to physical and mental discomfort for the students to the point where many have described 'hitting rock bottom' or 'having a breakdown' due to the lack of their otherwise everyday comforts that the students may identify themselves with – comforts that perhaps the Bahamians do not have access to. The feedback I receive in the final reflections strongly points at this lack of luxuries as a major 'wake-up call' for my students. Although the conditions at the field station do not represent an environment that most Bahamians on Andros Island experience (e.g. air conditioning is available to many people, and most residents have refrigeration, internet and cellular phone access), the students do have to deal with the cultural change of living at the station. One of the common responses I receive is that students do not realize how much they think they need comforts afforded to them, such as ice or internet access, especially after seeing local Bahamians living in the conditions that they do.

Dislocation is defined as both a change in physical location and how students locate themselves within group dynamics (Sharma et al., this volume). For the first part of this definition, the students come on the trip with the idea that they are visiting a tropical paradise, but they quickly realize that the part of the Bahamas we visit, although is certainly a paradise in its own right, is not the stereotypical vision they may have of a Caribbean island and the resorts that are depicted in the media. This is immediately brought to the foreground when we arrive in the country. We leave Nassau on a regional plane, and figuratively and literally watch out the window as we leave the comfort we are used to for a place where amenities are few and far between. Their view of paradise is also tarnished when they learn that because of colonialism historically, and now the trade and the tourism industry, much of the vegetation present consists of invasive non-native plants that are detrimental and disrupt the ecosystems.

Addressing the second part of the definition, the identity of the group dynamics tends to shift throughout the trip. The students who have previously experienced a study abroad trip, or a self-imposed lack of comfort for a period of time, through extensive primitive camping, backpacking or other experiences, become leaders who help others deal with their mental and physical discomfort. This shift in the group dynamic is apparent during the first days of the trip when students who have not previously experienced this austerity rely on those who have in order to get over the discomfort and initial shock of being away from home. One student mentioned that the discomfort was shared throughout the group during those first two days. The group was brought together when a leader became apparent in the group. I believe the students who become the early leaders of the group have experienced a prior disruption, had already shifted their perspectives and were readily adaptable when they experienced these subsequent disruptions and discomforts. Once a leader assumes this position as a role model, the uncomfortable students then begin to enjoy the trip and are more involved. This power shift presents itself again about halfway through the course, when the toll of laborious days, the constant attack by biting insects, the heat and other gruelling environmental conditions begin to break down the students, and these leaders emerge to help the others overcome this difficulty. A student who served the role as one of the leaders mentioned in her reflection that she 'did not want [the discomforts] to get in the way of my trip more than they already had … I had to ignore them otherwise they would wreck what was left of my trip'. Here she is psychologically overcoming the discomforts imposed upon her. Other students saw her push through and were then empowered to do the same.

The power dynamics also shift as we interact with the Bahamians. The power dynamic, at least from the Bahamian point of view, based on the comments from people I interviewed while I was there, is not white versus Black but more foreigners versus locals. There is contention between Bahamians and immigrants, particularly those who come to the Bahamas to exploit jobs and natural resources; however, white visitors tend to bring a racial power dynamic with them when they visit. Being white in the Bahamas, especially on Andros, is a geographic marker, not necessarily a judgmental characteristic, but a characteristic that can define a person's origin. Aside from mostly expatriates or temporary residents (i.e. 'snowbirds' who only live in the Bahamas throughout the winter, or the rotating military personnel who work on the US Navy base), white people on Andros are visitors. In 2018 it was reported that most of the 6 million annual visitors in the Bahamas, of which about 11,500 travel to Andros, come from the United States or Canada (Bahamas Ministry of Tourism, 2018). One student mentioned that she initially felt uncomfortable because she felt as if she was intruding, but this discomfort waned as another student filled the role as a leader. As we travel through the country, and visit settlements, including Red Bays, the person with the most international travel experience, who seemed to have developed more of a global perspective prior to taking this course, typically becomes the leader when interacting with local Bahamians. I feel this leadership role has less to do with the student's socio-economic background connecting them with the Bahamians, and more to do with their change in perspective from having been previously subjected to a disruptive experience and being able to adapt or acclimate to the new situation. They are often the first to approach people in the Bahamas or initiate conversations. These students with prior travel experience tend to talk or interact with the residents of Red Bays the longest and have richer conversations. One particular student who has taken this course two times displayed this phenomenon. The first time she took this course, she was passive or, in some instances, a submissive participant. The second time she took this class, she served the role as a leader and was the conduit between the group and the Bahamians.

Displacement, in the context of the DLN framework, is 'a psychic event where there is a shift in action from a desired target to a substitute target. It is an internal struggle' (Sharma et al., this volume). This displacement is apparent in the looks on students' faces as they step out of the van into Red Bays. The look is a mix of emotions. It is discomfort at first, and then often a look of melancholy. Emotions are shaken off and we begin the tour. The students experience dissonance and tension as they process the initial sight. We talk a lot throughout the course about what consequences our actions have globally, and this moment is when the students see the faces of the people who are directly or indirectly affected by these actions.

This, I believe, is where some looks of shame and guilt may be derived. The students feel guilty and often blame themselves for the conditions people in Red Bays are facing. The students become submissive or display overcorrective or overly sympathetic behaviours towards the residents as they interact with them – a misguided behaviour to address racial inequality that stems from the students' misplaced guilt. Students mention that they reflect and work through this guilt, and often use Red Bays as an experience that they can directly say changed them.

In an opposite sense, students also seem to experience a cognitive discordance that stems from a perception that they themselves self-identify as 'poor' or not well off, but when they see the residents of Red Bays they see themselves with a reconstructed identity. If the data contained in the University surveys mentioned above are representative of those who take this course, many of the students are from lower- to middle-income groups, which many of the students perceive for themselves as 'poor' or at least 'not well off', but the students in this course are not impoverished and do not have issues with food security or housing. They come to the realization that, although they originally see themselves as poor, they are, in fact, quite affluent relative to those in the Bahamas who do suffer in some instances with food security or inadequate housing. 'Seeing how differently people live there, I found a new appreciation of how and where I live,' said one student about the visit to Red Bays. Another student stated, 'Learning about what their [Red Bays residents] life is like compared to mine, their traditions, and hearing their stories, was one of the most moving and powerful experiences I've ever had.' The students are attributing their growth to this specific experience, whereas it is most likely the combination of all the activities and experiences that led to their development. This disruptive narrative, at least temporarily, changes the students' perspectives about themselves and others.

Environmental displacement is often more apparent. Frustration and sometimes anger due to lack of comforts the students are used to spring up throughout the trip. The most contentious issue during each time I have taken groups to the Bahamas is the lack of ice at the field station. A lot of students' frustrations about not having amenities, such as internet or air conditioning, are taken out on the lack of ice. The common idea within the group is that if 'they only had ice, things would be better'. This blame placed on the lack of ice, or at least an idea of ice being readily available to them once the trip is over, is an example of students displacing their disidentification and dislocation during the trip on a tangible entity to help them overcome their discomfort. After approximately a week after arriving, there is typically one student who has a verbal and physical outburst over the lack of ice. This suggests an internal struggle that these students are unable to emotionally process or cope with at the time. The students who have these outbursts shift the target off themselves onto the ice. The students submit to the idea that ice has this power over them.

Addressing Concerns with the Disruptive Learning Narrative Framework

The DLN framework has useful pedagogical implications, especially as these uncomfortable experiences or situations help develop a student's identity. Students may develop into leaders and, at the very least, change their global perspectives. This framework can help the instructor assess and adjust, if necessary, according to the needs or the reactions of the students. These uncomfortable moments are teachable moments, and I am reluctant to warn students about them prior to the trip in order to keep these experiences impartial. But I do have conversations with them pertaining to tough issues when necessary, especially if I sense they may be causing internal turmoil. Because of this, I feel students become more introspective during these experiences, and this may have lasting effects. One student, an Elementary Education major, stated that her now open mind 'is something I wish to pass onto my future students' and she wants them to realize that 'no matter what [their] abilities are or where [they] come from, [they] can always put in efforts large or small to help the planet.'

What instructors need to also be cognizant of, however, is how they interact with or view the people in the country they are visiting. I did a lot of introspection while developing the course, and over the past few years. I also spoke with many Bahamians in the communities we visited, with staff at the field station and with the people in the federal agencies we work with, about some of the concerns that I envision could arise by utilizing this DLN framework. In terms of using these uncomfortable situations or experiences during a study abroad course, I have deliberately developed my class so that it hopefully does not take a colonial, white saviour approach to restoration. My goal is to help the communities that we visit on Andros with their ecological restoration projects rather than take charge and ownership of these efforts. This, I feel, was accomplished for me, and is necessary for instructors who wish to use this framework to be mindful of. By having a direct dialogue with each group that visited, no matter the academic objectives of the course, the issues with the white saviour approach can be mitigated.

I also attempt to avoid a tourist model that uses peoples' struggles or trauma as a venue for our educational experience. It may not be apparent that trauma or struggles exist, so precautions need to be taken. Recognizing this can be a challenge in the Bahamas, for example, because the residents rely on visitors for their economy and they will most likely not be confrontational if they are taken advantage of by visiting groups. Tourism accounts for approximately 50 per cent of the Bahamian economy; so any negative responses to visitors tend to be outweighed by the financial value tourists add to the community. This exact sentiment was also shared with me by the two taxi drivers I spoke with while travelling to and from the airport. If it was not for the primarily white tourists, many Bahamians would not be paid at the end of the week and would not be able to afford food. There are examples of groups and their guests (completely unassociated with and unrelated to the field station at which we stay) who have had long running programmes on Andros that often conflicted with the residents. One group, for example, consisted of young, white, wealthy teens who had a reputation for drinking heavily and being rowdy. Despite the group's bad reputation, the residents felt they were unable to address the issue because they depended so heavily on that tourism. This programme dissolved, and immediately the economic impact has been felt throughout the community. About 15 per cent of Bahamians are unemployed and the poverty rate, at the time this chapter was written, is at 12.5 per cent. This extreme poverty, especially as previously discussed occurring on the family islands, drives the local Bahamians' desire for more visitors to the island. Traditional livelihood on Andros includes sustenance farming and fishing. In some cases, if a person does not catch a fish or crab on any given day, they may not eat that night. The residents are finding themselves relying more so on tourism for their livelihoods than they have in the past.

Although it is not a specific goal of the course, an indirect consequence of this educational model is that it does help the economy of the community visited. Students buy handmade crafts and food prepared by locals, the course relies on taxis for transportation and locals are employed by the field stations that host the class. As part of this course, a local basket maker is paid to provide the students a workshop on how to make palm-thatch baskets. The field station and the visitors it hosts contributes nearly half a million dollars to the Bahamian economy each year. This is through employing locals at the station, contracting locals for needs, and purchasing other goods and services. A lot of money is also spent by guests in purchasing crafts and other souvenirs from the shops near the station. This may be true for the communities that are the focus of other courses that attempt to use the DLN framework. An awareness and a proactive attempt by the instructor to resist the temptation of viewing communities and people through a tourist lens will help avoid the exploitation of marginalized groups of people.

Conclusion

On reading the reflections and feedback from the course, it seems that staying in the Bahamas for a full two weeks is enough time to give students an opportunity to experience uncomfortable moments, reflect on them and address them in a meaningful manner. Stereotypical perceptions of Bahamians and the country in general are challenged. Students in this course do not see the resorts, casinos or beaches typically visited by vacationers. We avoid these places and are immersed directly into a community removed from many services and conveniences.

Upon our return, students suggest that they valued the uncomfortable situations they experienced. This 'study abroad experience allowed me to learn a lot about myself, my place in the world, and how I want to give back to the world,' one student responded. Another stated that their 'perception of my role of being a citizen of this planet has changed in the sense that I know each and every single one of my actions/choices has a ripple effect'. These statements suggest to me that the disruption the students faced during this trip had an effect, hopefully a lasting one.

9

Winterim in Cuba: Unlearning and Disruptive Moments

Simon A. Akindes

When Roberto, an Afro-Cuban man in his early thirties, visited our study abroad group in Sueños, Santiago de Cuba, the middle-class neighbourhood where we were accommodated, the instinctual reaction of the first students he met was panic. Why would an uninvited man visit us? What was he looking for? We should be on the alert. An Afro-Cuban man that we had hardly met was invading our intimacy, our privacy. I, the faculty leader, was informed of his visit, but was not alarmed, having had a conversation with Roberto one or two days before, when we visited La Gran Piedra in the Sierra Maestra, the mountain range that surrounds Santiago de Cuba. I had learnt about his family and life in Cuba of a working-class man. Roberto wanted to know more about me, about the place in Africa I came from. A student in the group shared our address with him and he followed up with an unannounced visit, a common practice in my home country of Benin, the ancestral origins of many Afro-Cubans. Roberto, I was told, had had mild mental illness issues.

As it happened, Roberto paid us a few other visits. He brought us gifts of freshly picked mangoes, *guanábanas* (soursop) and bananas, and Cuban cigars. Students' initial reactions to Roberto epitomized the preconceived ideas many US Americans uncritically espouse when dealing with a Black male – fear, suspicion, defensiveness – and when Cuba is mentioned – dogma, dictatorship, human rights violations, poverty and deprivation. As a dark-skinned Cuban man, Roberto symbolized Cuba, and many of my students responded in predictable ways. As time passed, students learned to see Roberto differently. Roberto was one of the many lessons my students would learn during our visit.

We were now in Cuba; the norms were somehow different: kindness, friendship, the joy of life abounded. The purpose of the trip was to study what we could in twelve days, by seeing, listening to and experiencing Cuba. Cuba, for a long time, has captured the imagination of US citizens – first, by being the Caribbean island with plantations that made part of the US economy prosper; second, by being the place of joy and libertinage for the mafia and the powerful; third, by resisting the domination of its big neighbour for sixty-one years now and fourth, by implementing a socialist system in the 'backyard' of the United States, the most powerful capitalist country in the world. The mystique of Cuba is heightened by personalities such as Che Guevara and Fidel Castro, who have had a major impact on political and cultural life in the Americas and worldwide, and the influence of Cuban music on American jazz. One is not indifferent to Cuba, and the Winterim Study Abroad to Cuba organized by the University of Wisconsin-Parkside was meant to situate that mystique into other perspectives, and to understand Cuba. This trip was my fourth visit to Cuba and, having visited both Havana and Santiago, it was Santiago that earned my affection.

In this chapter, I purport to make meaning of how the University of Wisconsin-Parkside (UW-Parkside) students living in the Midwest in the United States were able to navigate the continuum from their own preconceptions and prejudices to the Cuban 'reality' they encountered after a twelve-day trip to Santiago de Cuba and Las Tunas. Santiago is the most Afro-Cuban town of the island, and Las Tunas, the Cuban capital of sculpture.

In this chapter, I use the Disruptive Learning Narrative (DLN) framework, a theoretical framework 'developed out of an urge to understand and seek clarity about intense and uncomfortable experiences' (Sharma et al., this volume). Focusing on three components of disidentification, dislocation and displacement, I examine how students may begin a process of self-transformation after being immersed in a rich, authentic and challenging study abroad experience that unsettled their sense of identity and resulted in various major and minor forms of dislocation and displacement. I primarily use students' texts provided in their final projects, writing assignments, podcasts and movies.

I focus on students' identities, on their interpretations of their interactions with Cubans, the lenses through which they viewed themselves and the short- or long-term transformations resulting from immersion into the Cuban society in Santiago and Las Tunas. I attempt to evaluate the extent to which this brief experience in Cuba, a country that, for sixty-one years, has dared to imagine a polity based on equality and justice, with institutions that cultivate values of solidarity, reciprocity and mutuality, has unsettled them.

In the first section, I begin with the rationale and intent behind the study abroad: how it originated, why and how it was set up and what it intended to achieve. In the second section, I deal with how students had to confront their ethnic, racial and gender identities in a situation where racism, contrary to official narratives, still exists – where ethnicity takes on different meanings, especially in a context where cultural identity and nation mean the same officially. The notion of 'cubanidad', what it means to be Cuban, has itself changed over time given the innumerable challenges the society has faced and the cultural currents coming from outside. In this section, identification and disidentification among students themselves are deconstructed and analyzed. Students belong to 'racial groups' that, in Cuba, differ from the ones ascribed to them in the United States. Disidentification (Sharma et al., this volume) refers 'to the process of becoming either increasingly or dramatically less identified with one's own familiar social and cultural norms'.

In the third section, which takes on a specific significance, I discuss dislocation in Cuba. In addition to its physical component, it has an ideological and political dimension that students had to make sense of. The exoticism of being in Cuba was always present as an additional layer of complexity. They were visiting a socialist country that promotes societal values antithetical to the ones they are familiar with in the United States. As Sharma et al. (this volume) point out, 'To gain an understanding of dislocation, it is important to pay close attention to how power moves within and across people on an individual and group level'. Cuba offered numerous opportunities for students to experience a social geography whereby, for most of them, it became essential to reinterpret the power associated with pre-established identities and the comfortable or uncomfortable 'cultural boxes' that had informed their lived experiences in the United States.

In the fourth section, I tackle the concept of displacement. Sharma et al. (this volume) argue:

> Displacement deals mostly with the psyche: an intense moment of rendezvous between disidentification and dislocation. ... Displacement is seen as a psychic event where there is a shift in action from a desired target to a substitute target. This 'displacement' happens when the desired target is not reachable or unacceptable and the substitute target emerges as acceptable or less threatening.

This study abroad experience offered few instances of intense dislocation and displacement. When dissonance occurred, it did not create severe emotions that would make students look to escape, but the negotiation between dislocation and disidentification had to be conducted again and again to avert crises.

In the fifth section, I place the whole trip within the context of learning. In a short study abroad experience of twelve days in a developing country, what does learning mean, and how much impact can it have? What kinds of transformation do we expect of students, if any? Or do we simply have them go through exciting or exotic experiences that produce no other result than to solidify their world view, and that comfort them in established hierarchies and dichotomies, with associated behaviours, attitudes and practices? Or does the impact and change happen only long after the trip, when students revisit their experiences, pictures, encounters and discussions among themselves, when they put things in perspective?

Of course, this study abroad trip to Santiago does not constitute a sufficiently long exposure capable of engineering a long-term self-transformation or a radical change of their own beliefs. Nonetheless, as a high-impact practice, it may be the first of a series of future transformative experiences. As teachers, we know that writing objectives and mindlessly getting students through specific activities does not suffice for a rich and empowering educational experience.

Learning is complex, unpredictable and, as my students and I discovered, it depends on personal histories, trajectories and interests. It also hinges on collective experiences and habits of minds students have cultivated over the years. In compact encounters, learning can simply be a string of 'accidents' and 'moments' with short- or long-term implications. The quality of these accidents or moments reveals itself through their disruptive nature. An upsetting and emotionally charged experience or episode can be a precursor to powerful self-reflections and new behaviours. However, a comforting experience could also lead to transformative futures.

Why a Winterim Study Abroad in Cuba: Rationale and Description

The Winterim Study Abroad contingent to Cuba, 16–28 January 2019, comprised two seniors, three juniors, two sophomores and myself, the faculty member. According to the rules of the United States Census Bureau (2020), racial classification is based on self-identification rather than on an objective classification anthropologically, genetically or biologically defined. In addition, race is often defined in terms of 'colour', and ethnicity in terms of culture and language or place of origin. The US Census Bureau assumes that the categories it uses correspond to the ones most widely accepted, and this chapter uses them, for lack of less confusing terminology. Three students, two males and one female (Peter, John and Anna), identified themselves as white. One of them often mentioned his Polish ancestry. For the two African American students, Serena and Cory (one female and the other male), no ambiguity existed in their 'racial' self-identification, and ethnicity was not a factor. The last two students, Sonia and Dolores, proudly claim their Latina and Hispanic descent. Dolores had often visited Honduras – her father hails from Honduras and her mother from El Salvador. The second student, Sonia, was born in Mexico, but came to the United States at a young age. She sometimes visited Mexico. Both Sonia and Dolores were less shocked or surprised by everyday life and struggle than their counterparts. They both spoke Spanish but did not feel comfortable doing so, at least in the first few days of our stay. They did not think they had the appropriate fluency; furthermore, Cuban Spanish has its own idiosyncrasies. I, the faculty leader, was born in the Republic of Benin in West Africa. I identify myself as African American or Black, which is how most people would characterize me. Ethnically, the picture could be a lot less clear. I could be Yoruba, Goun or even Fon.

Gender-wise, the distribution was balanced: four identified as female and four as male, including myself. The students, in their vast majority, knew little or nothing of each other, and came from various disciplines including Political Science, Communication, Business, Psychology and Biology. Their ages ranged from nineteen to forty. Four of them were travelling out of the country for the first time, one of whom did actually fly for the first time in her twenty-four years. The variety of backgrounds, socio-economic statuses, ethnic or racial origins, as well as the diversity of their lived experiences turned out to be the catalysts of compelling learning experiences that constantly disrupted their sense of comfort, their prior knowledge and the prejudices they had internalized. It also diluted, to a certain degree, the process of racial and ethnic identification, at least during the twelve days spent together.

I, the leader of the group, conceptualized the programme, but the details were arranged in Cuba by a Cuban organization, through Common Ground Education and Travel, based in Miami, Florida. The trip could not be organized directly with a Cuban institution according to local policies at the University of Wisconsin system. In Cuba, we interacted with respected scholars, journalists, artists, professionals and intellectuals to comprehend the complexities of Santiago, Las Tunas and Cuba. This programme was not a humanitarian effort to 'save' or help Cubans. It was conducted on the basis of the concept of equal, respectful, people-to-people interactions, which was pivotal to our critical understanding of the Cuban experiment in which two economies – one for tourists and foreigners and the other one for nationals – operated side by side.

Our main goal in the programme was to analyze the intricate complexity and invisible layers of a society that, for the past sixty-one years, had endeavoured to model an original polity based on equality, independence, and resistance to dominant capitalist ways of thinking and operating. Cuba has managed its economy within an international context of hostility characterized by sanctions and an economic embargo exerted by its powerful neighbour: the United States of America.

The course principally aimed at

1. Understanding the complexity of the political culture of individuals, communities and nations that have been colonized and globalized.
2. Critically examining the theoretical and historical underpinnings of political, social and cultural practices and policies of Cuba.
3. Evaluating the nature of Cuba's relations with the United States.
4. Developing intellectual/analytical skills necessary to make meaning of a 'developing' country like Cuba.
5. Cultivating dispositions and attitudes required to function in a 'developing' country like Cuba.

Setting up the programme ended up being an exciting endeavour. I am fluent in Spanish, and I had visited Santiago and Havana three times before. I knew multiple facets of Cuban social, political and cultural life that I wanted students to be exposed to. I intended them to experience discomfort and surprise, dislocation with language, culture, economy, religion, politics and the 'colour' of Santiago: They needed to witness a different way of life.

Above all, I wanted them to see that life was worth living elsewhere (especially in socialist and developing countries), and that human struggles, to a large extent, were universal. I hoped they would see how the United States was implicated in Cuba's fate of suffering and deprivations. Understanding how wealth and poverty are interconnected and explained by each other was of paramount importance. In other words, no country is poor or rich in isolation, and the majority of poor countries were formerly colonized by Western European countries or occupied by the United States at some point in their history.

As I teach courses such as Introduction to International Studies; Politics of Developing Countries and the Latin American Left, I wanted Cuba to serve as an example of exposition to life and culture in a Caribbean country. However, was Cuba the best example, given all that it triggers in the collective imagination of US Americans? Was it the appropriate country, as people, like the older generation of whites and wealthy Cubans who immigrated to the United States, hated it and viewed it as an unwanted symbol of communism in the Western Hemisphere?

The political dispensation inside Cuba itself, the historically edgy nature of its relationship with the United States characterized by hostility, an economic embargo and different types of anomalies, prevent clarity, blur the lines and cloud people's thinking.

For many years, the narrative of a dictatorship that is controlled by a single man, Fidel Castro, of a country that constantly violates human rights, and where freedoms do not exist, of a poor country totally lost in communist ideology and rigidity, has prevailed. Cuba, as is imagined by the neophytes or the common person, is a country of total misery. It is a country crippled in time with mid-twentieth-century cars, one that refuses progress and normality.

As one student, John, mentioned in his final paper on stereotypes and myths about Cuba, he had to verify the truthfulness of the following stereotypes: old cars, communism and equality, pickpockets, rum and cigars. John (15 February 2019) stated:

> It is incredibly difficult to enter the country leaving people to blindly form opinions of the country. Even worse many people fall for the anti-Cuban propaganda that has been spread through American media since the Cold War. Perhaps the most interesting thing I personally experienced on the trip was seeing which of these formulated ideas are reality, and which ones are far from the truth.

I was aware that students would be dislocated, and would enter an unusual location where the trappings of capitalism would not be in their face. I was conscious that they would be confronted with a mix of interdictions, delighted by exotic and pleasurable moments, Cuban friendliness, simplicity, spontaneity and humility. The trip was risky in that it could yield unpredictable results opposite the ones I intended to achieve.

Sonia's family was paranoid and scared, with no known reason. Sonia had a sister who had lived in Mexico and claimed Cuba was not a safe place to travel to. The trip was conceptualized around the strengths of Cuba, as recognized around the world: free universal health care and education, vibrant and creative cultural production as well as unique religious practices of *Santería*, the religion that adapted from the pantheon of deities that arrived in Cuba with African slaves, mostly from West and Central Africa.

Displacement and a heightened sense of loss can actually shut off the individual and block learning. A big question that tormented my mind revolved around the relevance and usability of the experience. The trip was not going to be the search for the comfort of home away from home. The rich, authentic and organic experiences would certainly lead to some form of dislocation, displacement and disidentification. What would then be the point?

Since the success of the Cuban Revolution on 1 January 1959, a lot of remarkable and adaptive changes have taken place regarding legislation, rule of law, human rights, gay rights, migration laws, the economy and especially the more recent but slow reforms regarding the privatization of part of the economy. The barrage of propaganda about Cuba complicates matters, when it comes to understanding these evolutionary changes.

It is a herculean effort for individuals who have grown up in the United States to encounter poor people from the Global South, especially Africans, Latinx and Asians, without succumbing to the 'charity' narrative and burden of wanting to help out, what I would call the humanitarian trap. No matter who they are, what conditions they themselves live in, the challenges they are facing and the troubles they go through, at the back of their heads, US Americans in general entertain the idea that they must empathize and help others out of their misery. Such deficit frames of mind are reinforced through churches and the numerous missions abroad for the purpose of helping out, and eventually spreading the gospel. Sometimes the dislocation resulting from such humanitarian or missionary trips is so strong that those who set out to help get transformed.

At the beginning of the experience, I made it clear to my students that they were not going to help Cubans, but rather were going to experience their lives. We intended to create a more horizontal and flat interaction with Cubans. They had to avoid this trap, but how was it possible when numerous households across the island lack basic amenities and are engaged daily in 'la lucha', or 'the struggle'? For Santiagoans, 'la lucha' means hustling and bustling to make ends meet, to eat, dress and accomplish most of the things human beings should do every day. How can students, who believe they live in the greatest country in the world, make meaning of that? How do they understand that 'la lucha' can be applied to their lives too? Their parents struggle to make ends meet, albeit to a lesser degree. How do they understand that part of the wealth that was created in the United States was acquired through plantations elsewhere and in Cuba, as is demonstrated by the documentary, *Traces of the Trade: A Story from the Deep North* (Browne, 2008)?[1] Only a clarity about their own lives will provoke such thoughts. The US context of media manipulation and hidden curriculum renders it even more difficult to conceptualize (Benkler et al., 2018; Valenzuela, 2019).

What kind of transformation did I want to see in students after the trip, when they return home, and re-engage with their families, communities and workplaces? How do I align class activities to create the 'right' context for the course? Going abroad for many is often regarded as an 'escape' from a stressful life to ecstatic moments, whatever the latter are. Discomfort, disturbance and malaise should not inhabit physical spaces, personal conversations, encounters and group dynamics.

Trips to developing nations risk reinforcing the view they are lucky or blessed US Americans who have freedoms other nations do not have. Any adventure should be 'safe'. For instance, the office of 'Risk Management' at the University of Wisconsin-Parkside wanted me to guarantee that, in Cuba, students would be using their seat belts in buses, which is not even the case when I travel to the airport in Chicago in a Wisconsin Coach bus. People are blinded towards their own reality, develop stereotypes about themselves and others, and, as Adichie (2009) puts it, this creates a dangerous 'single story' about others.

In terms of assessment for this elective course, participation accounted for 25 per cent and was based on attendance, reading materials, and participating in pre-trip meetings and debriefing sessions every day or two in Cuba. The pre-trip sessions proved to be very enlightening for students' interpretations of various gestures, lectures, acts and writings they would be exposed to. Ways of seeing, knowing and hearing were constantly challenged so that students could develop a better grasp of the Cuban reality. Assessment also included one-page reflective papers or podcasts every two days.

Before departure to Santiago, they read a few articles, watched two feature films and two documentaries, and wrote three-page-maximum papers (summary and reflection) on the materials mentioned above. The final project was flexible. Students were expected to demonstrate, in a reflective and critical manner, the knowledge they had acquired about Cuba, and the links they could establish between the lectures by guides and professionals, their readings and their personal experiences on the ground. They reflected on the themes we explored. The project could be in any of the following formats:

- Monologue on Cuba (videotaped or narrated);
- Fictitious dialogue between two people arguing about Cuba on specific areas;
- Digital photo project;
- Digital storytelling;
- Photoessay;
- Short movie or 'Youtube' video;
- Podcast project (with interviews);
- 'Pecha Kucha' – presentation using your own pictures;
- Sketch notes, etc.

On their return, they were scheduled to present what they had learnt on campus, which gave them the opportunity to show how much dislocation and disidentification they experienced in a visual and oral manner.

Process of Disidentification in an Officially Racism-Free Society

Disidentification, as formulated by Sharma et al. (this volume), refers to 'the process of becoming either increasingly or dramatically less identified with one's own familiar social and cultural norms'. The United States has official categories for people to identify themselves, and their choices go into official census data records. In Cuba, official documents do not mention race or ethnic backgrounds because the state has cultivated a powerful nationalistic discourse grounded in the creation of a national Cuban identity that takes precedence over all other identities. One is Cuban before anything else.

On this trip, African American students had a few moments that heightened their racial self-awareness. Cory, who is of lighter complexion, was often regarded as 'Blanco', whereas in the United States, he identifies as Black or African American without hesitation. Serena who is of darker complexion and myself were certainly 'Negros', and were treated as such. Cuba has a very long history of racism that has not entirely disappeared despite greater equality and opportunities created by the Revolution for Afro-Cubans. Moore (2019) argues that Fidel Castro's attitude towards racism was characterized by two dimensions: an integrationist approach grounded in whiteness and a refusal to table the issue of racism in Cuba. The dissenters were repressed. For a long time, the race question was not officially tackled.

Serena and I did experience such racist attitudes in the following instances. Usmany, our guide, took a picture of me in bright backlight that darkened the picture. He then laughingly made comments in Spanish to his colleague about my skin colour, thinking I would not understand. I then made it clear to him it was an unacceptable racist comment. He started describing himself as a 'Blanco', but later, towards the end of our twelve days in Cuba, he ironically identified himself as a 'Negro'. Was it because of the presence of Cory, the 'Negro' who is lighter than him, or the dilemmas that have inhabited him for a long time and that were brought to the surface in the presence of our 'racially' diverse group, and our comments on racism? He exemplifies the fact that disidentification may be a matter of a moment, but a moment that is inscribed in the *longue durée*, in the contradictions embedded in political and economic structures of our time. Both identification and disidentification do not form in a simple moment. They are historical processes, personal and collective, and are passed on and modified in accordance with dominant forces in society.

Serena, who does not speak Spanish, was shocked, when an employee of the hotel where we lodged in Las Tunas, rudely asked her to leave the hotel because he suspected her of loitering or of being a prostitute; fortunately, another employee courteously addressed the situation explaining that Serena was part of the university group. The incident, which could be regarded as anodyne in other circumstances or for a Cuban, rang very deep in Serena's racial experiences in the United States. Its most unsettling nature related to the total lack of courtesy towards her. She was not asked who she was, what she was doing or why she was in the hotel. It is the type of treatment Blacks receive in Cuba, where the police harass them in the name of law, order and 'nation'. I have personally witnessed and been victim of similar incidents on my previous trips to Cuba.

Another important moment occurred at Hotel Meliá in Santiago, a five-star hotel where we had just had a lecture on the Cuban health care system. We decided to take a picture in the lobby with the two female doctors who spoke to us. The walls of the lobby displayed Blackface pictures of Black men and women, grotesquely painted with exaggerated features, and in indecent and lascivious postures. Serena refused to take a picture along those walls, and we all concurred. I explained to one of the female doctors, a 'mulatta', that the wall paintings prompted us to change the location because the pictures along the wall were derogatory and racist. In disbelief, she commented they represented Cuban culture. She could not give me an answer when I asked her why white people were not represented the same way on public walls with blown-up physical traits. In its obsession with nationalism and unity, the government did not address such cultural remnants of slavery upfront, focusing on inequality and believing its elimination would eradicate other expressions of racism. As Benson (2016) underscored:

> Despite these gains, the premature proclamation that the new government had eliminated racism and the uncritical acceptance of 19th-century raceless ideologies failed to dismantle racial prejudices. In fact, revolutionary visual materials contradicted themselves by reinforcing ideas of Afro-Cuban immaturity and positioning Blacks as clients of the new state. (p. 29)

Santiago may have a large population of Blacks, but the Cuban Revolution, in its effort to create a new Cuban person, Che's 'new man'[2] proud of his or her motherland, has not encouraged narratives of other identities for the sake of unity. Cuba received more slaves than the United States, more than a million Black slaves, which changed its population make-up. It was a colonial society, with a plantation economy. The most contradictory aspect of race in Cuba today is how such a highly hybridized society, oriented towards social justice and equality, does not feel comfortable admitting that racism has been prevalent, especially since the Special Period, when Cuba was forced to open its country to international tourism to earn the foreign exchange it needed to continue providing services to its population.

Tourism has provided a new foundation for racist attitudes to re-emerge and flourish with weak official action to curb or stop it. In popular parlance, a common saying states that 'Aquí el que no tiene de Congo tiene de Carabalí' (Here, he who is not partially Congolese, is partially Carabalí), denoting the African character of Cuba. Serena, who, in other circumstances had more positive experiences with Black students from the University of Oriente, discovered that her Black identity was subjected to the same stereotypes in Cuba, far from home. The globalized and historical nature of racism hit her, in a society that claimed it had almost eliminated racism by opening up education, housing and health care to all, and by making private institutions and spaces public and inclusive. She did not know how much sense she should make of it, but disidentification did not occur. She was simply 'Black' in the United States and Cuba. Her experience did not call for a deep re-evaluation or reconstruction of her identity. That could have changed if she had stayed in Cuba longer, or at least it would have been more nuanced.

The Latina students, Sonia and Dolores, had unique experiences in Cuba. They felt a little intimidated by Cuban Spanish, and their confidence in speaking

Spanish took a few days to build. One of the reasons lies in the fact that, in the United States, they do not speak Spanish every day. After the long attempt to stifle the growth of Spanish, which is itself a colonial language in the United States, its use is spreading quickly, in workplaces, media landscapes, popular music and the business world at large. The number of people from Latin American descent also, especially from Mexico, is rising. For businesses, the growth represents a bigger segment of the market to tap into. The Latinx identity, despite its contradictions, layers, sublayers and anomalies is reconfiguring itself, gradually swallowing other linguistic and cultural identities.

For reasons of authenticity, Sonia did not feel comfortable speaking Spanish at first, but she soon discovered that speaking it brought her interlocutors closer to her as a Mexican or as an American woman, two identities Cubans in Santiago are familiar with and appreciate. As she put it, 'What a struggle it was, communicating, even though I could speak and understand Spanish. They have a different accent. They would mumble and drop the s. ...They were so excited to communicate when they realized I spoke Spanish' (personal communication, 15 February 2019). As she was told, 'we love Mexico because only Canada and Mexico helped Cuba during the blockade. Mexican culture is widespread: music, movies. We like Mexicans' (personal communication, 15 February 2019).

The United States has historically played a big part in the formation of Cuban identity. The North American factor has been preponderant in the formation of Cuban identity, either through the military presence of the United States for their independence from Spain and, later, through the plantations owned by American multinationals before the Revolution, their industrialized products or through its cultural practices, ways of thinking, and the way Cuba became a popular tourist destination for US Americans, a place of escape, gaming and pleasure.

In these new times of economic struggle, we were treated primarily as tourists by our hosts and regarded as 'tourists' by people we came across. The United States still lingers in the mind of Cubans, many of whom still dream of emigrating to the North, to rejoin the 'Cuba' that immigrants have recreated in Miami, keeping the culture of the island (food, music, language, religions, cultural norms, etc.) as a way of maintaining their Cuban identity. The economic precariousness that exists on the island itself facilitates specific mental frames of exiling oneself to survive. Survival, which in Cuban jargon, is understood as 'la lucha' determines relations between people and foreigners, and among themselves. This did not escape our students' notice. 'We in the USA [sic], do not lack social amenities, we have our hygiene products, we have our chocolate, our *nutella* and Cubans do not' (personal communication, 15 February 2019). As a consequence, it becomes easy for both citizens of the United States and Cuba to be fixated by the material gulf that separates both countries.

This situation takes a prominent place and makes it difficult for students to see that struggles in the Cuban society can be similar to that of US Americans. Commonalities, as well as the universal dimension of their own tribulations, escaped their notice. Therefore, they got stuck in humanitarian modes of empathy and sympathy, of 'I want to help.' They do not see the connection that may exist between US imperial practices and the situation on the ground.

Students do not experience Cuba in the same way. Given the strained relationship between the United States and Cuba, Peter would have loved to completely disidentify himself as a gringo or a Yankee to be able to blend in and not be regarded as the 'white imperialist'. He was afraid for his security and thought Cubans could mob him, simply for coming from the United States. That anxiety quickly disappeared as he discovered that Cubans were respectful, gentle, appreciative of his presence and welcoming. Sonia remarked,

> When we were down there, we were basically treated like royalty. I felt terrible, they kept feeding us, offering to do our laundry, in the schools they gave us the warmest of welcomes. I am not used to that treatment, so I did not know how to take it. But I felt great. It was refreshing. (Personal communication, 15 February 2019)

Anna was the only white female; she was extremely curious to be in Cuba and to know. She bought both recommended books, meticulously read the assigned chapters, watched the videos and participated actively in every single visit, conversation, lecture or event we were involved in. She suffered very little identification/disidentification, but adapted herself very easily to life in Santiago and to interacting with students twice as young. She primarily focused on Cuban women. In her final project, a photoessay, Anna reflected:

> Think about this – in 1975 Cuba enacted a law which required men and women to share the housework and to both take equal time to care for the children. They were both responsible to bring in the money to support the family. The law covers marriage, divorce, marital property, relationships, equal recognition of children whether their parents are married or not, obligations for children's care and education, adoption, and guardianship. Under this law, custody of children was not given to one parent over the other. Child support was not automatically expected to come from the father, but the dynamic of the family was inspected and a decision made for the best interest of the child. We still don't have this in

the US [sic] and Cuba had it figured out in 1975. (Personal communication, 10 February 2019)

Nevertheless, Anna discovered that a gap existed between the family code and social practices. For example, she noticed that old white male tourists were dining with young women of various races, and asked our guide Usmany about it. He denied that prostitution existed, but she insisted. Eventually, he admitted to it. Robaina (2019) characterized pre-revolutionary Cuba as 'the brothel of the Caribbean' (p. 257). As Lewis et al. (2003) pointed out, the revolutionary government, right from the beginning in 1961, considered prostitution 'a symbol of Cuba's degradation, a playground for tourists and of women's lack of opportunity under the old order' (p. 395). Actually, Havana, the most popular destination, was known as a place of pleasure and lust. Hodge (2019) remarked that 'Havana before the Revolution was little more than a casino and brothel for wealthy U.S. capitalists in search of exotic pleasures. And the use of Cuban women was ideologically in keeping with U.S. economic colonialism' (p. 548).

Cuba outlawed prostitution in 1961 and established remedial solutions to rehabilitate prostitutes and provide them with education and jobs. As Anna concludes, 'And so it seems in the twist of fate that Cuba had to once again rely on tourism money to fund the government that prostitution has also become big money for the citizens of Cuba and the women in particular' (personal communication, 10 February 2019).

Anna was rather introspective and understood that the government had to close its eyes on the phenomenon for realistic reasons of survival. For many women, deep into everyday 'lucha,' it was practical. Anna argued that there was

> a certain strength and confidence that radiates from any and all of the women that I had the pleasure of meeting in Cuba. With all of the problems and issues that the women of America have been facing this past year, I wondered what the secret was for the women of Cuba. (Personal communication, 10 February 2019)

Anna concludes her photoessay stating:

> Eleven days isn't much time to learn about a country, but I feel so connected to Cuba and its women with just the little amount of time that I spent there. There is a spirit of resilience, happiness, and confidence that radiates from their souls. My goal is to be able to return time and time again to be able to learn more about the people of Cuba – especially the women. (Personal communication, 10 February 2019)

A strong identification occurred between Anna and Cuban women, based on the insightful comparison she was making with women from the United States. She saw struggling women on both sides, but at different levels. She understood what Cuban women were going through and saw the beauty in their effort. She refused to look at them as pitiful souls to be redeemed. She did not grow up in wealth, not in the upper echelons of society, and she happens to have a Black husband.

Dislocation/Displacement: Religious and Political Dimensions

The *Santería* religious ceremony we attended three days after our arrival in Santiago ranks as one of the most dislocating experiences. Most students felt out of place. African slaves brought along their system of faith and worship based on a hierarchy of deities, each of whom attends to particular needs of their lives. Because they were not allowed to practice their religions openly, they incorporated in them other traditions from other parts of the continent, especially Central Africa, but also from Catholicism. However, the core of *Santería* remained African, especially rooted in Yoruba traditions of Benin and Nigeria. *Santería* symbolizes the presence and vibrancy of African cultures in Cuba. As it is with the diversity of the Cuban population and other forms of cultural production, many whites as well as people of Asian descent have joined *Santería*. Its appeal resides in its pragmatism, its focus on healing, mind and body health, and well-being. It helps people solve practical problems and has a therapeutic function.

Our ceremony took place in the living room of an apartment with two bedrooms, a kitchen and a bathroom. There seemed to be no boundaries between each unit, or rather every room could be used in various ways. Nevertheless, a couple of them had more specific functions, the kitchen and the bathroom. The living room served as prayer room filled with various shrines belonging to a pantheon of deities that one also finds in Nigeria, Benin and the Congo/Angola, the African countries the majority of Cuban slaves originated from. This space also serves to host guests, visitors and other members of the extended family. While we were in attendance, a few visitors came by, all of them Afro-Cubans. A woman, well versed in the religious practice, herself a priestess, gave us a passionate lecture about *Santería*, stressing that its practices had very specific purposes. They sought to achieve peace, harmony, tranquillity, stability and prosperity. The ceremony itself was a participatory event. We all had to make a wish, before a hen was sacrificed and all the ingredients that were used were taken to the sea so that our prayers can be heeded. The *babalao* or priest was a relatively young man who had studied *Santería* rituals and rites for years. He performed the rituals in an esoteric language. I could personally identify phrases in Yoruba, a language I speak. It was an unsettling and dislocating experience for students but, for me, it brought back images of my native country Benin. For students however, the ceremony certainly echoed images of paganism or traditional African religions that have received derogatory comments and were regarded as idolatrous or simply primitive.

After the ceremony, some of us decided to have private spiritual readings done. The two Latinas, Sonia and Dolores, Anna and myself elected to go through it in the *babalao's* bedroom. All the white males and the African American students decided to stay away. Most rooms in the apartment had multiple purposes. It was a small apartment with fluid shared spaces that function indiscriminately for performance of religious rituals, an indication that *Santería* was at the very centre of their lives. The walls of the bedroom adjacent to the living room were all decorated with blue-and-white fabric. The room was dedicated to *Yemayá*, the goddess of the Sea. For most students, dislocation took place at two levels: at the cultural/linguistic/religious level, but also at the political level.

Displacement/Dislocation: The Cultural Dimension

The cultural dislocating/displacing character of this ceremony occurred at three levels. The location itself was one, with the relatively thin or inexistent boundary between the private, the public, the religious and other parts of life. Students are used to the idea that you go somewhere to pray, a church, a temple, a mosque. The whole ceremony took place in an apartment. This *Santería* practice itself is rooted within a mental framework that students had to move into. Second, the idea of a supreme God at the bottom of the sea heeding our prayers is absolutely antithetical to the idea of an invisible God above, to whom one goes after death. Conceptualizing this event required a mental shift, a form of displacement. Third, the mixed language of prayers and rituals was rather esoteric, not exclusively in Spanish but in a language that Cuban and the uninitiated themselves did not fully understand, a combination of old African languages. For most students brought up in modern Christianity, praying is done in a language one understands.

Displacement/Dislocation: The Political Dimension

Being out of place, in unfamiliar and uncomfortable territory, is a condition for displacement to occur. The physical and cultural aspect, common in DLN theory, can be complemented with the political one. Cuba is not a liberal democracy like the United States or many other countries in the Global South. The students experienced life under an authoritarian government with little tolerance for political dissent. They navigated a landscape where the traditional big billboards advertising goods gave place to billboards advertising ideas, personalities and symbols of patriotism or revolutionary spirit. The billboards had an educational and ideological purpose, and are meant to foster conformity, continuity and unity. The message being promoted and the corresponding behaviour were clear. In the United States, commercial boards also have a political purpose, which is to reduce citizens to their consumer worth, and to promote values of individualism and self-indulgence. Such public boards, subtly ideological, occupy big physical spaces and carry powerful messages of patriotism too. In Cuba, the signs and billboards seek to obtain fidelity to the Revolution, and to teach in the most traditional, teacher-centred manner. The state and the government determine what the population needs and 'imparts' that knowledge to them, a form of teaching that prevails in many parts of the world.

Political dislocation also happened with Usmany's narrations. The discrepancy between his narration and students' experiences resulted not only in some form of discomfort, disorientation and loss, but also some form of surprise. In our debriefing sessions, we reflected upon what tourist guides tell visitors in the United States and in some other parts of the world. We then came to the conclusion that their praxis was about the same everywhere: to use an attractive, embellished and pleasing narrative to entice. In Cuba, it was important to do so not only for obvious historical and economic reasons, but also to present a positive image of the country.

Students learnt quickly how to deal with the information gap but, quite contradictorily, the lack of trust in Usmany's words did not stop them from developing quite an endearing relationship with him. They trusted him for his knowledge of the city and events that have marked political life in Cuba. Also, politically, they found themselves in a situation whereby they were the political 'other,' not obligated to navigate towards the Democratic or the Republican Party as in the United States. Reacting to the fact that the United States was constantly singled out as the source of all evils in Cuba, Peter mentioned:

At certain points I felt as though we were used as propaganda for the Cuban government. ... I also feel as though we were used to paint the US [sic] in a much more negative light. It was very common for the specialists that we had interviewed to mention or to bring up the word 'free' in terms of healthcare and education, to the point that I found it very annoying, as a response to their free education, we would often tell stories of the cost of school here. Granted, the cost of schooling in the US [sic] is absurdly expensive, but our facilities can be very nice and there are certainly perks to going to school in the US ... America certainly has its shortcomings, but it has its bright sides too. ... If I were to return, my main priority would be to talk more with the people. (Personal communication, 13 February 2019)

As a conclusion to this section, the levels of dislocation/displacement were, to a certain degree, reduced for the group. Disconnection was not total. Students shared apartments with Cuban hosts who may not have spoken English, but tried to speak it. Luxury hardly existed, but the *casas particulares* provided safe places and a valuable window into life in Cuba. The students had internet connection and were constantly exchanging messages, talks and video chats with family and friends in the United States in the evening. Both the dislocation and the discomfort were all the more bearable as we were warmly welcomed in schools, at the Universidad de Oriente, academic institutes, or musical academies, hospitals, religious places and almost every place we went. Students' comfort benefitted from the fact that people still have some admiration and respect for US Americans and the fact that their security was guaranteed. On the contrary, Cubans did not learn much from us. Almost nothing. No reciprocity, except when our students met privately with students from Universidad de Oriente.

Consequently, the sense of isolation was reduced. For those who were going out of the country for the first time, for those who had never flown on a plane in their lives, it was a real jump into the unknown. Watching and discussing movies and documentaries on Cuba, and reading articles, could not replace their actual presence in Cuba. Our pre-trip preparation, the fact that they were travelling with a faculty member who had vast experiences with travelling in general, and had visited Santiago twice, contributed immensely in allaying their fears of displacement and discomfort.

As soon as we landed, we talked to a family that was visiting Santiago. The father, who was born in Santiago, had never visited it since the Revolution in 1959. Neither had his children who were all born and raised in the United States and were in their forties and fifties already. This was a clear example of how Cubans had been politically displaced, lost contact with home over the decades of the Revolution. Cubans living in the United States of America have striven to recreate 'Cuba' in Miami. As they continued longing for a glorious return home, they lived in a universe of displacement.

Although the Cuban case is unique, this story would be familiar to many immigrants from other countries in the United States. The Latina students in our group, as second-generation US citizens, had experienced similar situations in their families. Their consciousness of displacement was high, and they had the tools to deal with it.

Disidentification, Dislocation and Displacement: For What Kind of Learning?

In this section, I focus on what type of learning occurred in Santiago and Las Tunas, after a twelve-day study abroad experience: What is the potential learning impact? What kinds of transformation may have happened, if any? What part did DLN play in it? Learning is a complex phenomenon. It happens in different contexts. Traditional forms of learning, based on rote memory and regurgitation, are valid in specific contexts and serve their purposes. When soldiers or workers are trained to execute specific tasks, learning occurs. When students go on a study abroad trip, learning occurs, but which kind?

Every two days during the trip, after or before dinner, we got together and every student gave an account of what they had observed and the reflections they had developed, not only in relation to what we had read, watched and discussed before the trip, but also in relation to the topics and format of their final project. They had the choice of producing a 250–400 words reflection paper or a five-minute podcast during the trip, but conditions of the trip did not allow this activity to be conducted easily. Instead, in the evening, we discussed notes and photos taken during lectures and visits.

The other major assignment consisted in producing a final project (previously discussed) intended to demonstrate what they had learned about specific aspects of Cuban life. They produced the following: an eight-page photoessay ('Women in Cuba'), a one-hour podcast (about all the various themes of the course), a movie on the Revolution, three PowerPoint presentations, two of which were accompanied with reflection papers.

The final projects students turned in demonstrated that some learning had taken place. Eyler (2018) specifies the conditions that allow sustainable learning to occur: curiosity, sociality, emotion, authenticity and failure. All of these conditions were amply met throughout the trip, not with the same intensity. The group was active throughout. The learning occurred through observations, lectures by Cuban scholars, discussions with Usmany and other citizens. Intentionality helped design the study abroad and determined the places we had to go. Nonetheless, with Usmany's complicity, we visited places that were not scheduled, for instance *La Gran Piedra* in the *Sierra Maestra*, the mountains where Fidel Castro and his comrades trained for the Revolution. UNESCO has listed *La Gran Piedra* as a World Heritage site (UNESCO, 2020). It comprised the ruins of coffee plantations created by French *planteurs* that migrated from Haiti after the Haitian Revolution, and a museum that includes slave quarters and their owners' mansion. This visit demonstrated to us how slaves were treated and controlled in slavery days and the material gap that existed between the owners and the slaves. Reflecting on the samples of the 'tools of slavery' on display, Peter states:

> The mountains gave me a deeper appreciation for the island's history of resistance. Beyond Castro, the mountains also were home to runaway slaves and independence movements against the Spanish. It is one thing to read about Cuban history and learn about the importance of the mountains to the island, but witnessing the actual landscape that played such an important role is completely different. I feel like seeing the place where history took place gave me a deeper appreciation of how it was able to take place and its deeper significance. (Personal communication, 15 February 2019)

Being in the *Sierra Maestra* was equally a pleasurable experience. Anna, and all of us, agreed that, there, we enjoyed one of our best meals of the trip: fresh pork cooked (fried) from scratch in the most ecological and healthiest circumstances.

The activities, as described in sections on disidentification and displacement/dislocation, produced various degrees of discomfort and disruptions. However, the levels remained low, and the pleasurable moments abounded. The positive experiences occupied a wide range: interactions with hosts in *casas particulares*; learning how to dance salsa in Bayamo and in Hotel Meliá in Santiago; going out to dinner and clubs; experiencing the frantic celebrations of the victory of Las Tunas Baseball team in the Cuban league for the first time in forty-seven years; seeing the fervour behind the celebration of José Martí's birthday; visiting the *Sierra Maestra*; spending time on the beach; visiting the astonishing pieces scattered all over the city of Las Tunas, the Capital of Sculpture; walking safely in the street with no fear of being attacked, even as tourists; and spending time with famous Afro-Cuban rappers and students at the Universidad de Oriente. Only a few negative experiences. Some of them took place in a *casa particular*.

A combination of DLN activities and smooth, enjoyable experiences produced the knowledge students acquired and their takeaways. They resulted from special teaching moments. Heath and Heath (2017) identify four elements for defining moments:

1. Elevation: They 'rise above the everyday. They provoke not just transient happiness, like laughing at a friend's joke, but memorable delight' (p. 12).
2. Insight: They 'rewire our understanding of the world' (p. 13).
3. Pride: They 'capture us at our best – moments of achievement, moments of courage' (p. 13).
4. Connection: They 'are social. ... These moments are strengthened because we share them with others' (p. 14).

The impact was compacted in the above four categories, in addition to DLN (Sharma et al., this volume). The students were at their true best in terms of mood, generosity (we shared all the pictures we took), solidarity, watching for and making fun of each other, caring for each other when some fell sick. They elevated themselves. Peter's example and other students' reflections indicate they have questioned the propaganda against the island and its demonization by meeting real Cubans; they have also looked back at life in the United States, and wondered why they had to pay so much for education in a rich country, and why their health care system bankrupted so many of their relatives. Because they had time on their own, they were able to meet people and create their own relationships. I remember the sense of achievement and pride Sonia revelled in when she struck amazing deals on items she bought for family and friends back home, especially cigars.

The biggest beauty of this Winterim was togetherness. We lived one or two houses from each other, experienced everything together and shared all our moments. Happy and difficult moments were shared. The insightful and reflective work produced by students at the end of the trip demonstrates the learning that has taken place, its variety and authenticity, beyond the pre-written objectives of the study abroad. The DLN framework does help students produce deep insights into their learning. It could be enough in some cases, but in the case of this Winterim study abroad to Santiago, Cuba, the DLNs were not the only factor that produced learning. Positive experiences also helped create learning opportunities.

As a conclusion, I would argue that the following aspects of this trip – the Cuban political experience, religious practices, identity issues related to race, linguistic differences and originality – did produce unsettling moments for students. They triggered deep reflections on Cuba and 'home'. The disruptive nature of these experiences did not lead to traumatic experiences. To a large extent, trauma and shock were minimal, given the harmonious conditions under which the study abroad was put together and Usmany's, our guide's, flexibility. The stress levels were low as the Cuban party organized the trip with detail and attention. Students' narratives, as they appear in their projects, podcasts, mini-papers and the numerous debriefing sessions we formally had at the end of the day or informally on the bus, provided the materials used as data to analyze this study abroad journey to Cuba.

Being in Cuba itself amounts to a form of disruption, but specific processes of disidentification and dislocation in various spaces disrupted and sometimes disturbed a few students, as they were confronted with forms of uncertainty and discrimination in a foreign land. Being African American in the United States can mean being white in monolingual Cuba. Racism is not officially acknowledged in Cuba, but it exists despite appearances of a 'post-racial' society where being Cuban trumps all other forms of identity. The disruption was not traumatic but provided powerful learning and unlearning moments. At any rate, sixty years of revolution cannot eliminate more than three hundred years of racism deeply entrenched in people's minds and various institutions. Dealing with the issue of racism in Cuba prepared students for the global world that is still informed by racism in many ways and areas. Young et al. (2014) suggest 'that identity for global citizens is in a constant state of flux. Rather than being stable, identity is a continual process of integrating new experiences and molding values, roles, and self-images based on context' (p. 11). Accordingly, the study abroad course for students represented a big jump into the world, not only because most were travelling abroad for the first time, but also mainly because of the various instances of displacement, disidentification and dislocation they experienced in the mythical land of Cuba. As John put it:

> Relationships between the United States and Cuba don't seem to be improving despite efforts of our previous president. It is very likely that most Americans will never be given the chance to experience or even learn about the real Cuba outside of resorts and tourist hubs. We were given a unique opportunity and we will never be the same for it. (Personal communication, 15 February 2019)

Conclusion

Manu Sharma

This collective volume on understanding 'what our doing does' (May, 2006) when educators take their post-secondary students on intentionally critical international service learning experiences that offer disruptive narratives is unique. The usefulness and comprehensiveness of the Disruptive Learning Narrative (DLN) framework are evident in the eight thoughtful contributing chapters that have applied the DLN framework as a guiding framework to analyse the varied disruptive narratives shared throughout the respective chapters.

There are many significant learnings that emerge from the contributed chapters which extend the original understanding of three interdependent elements in the DLN framework. Some of the key learnings that emerged in this volume which I would like to draw your attention to are (1) understanding that the racial identities of racialized students entering into mostly racialized countries abroad has an influential impact on comprehending the way privilege and power are understood in the country from which they departed, (2) there is a crucial responsibility of the educator who is supervising students abroad to do their best to ensure no deficit thinking or stereotypical affirmations are taken away from such experiences by educating students before, during and after such excursions, and finally (3) acknowledging the political, historical and social circumstances of the international country.

First Learning

The first key learning is very well illustrated in one of the chapters that demonstrates a greater disruption upon the return of students to Canada, instead of the disruption happening abroad. In Chapter 4, Njoki Wane and Hermia Anthony describe how the most impactful disruptive narrative occurred upon the return of racialized students to North America, as it reformatted how they understood themselves and their cultural identity with a focus on reclaiming a positive and unifying education about their African identity. This focus on the disruption occurring upon return gives particular attention to the flow of power and the richness of acknowledging the miseducation of racialized people in a Canadian context. In other chapters there were narratives that exemplified a healthy tension between non-racialized students and racialized students or between non-racialized students and local racialized people in the international country, which also helps bring forth conversations about race. Thus, the consideration of racial identity is pertinent to the DLN framework because it draws out the disruptive nature of conversations and interactions that are soaked in race, which are very rarely spoken about openly in the North American context. The hesitancy and serious implications of politics based on racial identity in North America is currently demonstrated by the continued efforts of the Black Lives Matter Movement during the summer of 2020.

Second Learning

The second key learning from the contributing chapters highlights the responsibility of the supervising educator to ensure that such international experiences do not replicate deficit-minded attitudes, thoughts or actions towards racialized people in international settings. Many of the chapters focused on the level of preparation prior to going on the international experience and on maintaining regular check-ins during the trip, as well as offering debriefing activities after the travel abroad to allow for the educator who supervised the trip to help facilitate learning to ensure that disidentification did not lead to deficit thinking.

For example, some chapters discussed having alumni from previous trips inform future students who are going on such an international experience as to what to expect from the locals and the experience in general. In other chapters, the focus was on teaching about cultural norms, basic language for that international country, and going in with a positive and open mind. A few authors drew their narratives directly from assignments after the international course was completed or from email exchanges years later.

Thus, the emphasis of being ready to receive learning in a positive, constructive and enlightening way is the responsibility of the educator taking the students abroad as they have the larger perspective on the critical purpose of the trip. These chapters make evident that much harm can be done when the supervising faculty member(s) do not ensure that learning experiences bring forth an asset-minded approach and respect when responding to disidentification. Thus, it is an essential learning to pay heed to. Hence, the DLN framework requires a strong sensitivity to the purpose and level of criticality in understanding the international experience.

Third Learning

The third key learning that emerged from the contributing chapters is acknowledging the political, historical and social circumstances of the international country. For example, the chapters that examined American students taking a course in the international setting of Cuba went into depth about how the politics, history and social circumstances of Cuba are different from that of the United States. Moreover, reflecting on these circumstances sometimes revealed misinformation, assumptions or preconceived thoughts that were inaccurate about Cuba. Communism in Cuba in contrast to capitalism in the United States brings forth different foundations on which residents of each respective country enact different lifestyle choices and face different sets of challenges, and these differences are in response to the existing form of government. Thus, the DLN framework provides space to bring into conversation the political, historical and social circumstances of the international country and this, in turn, helps to better contextualize the international experience.

Future Possibilities

The aforementioned third learning starts to offer a new interesting research question: How does the DLN framework become influenced by the local socio-political context in international countries? Moreover, how does the DLN framework, and its three elements of disidentification, dislocation and displacement, maintain sustainability or alternatively become modified vis-à-vis changing political, social and economic circumstances in which the international experiences occur? Do the shifting political landscapes of international countries create new and unexpected challenges for educators taking their students abroad?

Another interesting extension of the DLN framework would be examining the long-term impact of such disruptive narratives in a comparative study that not only looks at the lens of the student, the supervising educator, but also of the local international community members. It would be helpful to learn how the international community members of the hosting country view North American students who are racialized or non-racialized and what their perspectives are on the purposes and impacts of such international experiences on their local community.

Finally, another area of future research may be as to how, if at all, do international students use the DLN framework and its elements to explain their experiences at North American post-secondary institutions. I wonder if the impact of each of the three elements would be experienced equally or would it vary? Are disruptive narratives, as characterized by the DLN, experienced by international students in North America or would they describe them differently?

It is with the personal vision to inspire people from all around the world to become part of a shared conversation around race and power and privilege through international post-secondary experiences that I believe this collective volume, using the DLN framework, has paved multiple entryways into this much-needed timely and pertinent discussion.

Notes

6 Navigating the Discomfort of International Teaching Placements: Resistance or Flexibility?

1 The online course on global citizenship consists of six modules and can be found at https://globalcitizenshipedu.weebly.com/ (retrieved 10 January 2017).

7 Helping Future Teachers Negotiate the Paroxysms of Patriotism at Home and Abroad: A Parallax View

1 For a thorough discussion of Immanuel Kant's theory of the antinomy of pure reason, see Kant (1781/1998).

8 International Experiences in the Bahamas: A Tropical Restoration Experience

1 According to the *Times Literary Supplement* (1995, 6 October) Schumacher's (1973) book is of the one hundred most influential books since the war.
2 The foundations of a plantation where sisal (agave) was grown and used to make rope in the 1780s can still be seen on the banks of Stafford Creek, Andros Island, Bahamas.
3 For information on the ecological restoration model see, Clewell and Aronson (2013).

9 Winterim in Cuba: Unlearning and Disruptive Moments

1 *Traces of the Trade: A Story from the Deep North* (2008) is a documentary directed by Katrina Browne about the prominent DeWolf family in Bristol, Rhode Island. From

1769 to 1820, James Wolf accumulated an enormous amount of wealth and power through the triangular slave trade. He acquired the slaves in Ghana and brought them to his coffee and sugar plantations in Cuba. Katrina Browne, a descendant of James Wolf, retraced the trade and debunked the myth that Northerners were hardly part of the slave trade. She also showed how the descendants of James DeWolf owe their current success to the trade.

2 In the early years of the Revolution, Che Guevara promoted the necessity to create a 'new man' to lay the foundations of a socialist economy and society where material incentives would be replaced by an anti-capitalist consciousness to spur economic production. That ethos, based on values of humanism, altruism and equality was supposed to prevail over all other forms of identification and considerations. Cubans were supposed to work for other Cubans in a selfless manner.

References

Introduction

Black, G. L., & Bernardes, R. (2014). Developing global educators and intercultural competence through an international teaching practicum in Kenya. *Comparative and International Education/Éducation Comparée et Internationale, 43*(2), 1–15.

Corkett, J. K., & Hatt, B. E. (2015). International practica and perception of pedagogy. *Teacher Education and Practice, 28*(4), 583–600.

Kovach, M. (2009). *Characteristics, conversations, and contexts*. Toronto, ON: University of Toronto Press.

Larsen, M. A., & Searle, M. J. (2017). International service learning and critical global citizenship: A cross-case study of a Canadian teacher education alternative practicum. *Teaching and Teacher Education, 63*(April), 196–205.

May, T. (2006). *Philosophy of Foucault*. Montreal, QC: McGill-Queen's Press.

Mwebi, B. M., & Brigham, S. M. (2009). Preparing North American preservice teachers for global perspectives: An international teaching practicum experience in Africa. *Alberta Journal of Educational Research, 55*(3), 414–27.

Scheurman, G., & Parliament, S. (2018). *Paroxysms of patriotism*. Unpublished manuscript.

Smith, L. (1999). *Decolonizing methodologies: Research and indigenous people*. London: Bloomsbury.

Wa Thiong'o, N. (1992). *Decolonising the mind: The politics of language in African literature*. Westlands, Nairobi: East African.

Žižek, S. (2009). *The parallax view*. Cambridge, MA: MIT Press.

Chapter 1

Bailey, A., & Fernando, I. (2011). Decoding voluntourism process: A case study of the pay it forward tour. *Journal of Experiential Education, 33*(4), 406–10.

Britzman, D. P. (2012). *Practice makes practice: A critical study of learning to teach*. Albany, NY: Suny Press.

Clandinin, D. J., & Connelly, F. M. (2000). *Experience and story in qualitative research*. San Francisco, CA: Jossey-Bass.

Crabtree, R. D. (2007). Asking hard questions about the impact of international service learning. *Conversations: On Jesuit Higher Education, 31*(2), 39–42.

Crabtree, S. A., Parker, J., Azman, A., & Carlo, D. P. (2014). Epiphanies and learning in a postcolonial Malaysian context: A preliminary evaluation of international social work placements. *International Social Work, 57*(6), 618–29.

Creswell, J. W. (2014). *A concise introduction to mixed methods research.* Los Angeles: Sage.

Foucault, M. (1986). Of other spaces (J. Miskowiec, Trans.). *Diacritics, 16*(1), 22–7.

Freud, A. (1974). *The ego and the mechanisms of defense.* New York, NY: International Universities Press.

Freud, S. (1955). *The interpretation of dreams.* New York, NY: Basic Books.

Greene, M. (1984). Excellence, meanings, and multiplicity. *Teachers College Record, 86*(2), 282–97.

Malewski, E., & Phillion, J. (2009). International field experiences: The impact of class, gender and race on the perceptions and experiences of preservice teachers. *Teaching and Teacher Education, 25*(1), 52–60.

May, T. (2006). *Philosophy of Foucault.* Montreal, QC: McGill-Queens Press.

Menter, I. (1984). Teaching practice stasis: Racism, sexism and school experience in initial teacher education. *British Journal of Sociology of Education, 10*(4), 459–73.

Pence, H. M., & Macgillivray, I. K. (2008). The impact of an international field experience on preservice teachers. *Teaching and Teacher Education, 24*(1), 14–25.

Quezada, R. L. (2004). Beyond educational tourism: Lessons learned while student teaching abroad. *International Education Journal, 5*(4), 458–65.

Solomon, R. (1997). Race, role modelling, and representation in teacher education and teaching. *Canadian Journal of Education/Revue Canadienne De L'éducation, 22*(4), 395–410. doi:10.2307/1585791

Willard-Holt, C. (2001). The impact of a short-term international experience for preservice teachers. *Teaching and Teacher Education, 17*(4), 505–17.

Chapter 2

Addleman, R. A., Nava, R. C., Cevallos, T., Brazo, C. J., & Dixon, K. (2014). Preparing teacher candidates to serve students from diverse backgrounds: Triggering transformative learning through short-term cultural immersion. *International Journal of Intercultural Relations, 43*(Part B, November), 189–200.

Aikman, S. (1997). Interculturality and intercultural education: A challenge for democracy. *International Review of Education, 43*(5–6), 463–79.

Allen, R. L. (2004). Whiteness and critical pedagogy. *Educational Philosophy and Theory, 36*(2), 121–36.

Armstrong, N. F. (2008). Teacher education in a global society: Facilitating global literacy for preservice candidates through international field experiences. *Teacher Education and Practice, 21*(4), 490–506.

Black, G. L., & Bernardes, R. (2014). Developing global educators and intercultural competence through an international teaching practicum in Kenya. *Comparative and International Education*, *43*(2), 1–15.

Buchanan, J. (2004). The Thais that bind: The contribution of an international practicum to students' intercultural understanding. *Pacific Asian Education*, *16*(2), 22–37.

Carr, P. R. (2017). Whiteness and white privilege: Problematizing race and racism in a 'color-blind' world and in education. In K. Fereidooni & M. El (Eds.), *Rassismuskritik and Widerstandsformen* (pp. 871–89). Wiesbaden, Germany: Springer VS.

Cushner, K. (2007). The role of experience in the making of internationally-minded teachers. *Teacher Education Quarterly*, *34*(1), 27–39.

Darling-Hammond, L. (2014). Strengthening clinical preparation: The holy grail of teacher education. *Peabody Journal of Education*, *89*, 547–61.

DiAngelo, R. (2011). White fragility. *International Journal of Critical Pedagogy*, *3*(3), 54–70.

Dunn, A. H., Dotson, E. K., Cross, S. B., Kesner, J., & Lundahl, B. (2014). Reconsidering the local after a transformative global experience: A comparison of two study abroad programs for preservice teachers. *Action in Teacher Education*, *36*(4), 283–304.

Finney, S., & Orr, J. (1995). 'I've really learned a lot, but …': Cross-cultural understanding and teacher education in a racist society. *Journal of Teacher Education*, *46*(5), 327–33.

Foucault, M. (1986). Of other spaces (J. Miskowiec, Trans.). *Diacritics*, *16*(1), 22–7.

Freire, P. (1996). *Pedagogy of the oppressed* (revised). New York, NY: Continuum.

Freud, S. (1955). *The interpretation of dreams*. New York, NY: Basic Books.

Gorski, P. C. (2008). Good intentions are not enough: A decolonizing intercultural education. *Intercultural Education*, *19*(6), 515–25.

Gregoire, M. (2003). Is it a challenge or a threat? A dual-process model of teachers' cognition and appraisal processes during conceptual change. *Educational Psychology Review*, *15*(2), 147–79.

Grierson, A., & Denton, R. (2013). Preparing Canadian teachers for diversity: The impact of an international practicum in rural Kenya. In L. Thomas (Ed.), *What is Canadian about teacher education in Canada? Multiple perspectives on Canadian teacher education in the twenty-first century* (pp. 188–211). Ottawa, ON: Canadian Association for Teacher Education.

Harris, M. D. (1992). Africentrism and curriculum: Concepts, issues, and prospects. *Journal of Negro Education*, *61*(3), 301–16.

Henfield, M. S., & Washington, A. R. (2012). 'I want to do the right thing but what is it?': White teachers' experiences with African American students. *Journal of Negro Education*, *81*(2), 148–61.

Holm, G., & Zilliacus, H. (2009). Multicultural education and intercultural education: Is there a difference? In M. Talib, J. Loima, H. Paavola, & S. Patrikainen (Eds.), *Dialogues on diversity and global education* (pp. 81–95). Berlin: Peter Lang.

Hutchison, D. (2015). Project-based learning: Drawing on best practices in project management. *What works? Research into practice*. Ontario Ministry of Education. Retrieved from http://www.edu.gov.on.ca/eng/literacynumeracy/inspire/research/WW_BestPractices.pdf

Jefferess, D. (2012). The 'me to we' social enterprise: Global education as lifestyle brand. *Critical Literacy: Theories and Practices*, 6(1), 18–30.

Kearney, S., Perkins, T., & Maakrun, J. (2014). A transformative experience: A short-term cross-cultural service-learning immersion to Kenya. *Issues in Educational Research*, 24(3), 229–40.

Krabill, R. (2012). American sentimentalism and the production of global citizens. *Contexts*, 11(4), 52–4.

Larsen, M. A., & Searle, M. J. (2017). International service learning and critical global citizenship: A cross-case study of a Canadian teacher education alternative program. *Teaching and Teacher Education*, 63, 196–205.

Lee, J. (2011). International field experience: What do student teachers learn? *Australian Journal of Teacher Education*, 36(10), 1–22.

Leeman, Y. A. M. (2003). School leadership for intercultural education. *Intercultural Education*, 14(1), 31–45.

Major, J., & Santoro, N. (2016). Supervising an international teaching practicum: Building partnerships in postcolonial contexts. *Oxford Review of Education*, 42(4), 460–74.

Martin, F., & Pirbhai-Illich, F. (2016). Towards decolonising teacher education: Criticality, relationality and intercultural understanding. *Journal of Intercultural Studies*, 37(4), 355–72.

Matias, C. E. (2016). 'Why do you make me hate myself?': Re-teaching whiteness, abuse, and love in urban teacher education. *Teaching Education*, 27(2), 194–211.

Maynes, N., Allison, J., & Julien-Schultz, L. (2013). An examination of longevity of impact of an international practicum experience on teachers' beliefs and practices four years later. *International Education Studies*, 6(4), 154.

McIntosh, P. (1989, July/August). White privilege: Unpacking the invisible knapsack. *Peace and Freedom Magazine*, 10–12.

Menter, I. (1989). Teaching practice stasis: Racism, sexism and school experience in initial teacher education. *British Journal of Sociology of Education*, 10(4), 459–73.

Merriweather Hunn, L. M. (2004). Africentric philosophy: A remedy for eurocentric dominance. *New Directions for Adult and Continuing Education*, 2004(102), 65–74.

Merryfield, M. (2000). Why aren't teachers being prepared to teach for diversity, equity, and global interconnectedness? A study of lived experiences in the making of multicultural and global educators. *Teaching and Teacher Education*, 16(4), 429–43.

Mezirow, J. (1991). *Transformative dimensions in adult learning*. San Francisco, CA: Jossey-Bass.

Mezirow, J. (2000). Learning to think like an adult: Core concepts of transformational theory. In J. Mezirow & Associates (Eds.), *Learning as transformation* (pp. 3–34). San Francisco, CA: Jossey-Bass.

Miller, L. (2006). Nipissing in Africa. *Professionally speaking*. Retrieved from https://professionallyspeaking.oct.ca/june_2006/nipissing_africa.asp

Moore, N. (2014). Me to we: Unpacking the realities of white privilege in development praxis. In A. Asabere-Ameyaw, J. Anamuah-Mensah, G. J. S. Dei, & K. Raheem (Eds.), *Indigenist African development and related issues: Towards a transdisciplinary perspective* (pp. 49–63). Rotterdam, The Netherlands: Sense.

Mwebi, B. M., & Brigham, S. M. (2009). Preparing North American pre-service teachers for global perspectives: An international teaching practicum experience in Africa. *Alberta Journal of Educational Research, 55*(3), 414–27.

Nakayama, T. K., & Krizek, R. L. (1995). Whiteness: A strategic rhetoric. *Quarterly Journal of Speech, 81*(3), 291–309.

Ntseane, P. G. (2011). Culturally sensitive transformational learning: Incorporating the Afrocentric paradigm and African feminism. *Adult Education Quarterly, 61*(4), 307–23.

Pellegrino, J. W., & Hilton, M. L. (Eds.). (2012). *Education for life and work: Developing transferable knowledge and skills in the 21st century*. National Research Council. Committee on Defining Deeper Learning and 21st Century Skills, Board on Testing and Assessment and Board on Science Education, Division of Behavioral and Social Sciences and Education. Washington, DC: The National Academies Press.

Pence, H. M., & Macgillivray, I. K. (2008). The impact of an international field experience on preservice teachers. *Teaching and Teacher Education, 24*(1), 14–25.

Portera, A. (2008). Intercultural education in Europe: Epistemological and semantic aspects. *Intercultural Education, 19*(6), 481–91.

Razack, N. (2005). 'Bodies on the move': Spatialized locations, identities, and nationality in international work. *Social Justice, 32*(4), 87–104.

Razack, S. (1998). *Looking white people in the eye: Gender, race, and culture in courtrooms and classrooms*. Toronto, ON: University of Toronto Press.

Ritchie, J., & Spencer, L. (1994). Qualitative data analysis for applied policy research. In A. Bryman and R. G. Burgess (Eds.), *Analyzing qualitative data* (pp. 173–94). New York, NY: Routledge.

Said, E. (1978). *Orientalism: Western representations of the Orient*. New York, NY: Pantheon.

Schwarz, K. C. (2015). Encounters with discomfort: How do young Canadians understand (their) privilege and (others') poverty in the context of an international volunteer experience? *Canadian and International Education, 44*(1), 1–15.

Sleeter, C. (2008). Equity, democracy, and neoliberal assaults on teacher education. *Teaching and Teacher Education, 24*(8), 1947–57.

Smolcic, E., & Katunich, J. (2017). Teachers crossing borders: A review of the research into cultural immersion field experience for teachers. *Teaching and Teacher Education, 62*, 47–59.

Sobel, D. (2004). *Place-based education: Connecting classrooms and communities*. Great Barrington, MA: The Orion Society.

Solomona, R. P., Portelli, J. P., Daniel, B., & Campbell, A. (2005). The discourse of denial: How white teacher candidates construct race, racism and 'white privilege'. *Race Ethnicity and Education*, 8(2), 147–69.

Study Group on Global Education. (2017). *Global education for Canadians: Equipping young Canadians to succeed at home & abroad: Executive summary and recommendations*. Retrieved 9 March 2019 from https://www.rolandparis.com/single-post/2017/11/15/global-education-for-canadians-equipping-young-canadians-to-succeed-at-home-abroad-study

Tallon, R. (2012). The impressions left behind by NGO messages concerning the developing world. *Policy & Practice: A Development Education Review*, (15). Retrieved 9 March 2019 from https://www.developmenteducationreview.com/issue/issue-15/impressions-left-behind-ngo-messages-concerning-developing-world

Tangen, D., Henderson, D., Alford, J., Hepple, E., Alwi, A., Abu Hassan Shaari, Z., & Alwi, A. (2017). Shaping global teacher identity in a short-term mobility programme. *Asia-Pacific Journal of Teacher Education*, 45(1), 23–38.

Taylor, E. W. (2008). Transformative learning theory. *New Directions for Adult and Continuing Education*, 119, 5–15.

Taylor, H. (1969). *The world as teacher*. New York, NY: Doubleday.

Trilling, B., & Fadel, C. (2009). *21st century skills: Learning for life in our times*. San Francisco, CA: Jossey-Bass.

Trilokekar, R. D., & Kukar, P. (2011). Disorienting experiences during study abroad: Reflections of pre-service teacher candidates. *Teaching and Teacher Education*, 34(1), 9–21.

Twine, F. W., & Steinbugler, A. (2006). The gap between *whites* and *whiteness*: Interracial intimacy and racial literacy. *The DuBois Review: Social Science Research on Race*, 3(2), 341–63.

Ullucci, K. (2010). What works in race-conscious teacher education? Reflections from educators in the field. *Teacher Education Quarterly*, 37(2), 137–56.

Warfield-Coppock, N. (1995). Toward a theory of Afrocentric organization. *Journal of Black Psychology*, 21(1), 30–48.

Wilson, A. H. (1982). Cross-cultural experiential learning for teachers. *Theory into Practice*, 21(3), 184–92.

Chapter 3

Bellamy, C., & Weinberg, A. (2006). Creating global citizens through study abroad. *Connection: The Journal of the New England Board of Higher Education*, 21(2), 20–1.

Bernard, H. R., Wutich, A., & Ryan, G. W. (2016). *Analysing qualitative data: Systematic approaches*, 2nd ed. Thousand Oaks, CA: Sage.

Bosley, H. E., & Brothers, G. L. (2008). Bridging an interdisciplinary gap: A case for uniting tourism and urban planning for a consistent understanding of the 'urban tourist bubble'. In D. B. Klenosky & C. LeBlanc (Eds.), *Proceedings of the 2008 Northeastern Recreation Research Symposium*, pp. 165–70, Newtown Square, PA: US Department of Agriculture, Forest Service, Northern Research Station.

Caton, K., Schott, C., & Daniele, R. (2014). Tourism's imperative for global citizenship. *Journal of Teaching in Travel & Tourism, 14*(2), 123–8.

Davis-Salazar, K. L. (2016). 'Glocalizing' the campus to advance global learning. *Liberal Education, 102*(2). Retrieved 14 June 2018 from https://www.aacu.org/liberaleducation/2016/spring/davis-salazar

Echtner, C. M., & Prasad, P. (2003). The context of third world tourism marketing. *Annals of Tourism Research, 30*(3), 660–82.

Foucault, M. (1986). Of other spaces (J. Miskowiec, Trans.). *Journal of Diacritics, 16*(1), 22–7.

Gibbs, G. (2008). *Analyzing qualitative data*. Thousand Oaks, CA: Sage.

Griffith, L. M., & Marion, J. S. (2018). *Apprenticeship pilgrimage: Developing expertise through travel and training*. New York, NY: Lexington Books.

Institute of International Education. (2017). Open doors 2017 executive summary. Retrieved from https://www.iie.org/Why-IIE/Announcements/2017/11/2017-11-13-Open-Doors-2017-Executive-Summary

Palacios, J. J. (2004). Corporate citizenship and social responsibility in a globalized world. *Citizenship Studies, 8*(4), 382–402.

Pan, B., Wasko, J., Smith, K., Litvin, S., Mueller, R., Li, Q., & Jie Zang, J. (2011). Cultural education through study abroad in China: A case study [Paper Presentation]. TEFI World Congress, Philadelphia, PA. Retrieved 1 July 2018 from https://www.researchgate.net/publication/255728908_Cultural_Education_through_Study_Abroad_in_China_A_Case_Study

Picard, D. (2011). *Tourism, magic and modernity: Cultivating the human garden*. New York, NY: Berghahn Books.

Rosaldo, R. (1989). Imperialist nostalgia. *Representations, 26*(Spring), 107–22.

Salazar, N. B., & Graburn, N. H. H. (2014). *Tourism imaginaries: Anthropological approaches*. New York, NY: Berghahn Books.

Schieffelin, E. L. (1985). Performance and the cultural construction of reality. *American Ethnologist, 12*(4): 707–24.

Simoni, V. (2016). *Tourism and informal encounters in Cuba*. New York, NY: Berghahn Books.

Skinner, J. (2008). Women dancing back – and forth: Resistance and self-regulation in Belfast salsa. *Dance Research Journal, 40*(1): 65–76.

Staten, C. L. (2015). *A history of Cuba*, 2nd ed. New York, NY: Saint Martin's Press.

Strauss, C. (2006). The imaginary. *Anthropological Theory, 6*(3): 322–44.

Tylor, E. B. (1871). *Primitive culture*. London: John Murray.

Urry, J. (1990). *The tourist gaze: Leisure and travel in contemporary societies*. London: Sage.
Urry, J., & Larson, J. (2011). *The tourist gaze 3.0*. London: Sage.

Chapter 4

Alfred, T. (2005). *Wasáse: Indigenous pathways of action and freedom*. Toronto, ON: University of Toronto Press.

Alfred, T. (2009). Restitution is the real pathway to justice for Indigenous peoples. In G. Younging, J. Dewar, & M. DeGagné (Eds.), *Response, responsibility, and renewal: Canada's truth and reconciliation journey* (pp. 179–87). Ottawa, ON: Aboriginal Healing Foundation.

Asante, M. K. (2002). Intellectual dislocation: Applying analytic Afrocentricity to narratives of identity. *Howard Journal of Communications, 13*(1), 97–110.

Asante, M. K. (2007). *An Afrocentric manifesto: Toward an African renaissance*. Cambridge, UK: Polity Press.

Battiste, M. (2013). *Decolonizing education: Nourishing the learning spirit*. Saskatoon, SK: Purich.

Clarke, J. H. (1991). *Africans at the crossroads: Notes for an African world revolution*. Trenton, NJ: Africa World Press.

Codjoe, H. M. (2005). Africa(ns) in the Canadian educational system: An analysis of positionality & knowledge construction. In W. J. Tetty & K. P. Puplampu (Eds.), *The African diaspora in Canada: Negotiating identity and belonging* (pp. 63–92). Calgary, AB: University of Calgary Press.

Garvey, A. J. (Ed.). (1968). *Philosophy and opinions of Marcus Garvey*. New York, NY: Arno Press.

Gibbs. C. R. (1995). *Black inventors: From Africa to America: Two million years of invention & innovation*. London: Three Dimensional.

Karenga, M. (2008). *Kawaida and questions of life and struggle: African American, pan-African and global issues*. Los Angeles, CA: University of Sankore Press.

Lorde, A. (2007). *Sister outsider: Essays & speeches by Audre Lorde*. Berkeley, CA: Crossing Press.

Omolewa, M. (2007). Traditional African modes of education: Their relevance in the modern world. *International review of education, 53*(5–6), 593–612.

Odora, C. (1994). Indigenous forms of learning in Africa with special reference to the Acholi of Uganda. *Indigenous Education in Africa. Rapport,* (7), 61–90.

Pete, S., Schneider, R., & O'Reilly, K. (2013). Decolonizing our practice: Indigenizing our teaching. *First Nations Perspectives, 5*(1), 99–115.

Smith, L. T. (2012). *Decolonizing methodologies: Research and Indigenous peoples*. London, England: Zed Books.

Syed, K. T. (2010). Canadian educators' narratives of teaching multicultural education. *International Journal of Canadian Studies, 42*, 255–69.

Tetty, W., & Puplampu, K. (2005). *The African diaspora in Canada: Negotiating identity and belonging*. Calgary, AB: University of Calgary Press.

Thabo Mbeki Foundation. (1 June 201). *I am an African* speech by President Thabo Mbeki – 8 May 1996. You Tube. https://www.youtube.com/watch?v=dCeLwTlTRoQ.

Truth and Reconciliation Commission of Canada. (2015). *Honouring the truth, reconciling for the future: Summary of the final report of the Truth and Reconciliation Commission of Canada*. Ottawa, ON: Truth and Reconciliation Commission of Canada.

Tuck, E., & Yang, W. K. (2012). Decolonization is not a metaphor. *Decolonization: Indigeniety, Education & Society, 1*(1), 1–40.

Tuck, E., McKenzie, M., & McCoy, K. (2014). Land education: Indigenous, post-colonial, and decolonizing perspectives on place and environmental education research. *Environmental Education Research, 20*(1), 1–15.

Ture, K., & Hamilton, C. (1992). *Black power: The politics of liberation in America*. New York, NY: Random House.

Wane, N. (2009). *Reflecting on race and racism in Canadian education* [Paper presentation]. Ontario Institute for Studies in Education, University of Toronto. Toronto, Canada.

Wane, N., & Simmons, M. (2011). Introduction. In N. Wane, A. Kempf, & M. Simmons (Eds.), *The Politics of cultural knowledge* (pp. 1–7). Rotterdam, The Netherlands: Sense.

wa Thiong'o, N. (2009). *Something torn and new: An African renaissance*. New York, NY: Basic Civitas.

Waziyatawin, & Yellow Bird, M. (2012). Introduction: Decolonizing our minds and actions. In Waziyatawin & M. Yellow Bird (Eds.), *For Indigenous minds only: A decolonization handbook* (pp. 1–14). Santa Fe, NM: School for Advanced Press.

Wildcat, M., McDonald, M., Irlbacher-Fox, S., & Coulthard, G. (2014). Learning from the land: Indigenous land-based pedagogy and decolonization. *Decolonization: Indigeneity, Education & Society, 3*(3), i–xv.

Chapter 5

Baxter Magolda, M. B. (2008). Three elements of self-authorship. *Journal of College Student Development, 49*(4), 269–84.

Dolby, N. (2004). Encountering an American self: Abroad and national identity. *Comparative Education Review, 48*(2), 150–73.

Lacan, J., (2006). *Ecrits* (B. Fink, Trans.). New York, NY: Norton (original work published in 1966).

Marginson, S., (2014). Student self-formation in international education. *Journal of Studies in International Education, 18*(1), 6–22.

Markus, H., & Nurius, P. (1986). Possible selves. *American Psychologist, 41*(9), 954–69.

Pizzolato, J. E. (2005). Creating crossroads for self-authorship: Investigating the provocative moment. *Journal of College Student Development, 46*(6), 624–41.

Trilokekar, D. R., & Kukar, P. (2011). Disorienting experiences during study abroad: Reflections of pre-service teacher candidates. *Teaching and Teacher Education, 27*(1), 1141–50.

Chapter 6

Batey, J. J., & Lupi, M. H. (2012). Reflections on interns' culture developed through a short-term international internship. *Teacher Education Quarterly, 39*, 25–44.

Beck, C., & Kosnik, C. (2000). Associate teachers in preservice education: Clarifying and enhancing their role. *Journal of Education for Teaching, 26*(3), 207–24.

Briscoe, P., & Pollock, K. (2017). Principals' perception of difference and diversity. *CAP Journal*, 10–14. Retrieved 8 June 2018 from https://www.edu.uwo.ca/faculty-profiles/docs/other/pollock/cap2017briscoepollock.pdf

Butin, D. W. (2003). Of what use is it? Multiple conceptualizations of service learning within education. *Teachers College Record, 105*(9), 1674–92.

Chapman, D. (2018). The ethics of international service learning as a pedagogical development practice: A Canadian study. *Third World Quarterly, 30*(10), 1899–1922.

Coles, R. (1993). *The call of service: A witness to idealism*. New York, NY: Houghton Mifflin.

Crabtree, R. (2008). Theoretical foundations for international service-learning. *Michigan Journal of Community Service Learning, 15*(1), 18–36.

Cushner, K., & Mahon, J. (2002). Overseas student teaching: Affecting personal, professional, and global competencies in an age of globalization. *Journal of Studies in International Education, 6*(1), 44–58.

Dillon, D., & O'Connor, K. (2010). What should be the role of field experiences in teacher education programs? In T. Falkenberg & H. Smits (Eds.), *Field experiences in the context of reform of Canadian teacher education programs* (pp. 117–46). Winnipeg, MB: Faculty of Education of the University of Manitoba. Retrieved 2 May 2018 from http://hdl.handle.net/1880/113304

Drolet, J. (2014). Getting prepared for international experiential learning: An ethical imperative. In R. Tiessen & R. Hush (Eds.), *Globetrotting or global citizenship? Perils and potential of international experiential learning* (pp.185–97). Toronto, ON: University of Toronto Press.

Gelmon, S. B., Holland, B. A., Driscoll, A., Spring, A., & Kerrigan, S. (2001). *Assessing service-learning and civic engagement: Principles and techniques*. Campus Compact. Providence, RI: Brown University.

Grierson, A., & Denton, R. (2013). Preparing Canadian teachers for diversity: The impact of an international practicum in Kenya. In L. Thomas (Ed.), *What is Canadian about teacher education in Canada? Multiple perspectives on Canadian teacher education in the twenty-first century* (pp. 188–211). Ottawa, ON: Canadian Association for Teacher Education.

Hurd, C. (2008). Is service learning effective? A look at the current research. In S. Shalini (Ed.), *Service learning: Perspectives* (pp. 44–60). Hyderabad, India: ICFAI University Press.

Hurtado, I. G., Coronel, J. M., Carrasco, M. J., & Correa, R. I. (2013). Internationalization of the practice in education degree: Students' intercultural experiences in the teaching and learning process at Saharawi Refugee Camps. *Journal of Education and Learning, 2*(1), 253–61.

Langdon, J., & Agyeyomah, C. (2014). Critical hyper-reflexivity and challenging power: Pushing past the dichotomy of employability and good global citizenship in development studies experiential learning contexts. In R. Tiessen & R. Huish (Eds.), *Globetrotting or global citizenship? Perils and potential of international experiential learning* (pp. 43–70). Toronto, ON: University of Toronto Press.

Larsen, M. A., & Searle, M. J. (2017). International service learning and critical global citizenship: A cross-case study of a Canadian teacher education alternative practicum. *Teaching and Teacher Education, 63,* 196–205.

Maynes, N., Hatt, B, & Wideman, R. (2013). Service learning as a practicum experience in a pre-service education program. *Canadian Journal of Higher Education, 43*(1), 80–99.

Mwebi, B. M., & Brigham, S. M. (2009). Preparing North American preservice teachers for global perspectives: An international teaching practicum experience in Africa. *Alberta Journal of Educational Research, 55*(3), 414–27.

Sarri, R. (1997). International social work at the millennium. In M. Reisch & E. Gambrill (Eds.), *Social work in the 21st century* (pp. 707–22). Thousand Oaks, CA: Prince Forge Press.

Scheyvens, R., & Leslie, H. (2000). Gender, ethics and empowerment: Dilemmas of development fieldwork. *Women's Studies International Forum, 23*(1), 119–30.

Smith, M., Jennings, L., & Lakhan, S. (2014). International education and service learning: Approaches toward cultural competency and social justice. *Counseling Psychologist, 42*(8), 1188–214.

Smolcic, E., & Katunich, J. (2017). Teachers crossing borders: A review of the research into cultural immersion field experience for teachers. *Teaching and Teacher Education, 62,* 47–59.

Thomas, L., & Chandrasekera, U. (2014). *Uncovering what lies beneath: An examination of power, privilege, and racialization in international social work.* In R. Tiessen & R. Huish (Eds.), *Globetrotting or global citizenship? Perils and potential of international experiential learning* (pp. 90–112). Toronto, ON: University of Toronto Press.

Tiessen, R. (2014). Career aspirations and experiential learning abroad: Perspectives from Canadian youth on short term placements. In R. Tiessen & R. Huish (Eds.), *Globetrotting or global citizenship? Perils and potential of international experiential learning* (pp. 71–89). Toronto, ON: University of Toronto Press.

Tiessen, R., & Huish, B. (Eds.). (2014). *Globetrotting or global citizenship? Perils and potential of international experiential learning.* Toronto, ON: University of Toronto Press.

Chapter 7

Bruner, J. (1960). *The process of education.* Cambridge, MA: Harvard University Press.

Carton, E. (2006). *Patriotic treason: John Brown and the soul of America.* New York, NY: The Free Press.

Fortas, A., & Supreme Court of The United States. (1968). *U.S. Reports: Tinker v. Des Moines School Dist., 393 U.S. 503* [Periodical]. Retrieved from the Library of Congress: https://www.loc.gov/item/usrep393503/

Foucault, M. (1986). Of other spaces (J. Miskowiec, Trans.). *Diacritics, 16*(1), 22–7.

Freire, P. (1997). *Pedagogy of the heart.* New York, NY: Continuum.

Freire, P. (1998a). *Teachers as cultural workers: Letters to those who dare to teach.* Boulder, CO: Westview Press.

Freire, P. (1998b). *Pedagogy of freedom: Ethics, democracy, and civic courage.* Lanham, MD: Rowman & Littlefield.

Jameson, F. (2006). First impressions. *London Review of Books, 28*(17), 7–8.

Kant, I. (1998). *Critique of pure reason* (P. Guyer & A. W. Wood, eds. & Trans.). Cambridge, UK: Cambridge University Press (original work published 1781).

Karatani, K. (2003). *Transcritique: On Kant and Marx.* Cambridge, MA: MIT Press.

Kuhn, T. (1962). *The structure of scientific revolutions.* Chicago, IL: University of Chicago Press.

Scheurman, G. (2017, March). *Ambassadors or apologists for American democracy: A new twist for student teachers overseas* [Paper presentation]. Annual Meeting of the Consortium of Overseas Student Teaching, Melbourne, Australia.

Scheurman, G. (2018, April). *How democratic is student teaching: Lessons for everyone from those who face such questions overseas?* [Paper presentation]. National Field Experience Conference, University of Northern Colorado.

Scheurman, G., & Parliament, S. (2018). *Paroxysms of patriotism.* Unpublished manuscript.

Thoreau, H. D. (1866). Civil disobedience. In *A Yankee in Canada, with anti-slavery and reform papers* (pp. 123–51). Cambridge, MA: Welch, Bigelow.

Žižek, S. (2009). *The Parallax view.* Cambridge, MA: MIT Press.

Chapter 8

Bahamas Ministry of Tourism. (2018). *Foreign arrivals summary report.* Retrieved 9 July 2019 from https://www.tourismtoday.com/sites/default/files/summary_foreign_air_and_sea_arrivals_january_to_december_2018_with_stopovers_1.pdf

Bloom, B. S. (Ed.). (1956). *Taxonomy of educational objectives. Vol. 1: Cognitive domain.* New York, NY: Longman.

Clewell, A., & Aronson, J. (2013). *Ecological restoration: Principles, values, and structure of an emerging profession*, 2nd ed. Washington, DC: Island Press.

Cole, T. (2012, 21 March). The white-savior industrial complex. *Atlantic.* Retrieved 9 July 2019 from https://www.theatlantic.com/international/archive/2012/03/the-white-savior-industrial-complex/254843/

Gooley, T. (2017). *How to read nature: Awaken your senses to the outdoors you've never noticed.* New York, NY: The Experiment.

Government of the Bahamas. (2011). *Forestry unit: About us.* Retrieved 9 July 2019 from https://bit.ly/3l3EFo8

Government of the Bahamas. (2011). *Forestry unit: Partnerships/projects.* Retrieved 9 July 2019 from https://bit.ly/3iWGGk6

Howard, R. (1999). *Promised is'land: Reconstructing history and identity among the black Seminoles of Andros Island, Bahamas.* Unpublished doctoral dissertation. University of Florida. Retrieved 9 July 2019 from https://ufdc.ufl.edu/AA00022324/00001

Maslow, A. H. (1943). A theory of human motivation. *Psychological Review, 50*(4), 370–96.

National Survey of Student Engagement. (2018). *NSSE 2018 frequencies and statistical comparisons: University of Wisconsin-River Falls.* Retrieved 9 July 2019 from https://www.uwrf.edu/Research/upload/NSSE18-Frequencies-and-Statistical-Comparisons-UW-River-Falls.pdf

Punyanunt-Carter, N. M. (2008).The perceived realism of African American portrayals on television. *Howard Journal of Communications, 19*(3), 241–57.

Saunders, G. (2016). *Race and class in the colonial Bahamas, 1880–1960.* Gainesville, FL: University Press of Florida.

Schumacher, E. F. (1973). *Small is beautiful: A study of economics as if people mattered.* London: Blond & Briggs.

Sirolli, E. (2012, September). If you want to help someone shut up and listen! [video file]. Retrieved 9 July 2019 from https://www.ted.com/talks/ernesto_sirolli_want_to_help_someone_shut_up_and_listen?language=en

Sweet, W. V., Kopp, R. E., Weaver, C. P., Obeysekera, J., Horton, R. M., Thieler, E. R., & Zeras, C. (2017). *Global and regional sea level rise scenarios for the United States* [Technical report NOS CO-OPS 083]. National Atmospheric and Oceanic Administration: Center for Operational Oceanographic Products and Services. Retrieved 9 July 2019 from https://pubs.giss.nasa.gov/abs/sw01000b.html

Times Literary Supplement. (1995, 6 October). The hundred most influential books since the war. *Times Literary Supplement, 4827*, 39. London: News International Associated Services.

University of Wisconsin River–Falls. (n.d.). About us. Retrieved 9 July 2019 from https://www.uwrf.edu/AboutUs/PointsofPride.cfm

University of Wisconsin River–Falls. (n.d.). *Enrollment report Fall 2017*. Office of institutional research: 2018–2017 enrollment reports: Enrollment by academic level. Retrieved 9 July 2019 from https://www.uwrf.edu/Research/upload/17-18-Enrollment-Report-by-Acad-Level.pdf

University of Wisconsin River–Falls. (n.d.). *Quick facts: Fall 2017*. Institutional research: Campus data reports. Retrieved 9 July 2019 from https://www.uwrf.edu/Research/upload/UWRF-Quick-Facts-Fall-2017.pdf

University of Wisconsin System. (n.d.). Education reports and statistics, student financial aid. Retrieved 9 July 2019 from https://www.wisconsin.edu/education-reports-statistics/download/educational_statistics/informational_memoranda/Student-Financial-Aid,-2017-18.pdf

Chapter 9

Adichie, Chimamanda. The danger of a single story. Filmed July 2009 at TED Global [Video File, 18:33]. Retrieved 8 August 2020 from https://www.ted.com/talks/chimamanda_adichie_the_danger_of_a_single_story?utm_campaign=tedspread&utm_medium=referral&utm_source=tedcomshare

Benkler, Y., Faris, R., & Roberts, H. (2018). *Network propaganda: Manipulation, disinformation, and radicalization in American politics*. Oxford, UK: Oxford University Press.

Benson, D. S. (2016). Not blacks, but citizens: Race and revolution in Cuba. *World Policy Journal, 33*(1), 23–9.

Browne, K. (Director). Kovgan, A., & Ray, J. (Co-Directors). (2008). *Traces of the Trade: A Story from the Deep North* [FILM]. USA: American Documentary.

Eyler, J. R. (2018). *How humans learn: The science and stories behind effective college teaching*. Morgantown, WV: West Virginia University Press.

Heath, C., & Heath, D. (2017). *The power of moments: Why certain experiences have extraordinary power*. New York, NY: Simon and Schuster.

Hodge, D. G. (2019). Colonizing the Cuban body. In A. Chomsky, B. Carr, A. Prieto, & P. M. Smorkaloff (Eds.), *The Cuba reader: History, culture, politics*, 2nd ed. (pp. 547–52). Durham, NC: Duke University Press.

Lewis, O., Ruth, L., & Susan, R. (2004). The rehabilitation of prostitutes. In A. Chomsky, B. Carr, A. Prieto, & P. M. Smorkaloff, (Eds.), *The Cuba reader: History, culture, politics* (pp. 395–8). Durham, NC: Duke University Press.

Moore, C. (2019). Silence on Black Cuba. In A. Chomsky, B. Carr, A. Prieto, & P. M. Smorkaloff (Eds.), *The Cuba reader: History, culture, politics*, 2nd ed. (pp. 380–4). Durham, NC: Duke University Press.

Robaina, T. F. (2019). The brothel of the Caribbean. In A. Chomsky, B. Carr, A. Prieto, & P. M. Smorkaloff (Eds.), *The Cuba reader: History, culture, politics*, 2nd ed. (pp. 239–41). Durham, NC: Duke University Press.

UNESCO. (2020). *Archaeological landscape of the first coffee plantations in the South-East of Cuba. World Heritage List section*. Retrieved 10 March 2021 from https://whc.unesco.org/en/list/1008

United States Census Bureau. (2020, 21 April). *About race*. Retrieved 31 July 2020 from https://www.census.gov/topics/population/race/about.html

Valenzuela, A. (2019). The struggle to decolonize official knowledge in Texas' state curriculum: Side-stepping the colonial matrix of power. *Equity and Excellence in Education, 52*(2–3) (August), 197–215. Retrieved 30 July 2020 from https://doi.org/10.1080/10665684.2019.1649609

Young, J., Natrajan-Tyagi, R., & Platt, J. J. (2015). Identity in flux: Negotiating identity while studying abroad. *Journal of Experiential Education, 38*(2), 175–88. Retrieved 5 June 2019 from https://doi:10.1177/1053825914531920

Conclusion

May, T. (2006). *Philosophy of Foucault*. Montreal, QC: McGill-Queen's Press.

Index

Note: Numbers in italics denote Figures.

addiction 80-1
Addleman, Rebecca et al. 43
African Americans 81-4, 143-4, 155, 179, 184, 191, 197
African Canadians 80, 83-4
African societies
    and community-oriented interdependence 52
    education and knowledge 76-9
    stereotypes of 18, 21, 61, 74, 75
    See also Kenya; Somalia; Tanzania
Africville, Nova Scotia 83
Akindes, Simon A. 7-8, 175-97
Allen, Andrew 3, 9-34, 50
Allen, Ricky Lee 50
Andros Island, Bahamas. *See* Bahamas
Anthony, Hermia 5, 91-116, 199-200
Asante, Molefi 78, 79, 88

Bahamas 7, 153-74, 203 n.2
    slavery and 153-4, 164
    tourism in 164, 168, 169-70, 172-3
Bailey, Andrew W., and Irene K. Fernando 10
Battiste, Marie 73
Baxter Magolda, Marcia B. 92-3
Beckford, Clinton 11-12
Bernardes, Rogerio 4, 35-54
Black, Glenda 4, 35-54
Blackness 81-7
Bosley, Holly E., and Gene L. Brothers 58
Britzman, Deborah 18, 19-21
Bruner, Jerome 150
Butin, Dan W. 119

Chapman, Debra 120
China 6-7, 92, 140, 141, 142-3, 145, 151-2
Christianit 16, 17, 191
Clarke, John Henrik 78, 79
Clovis, Chris 11-12

cognitive dissonance 11, 17, 20, 21, 23, 27, 28, 32, 49, 91-2, 149, 170, 177-8
    and heterotopias 45-6
    and the tourist imaginary 57-71
    and transformational learning theory 40-1
    See also Lacan, Jacques
Cole, Teju 154, 162
Coles, Robert 119
colourism 83, 87
Conjunto Folclórico Raices Profundo 63-4
Consortium of Overseas Student Teaching programme 141-2
Crabtree, Robin 14-15
Creswell (2014) 11
Cuba 4, 7-8, 55-72, 175-98
    American embargo against 58-60, 180, 181
    and cubanidad 177
    revolution in 58, 60, 204 n.2
    tourism in 186, 187-8, 189, 192, 197
Cuba Music and Culture Seminar 56-7, 63

decolonization, 73-4, 82, 83-9
deficit framing 43-4, 46, 48, 49-50, 53
DiAngelo, Robin 42, 47
Diop, Cheikh Anta 75, 78
disidentification, definition of 19-24
dislocation, definition of 24-9
displacement, definition of 29-32
Disruptive Learning Narrative (DLN) framework
    definition and formulation of 1, 2, 9-34, *31*
Dlamini, Nombuso 11-12
Dolby, Nadine 92
Du Bois, W. E. B. 78, 150

Echtner, Charlotte M., and Pushkala Prasad 61

ecological restoration 7, 153–74, 203 n.3
Ecuador 6, 140, 141–2, 143–5, 151
embodied learning 63, 64–6, 70–1, 87. *See also* experiential learning
experiential learning 4, 9–10, 28, 37–8, 39, 56, 59, 62, 123–37. *See also* embodied learning

Finney, Sandra, and Jeff Orr 35
foreign aid 15, 153
Foucault, Michel 18–19, 27–8, 45, 56, 145
Freire, Paulo 35, 152
Freud, Anna 18–19, 29–30
Freud, Sigmund 18–19, 29, 47–8, 95

Garvey, Amy Jacques 78–9
Garvey, Marcus 78
Gibbs, C. R., *Black Inventors Book: From Africa to America: Two million years of invention & innovation* (1995) 77
Global North 74, 118
Global South 118, 121, 182, 192
Greene, Maxine 21
Griffith, Lauren Miller, and Jonathan S. Marion 70
Guevara, Che 176, 204 n.2

Hartman, Saidiya 79
heterotopias. *See* Foucault, Michel
host communities, relationships with 52, 53, 117–18, 120–1
  in Cuba 56, 60, 70, 71
  in Kenya 36
  in Uganda 6, 118, 121–6, 129–32, 133, 137
Hurd, Clayton 119

Ibrahim, Awad 3, 9–34
imperialist nostalgia 61
Indigenous knowledges 37, 73, 74, 77–8
Indigenous peoples 37, 38, 73, 74, 77–8, 88, 153–4, 155
Institute of International Education 55
interculturalism 37–8, 40, 145
interdependence 4, 52–3, 160
international teaching placements. *See* practicums

interviews as methodology 11, 13, 106, 107, 125
Islam 16, 124

Jamaican Canadians 84–7
Jameson, Fredric 142
Juneau, Kevyn J. 153–74

Kane, Ruth 6, 117–37
Kant, Immanuel 150, 152
Karenga, Maulana 78, 79
Kenya
  colonial schools in 76–7
  dislocation on return from 5, 73–90
  international teaching practicum in 4, 35–54
Keto, C. Tsehloane 78
Kuhn, Thomas 150

Lacan, Jacques 5, 92, 93–6, 97–8, 100–1, 103–6, 107
Lampman, Aaron M. 4, 55–72
Langdon, Jonathan, and Coleman Agyeyomah 117, 120, 131, 133, 135
Larsen, Marianne, and Michelle J. Searle 119–20
linguistics 5, 91–116, 127
Lorde, Audre 87

maladaption 6–7, 142
Marginson, Simon 92–3
Markus, Hazel, and Paula Nurius 91, 93
Martin, Fran, and Fatima Pirbhai-Illich 39
May, Todd 2, 8, 27, 199
Maynes, Nancy, Blaine Hatt, and Ron Wideman 120
Mazama, Ama 78
Mazrui, Ali 77
Mbeki, Thabo 78
Menter, Ian 33, 34, 47
Merryfield, Merry 38
Mexico 148–9, 151, 179, 187
Mezirow, Jack 39, 40, 50, 51, 53

Nakayama, Thomas K., and Robert L. Krizeck 47
national identity 6–7, 92, 139. *See also* patriotism

Nkrumah, Kwame 78
non-government organizations
    (NGOs) 4, 36–53
Norway 146–8, 151–2
Ntseane, Peggy Gabo 40–1, 51, 52

Odora, Catherine 78
otherness, beliefs about 56, 57–8, 60,
    62, 64, 79
  and displacement 67–70

parallax views 6–7, 139–52
Parkinson, Michelle 5, 91–116
Parliament, Stephen 6–7, 139–52
patriotism 6–7, 139, 144–52, 192. *See also*
    national identity
Pence, Holly M., and Ian
    K. Macgillivray 9–10
Picard, David 57, 59–60
Pizzolato, Jane Elizabeth 91, 92–3
plantations 154, 176, 183, 186, 187, 195,
    203 n.2, 204 n.1
Portera, Agostino 37
power. *See* racism; tourist imaginary;
    whiteness; white savior complex
practicums 3, 9, 13, 29–30
  in Canada 21, 23, 32–4
  in Ecuador 6, 140, 141–2, 143–5,
    151–2
  in Kenya 4, 35–54, 88
  in Tanzania 9–34
  in Uganda 117–37
privilege. *See* racism; tourist imaginary;
    whiteness; white savior complex
psychoanalysis. *See* Freud, Anna; Freud,
    Sigmund; Lacan, Jacques
Puja, Grace 11

race
  avoidance of discussion of 11, 21–3, 31
  importance of critical reflection
    on 2, 20, 28. *See also* African
    societies, stereotypes of; Blackness;
    decolonization; racial identity;
    white fragility; whiteness;
    whiteness studies
race relations 1, 16, 28, 186, 200, 202
racial identity 2, 17, 20, 23, 24,
    29–31, 200

racism 16–17, 42, 47, 67, 82, 120,
    177, 184–6, 197. *See also* slavery;
    whiteness
Razack, Narda 45
resistance to challenging power
    dynamics 6, 26, 27, 28, 46, 47,
    53, 117–37
Ritchie, Jane, and Liz Spencer 41
Rosaldo, Renato 61
rote learning 42
Rouhani, Leva 6, 117–37

Said, Edward 38, 43, 46, 53
Salazar, Noel B., and Nelson H. H.
    Graburn 57, 58
Scheurman, Geoffrey 6–7, 139–52
Scheyvens, Regina, and Helen Leslie 120
Schumacher, Ernst Friedrich 153, 155,
    157, 203 n.1 (chap. 8)
Schwarz, Kaylan C. 47, 52–3
Schweitzer, Kenneth 4, 55–72
self-transformation. *See*
    under transformation
service learning 2, 3, 6, 14–15, 35, 43,
    117–37, 199
shadism 83–4, 87
Sharma, Manu 1–8, 9–34, 199–202
Sierra Leone 81–2
Simoni, Valerio 64, 65
slavery 79, 83–4, 85–6, 153–4, 164, 182,
    186, 190, 195, 204 n.1
Smolcic, Elizabeth, and John Katunich 38,
    40, 117
Sobel, David 53
Somalia 79–80
spirituality 5, 61, 65–6, 76, 85–6, 88, 191
study abroad programmes
  in the Bahamas 153–74
  in Cuba 55–72,
  in Europe 91–116
Study Group on Global Education 35
subaltern 43, 52
surveys as methodology 95, 98–9, 106

Tallon, Rachel 36, 43, 52, 53
Tanzania, international teaching
    placement in 9–34
  and heterotopias 27–8
  origins and structure of 11–15
Taylor, Edward W. 40, 51

The Catalyst (study abroad
    programme) 96–116
Thio'ngo, Ngũgĩ Wa 78, 79
Thoreau, Henry David 150
Tiessen, Rebecca, and Robert Huish 120,
    123, 130–1, 134–6
tourism 7, 10, 22, 25, 56
    in the Bahamas 164, 168,
        169–70, 172–3
    in Cuba 186, 187–8, 189, 192, 197
tourist gaze 56, 62, 71. *See also* tourist
    imaginary
tourist imaginary 7, 56, 57–62, 64,
    66, 70–1
transformation 1, 8, 53, 55–71, 73, 88, 194
    self-transformation 176, 178
    See also transformational
        learning theory
transformational learning theory 39,
    40–1, 51–2
Trilokekar, Roopa Desai, and Polina
    Kukar 92
Truth and Reconciliation Commission
    of Canada, *Honouring the truth,
    reconciling for the future: Summary
    of the final report of the Truth and
    Reconciliation Commission of Canada*
    (2015) 73
Ture, Kwame, and Charles Hamilton,
    *Black Power: The Politics of Liberation
    in America* (1992) 78

Tylor, Edward Burnett, *Primitive Culture*
    (1871) 61

Ubuntu philosophy 52, 88
Uganda
    international service learning
        practicum in 6, 118, 122–37
    schools in 124–5, 128
Ullucci, Kerri 50
Urry, John, and Jonas Larsen 56, 62

volunteer placements 10, 120–1, 124, 126,
    130, 131

Waller, Willard 19
Wane, Njoki 5, 91–116, 199–200
white fragility 19, 22, 29
whiteness 22, 30, 50, 75, 130, 135,
    184–5
whiteness studies 39–40
white saviour complex 7, 45–6,
    153–74
Wilcox, Kevin 4, 35–54
Woodson, Carter G. 79

Žižek, Slavoj 6, 139, 140, 142,
    149–50, 152